Asset Management and The Case of Turkey: Risk Adjusted Performance Evaluation of Turkish Mutual and Pension Funds

Tayfun Özkan and Hakkı Öztürk

Asset Management and The Case of Turkey: Risk Adjusted Performance Evaluation of Turkish Mutual and Pension Funds

PETER LANG

Bibliographic Information published by the Deutsche Nationalbibliothek
The Deutsche Nationalbibliothek lists this publication in the Deutsche Nationalbibliografie; detailed bibliographic data is available online at http://dnb.d-nb.de.

Library of Congress Cataloging-in-Publication Data
A CIP catalog record for this book has been applied for at the Library of Congress.

Cover illustration:
© NicoElNino/shutterstock.com

ISBN 978-3-631-87953-5 (Print)
E-ISBN 978-3-631-88155-2 (E-PDF)
E-ISBN 978-3-631-88156-9 (EPUB)
10.3726/b19820

Peter Lang – Berlin · Bruxelles · Istanbul · Lausanne · New York · Oxford

This publication has been peer reviewed.

www.peterlang.com

Abstract: The asset management industry is one of the essential sources of economic growth in a country since it functions as an intermediary between savings and investments. The asset management industry is also important for financial markets to ensure new funds and it helps investors to achieve their investment goals. Therefore, the aim of this study is to analyze the fund management industry in an emerging market. In this book, we first reviewed the fund performance measurement ratios and then we evaluated these performance measures of mutual and pension funds in Turkey between 2010 and 2019 to determine whether the funds generate alphas (excess returns). The risk-adjusted performance measures (Sharpe, Treynor, Information, Jensen's alpha, Sortino, and Omega ratios) were calculated to see if the funds generated excess risk-adjusted returns during analyzed period. We believe that the results have important implications for all investors, fund managers, regulators and as well as for the economy. In addition, the book can also be used as a supplementary textbook for both undergraduate and graduate students of finance.

Keywords: fund management, fund performance measures, risk adjusted returns, asset management, mutual funds, pension funds, excess returns, alpha

Preface

Savings and capital accumulation are insufficient in Turkey to grow its economy. Hence it requires foreign capital which renders it susceptible to economic crises. Another policy to fuel growth is to commingle small savings via fund management. This policy can work only if the fund management industry generates acceptable, i.e., above-market returns in a sustainable manner. In this empirical study, it is analyzed whether the fund industry generates such returns. This study is based on a chapter of Tayfun Ozkan's PhD dissertation under the supervision of Assoc. Prof. Hakki Ozturk.

The last decade (2010–2019) of Turkish fund management industry including both the mutual and the pension funds (which represent 90 % of the industry as of 2019) are covered. The analysis is performed by creating fund categories (in line with regulatory and international guidelines), selecting an appropriate category benchmark for each fund category, and measuring the risk-adjusted return performance of the fund categories.

Eight different mutual and thirteen different pension fund categories are defined. Performances are measured via six different risk-adjusted single-index models (namely Sharpe, Treynor, Information, Jensen's alpha, Sortino, and Omega ratios) both against the risk-free rate of return and a benchmark defined for the relevant fund category in four different time horizons (annual, rolling 3-yearly and 5-yearly, and decade-long) based on both equally and AuM-weighted weekly returns data.

The fund category analysis results in general indicate that out of 21 total mutual and pension fund categories analyzed (i) there is no fund category whose absolute risk-adjusted performance (measured by the Sharpe and Treynor ratios) is sustainably successful, i.e., which always beats the risk-free rate of return; (ii) there is no fund category whose relative risk-adjusted performance (measured by Information and Jensen's alpha ratios) is sustainably successful, i.e., which always beats its benchmark; (iii) there is no fund category which sustainably yields successful returns in terms of downside risk-adjusted performance (measured by Sortino ratio) and in terms of higher moments (measured by Omega ratio).

There is no evidence that the risk-adjusted performances are better in the long run. There is only one fund category out of 21 fund categories where longer period returns are better than the annual ones: equity pension funds category.

There are four fund categories which can be compared against each other in terms of mutual vs pension funds: gold, equity, fixed income, and money market fund categories. Gold, equity, and money market fund categories exhibit same risk-adjusted performance trends while fixed income fund category differs mainly based on more allocation to private sector securities in mutual funds (28 %) than pension funds (6 %).

Contents

Abbreviations

AuM	Assets under Management
CAPM	Capital Asset Pricing Model
CBRT	Central Bank of Republic of Turkey
CMB	Capital Markets Board of Turkey
CSD	Central Securities Depository of the Turkish capital markets
DPM	Discretionary Portfolio Management
ETF	Exchange Traded Fund
EU	European Union
FMI	Fund Management Industry
FoF	Fund of Funds
MF	Mutual Funds
PDP	Public Disclosure Platform
PEIF	Private Equity Investment Funds
PF	Pension Funds
PPP	Public Private Partnership
REIF	Real Estate Investment Funds
SME	Small Medium Enterprises
TCMA	Turkish Capital Markets Association
TEFAS	Turkish Electronic Funds Trading Platform
TL	Turkish Liras
TUIK	Turkish Statistical Institute
VaR	Value at Risk

Symbols

Average benchmark return for the period:	$\overline{R_B}$
Average portfolio (fund category) return for the period:	$\overline{R_p}$
Average risk-free rate of return for the period:	$\overline{R_f}$
Beta of portfolio:	β_p
Standard deviation of portfolio (fund category) returns:	σ_p
Standard deviation of excess returns:	$\sigma_{(R_p - R_f)}$
Total:	Σ

1. Asset management and the case of Turkey

Asset management and banking are like yin-yang medallion of financial intermediation. They complement each other and balance the markets. In Turkey, asset management is much smaller than banking. This imbalance hinders efficient and long-term allocation of funds and consequently growth of economy. The country lacks capital accumulation which is customarily filled in by foreign capital rendering the country vulnerable to external shocks, as painfully experienced in the last couple of years. A panacea may be commingling small savings into sizeable investment funds and channeling these funds (i) to purchase bonds and lease certificates of companies, especially SMEs, easing their burden of bank financing, (ii) to venture capital start-ups boosting innovation, entrepreneurship, and young employment, (iii) to invest in infrastructure projects alongside the government funds in PPP models, etc. In other words, small savings may become institutional investors via fund management. Turkey has experienced the advantages of the first sizeable institutional investors in the capital markets with the creation of voluntary pension funds. Institutional investors with long-term investment mandates provide stability in times of turbulence in the markets.

The sine qua non-condition for retail investors to commingle their savings into investment funds is a satisfactory risk-adjusted return they expect to receive in a persistent manner. This is also a condition for institutional investors to continue investing in the capital markets vis-à-vis the asset management sector. In this book, we analyzed whether the Turkish fund management industry, as a proxy of the asset management sector, could satisfy this sine qua non-condition for mutual funds, i.e., retail investors and for pension funds, i.e., institutional investors.

The weekly returns data of both mutual and pension funds for 10 years between 2010–2019 (examined in annual, in rolling 3-yearly and 5-yearly, and a decade-long time horizons) are analyzed in terms of absolute risk measures (i.e., vis-à-vis the risk-free rate of return), in terms of relative returns (i.e., via-a-vis the benchmark return), and in terms of higher moments (i.e., in relation to downside risk) by both taking into consideration the fund sizes (AuM-weighted) and not (equally weighted).

1.1 Asset management's role within economy and the financial system

Before delving into performance analysis, we would like to point out the place of asset management and its significance within the economies in general. The asset management industry emerges and grows with capital accumulation. The more available capital for financial investment, the more the asset management services is required as illustrated in Figure 1.1.

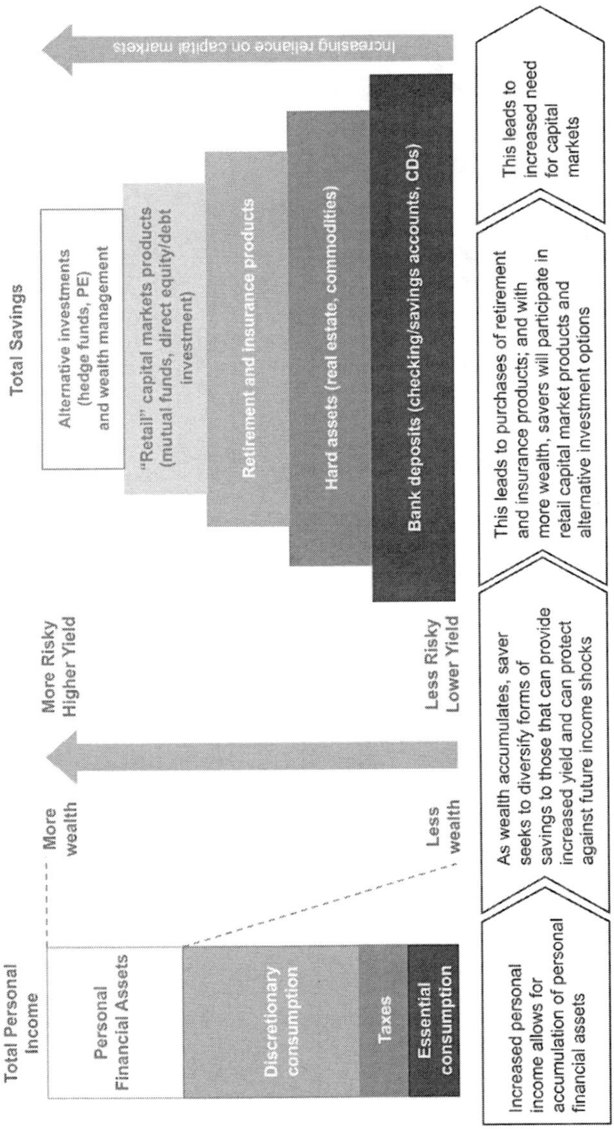

Figure 1.1: Illustrative evolution of capital savings and investment
Source: World Economic Forum

Therefore, we observe larger mutual funds in developed countries compared to developing ones in terms of the AuM/GDP ratio – as shown in Figure 1.2 for some selected countries.[1]

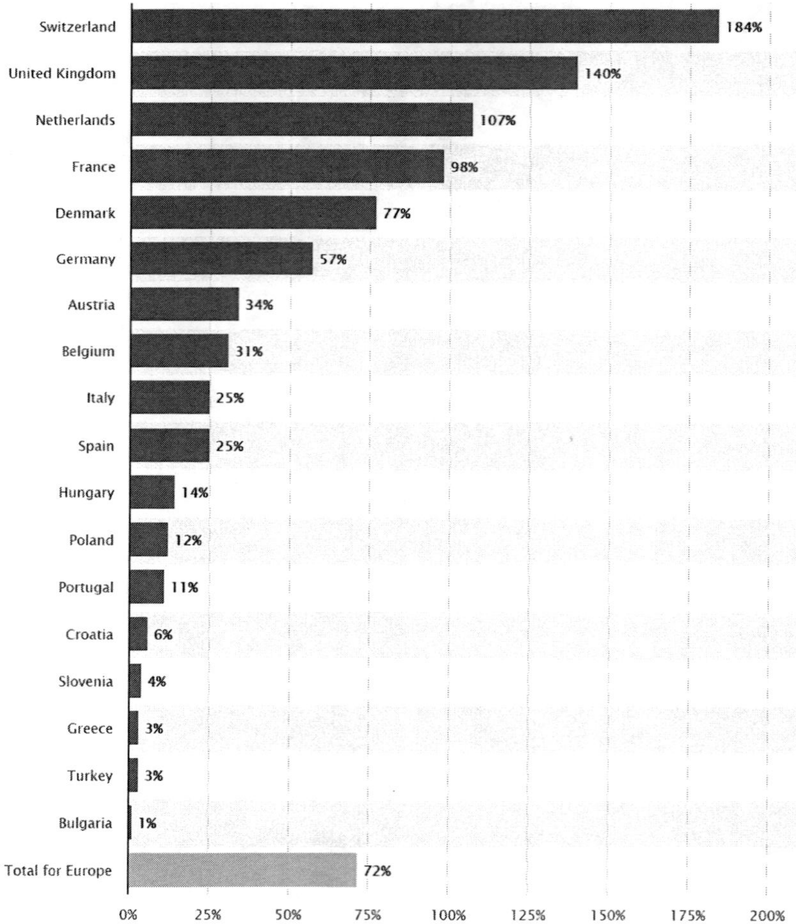

Figure 1.2: Ratio of mutual funds' size to GDP in selected countries (end of 2018)
Source: www.Statista.com

1 Amount of Funds Assets in Selected Countries of the World. 2020. https://www.statista.com/statistics/270289/amount-of-fund-assets-in-selected-countries-of-the-world/

The size of the mutual funds industry is also a function of the size of the economy and thence we observe large mutual funds in large economies of the world such as China, Brazil, and South Korea as well as in developed countries.[2] The size of pension funds is also an important component of asset management. Pension assets exceeded USD 50 trillion worldwide for the first time at the end of 2019 according to the latest report by the OECD.[3]

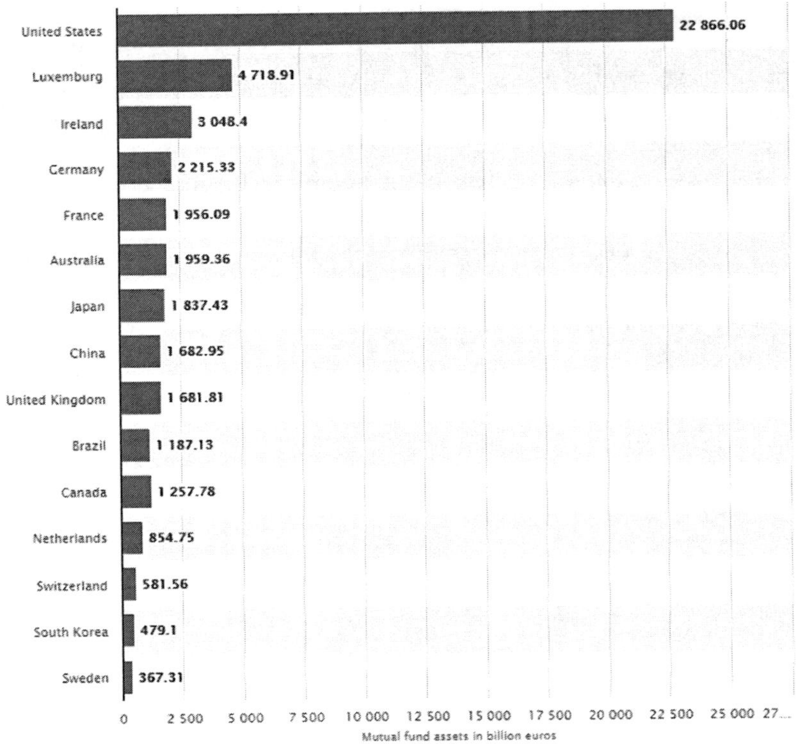

Figure 1.3: Mutual funds' size in selected countries worldwide in 2019 (billionEUR). Amount of fund assets in selected countries of the world. 2020. https://www.statista.com/statistics/270289/amount-of-fund-assets-in-selected-countries-of-the-world/ data released February 2020.
Source: www.Statista.com

2 Investment Fund Assets to GDP Ratio by Country. 2020. https://www.statista.com/statistics/368648/europe-investment-funds-assets-to-gdp-ratio-by-country/ data released November 2020..

3 Pension Markets in Focus, OECD. 2020. https://www.oecd.org/pensions/pensionmarketsinfocus.htm.

There are three dimensions to evaluate asset management's contribution to economies.

(i) Its performance relative to the market average,
(ii) Gross value added to economic growth via employment, taxes, and profits generated by the sector, and
(iii) Its role in channeling new capital to public and private companies, i.e., savings-investment channel.

The first step is that the industry should provide better performance than the market average for investors to entrust their savings into the professional hands. In this book, we shall analyze whether it does vis-à-vis the Turkish economy.

In the second dimension the gross economic value added by the asset management industry to the economic growth is calculated as the share of the industry's total value created in terms of employment (total salary payments), taxes, and profits to the GDP. Figure 1.4 depicts the industry's contribution to the Turkish economy for the years between 2013–2019.

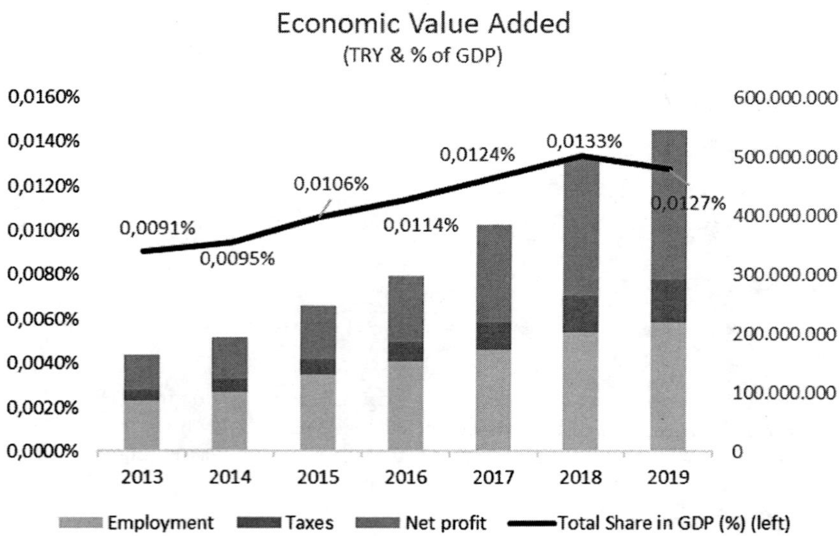

Figure 1.4: Economic value added by the asset management industry
Source: Authors' drawing based on data from Gösterge, the quarterly bulletin of the TCMA

As observed in Figure 1.4, the contribution to GDP is around 0,01 % in Turkey. The very same figure is 0,35 % in the European economy in total in 2014; and it is estimated to be closer to 1 % in the United Kingdom due to the country's international nature as an asset management services center (Oxera 2016, p. 7). It is obvious that the Turkish asset management's contribution to GDP is far behind (35 times less than) that of the European average. As a highly sophisticated services sector, asset management (i) employs very qualified work force (hence a high value added in terms of total salaries paid to number of personnel employed), (ii) cannot get involved in unregistered economy in any way, i.e., wholly taxed for its operations, and (iii) yields a high EBITDA margin in normal conditions, i.e., if operates within the internationally accepted set-up (the fee structures and all), all of which lead us to this conclusion: *the larger the asset management industry, even the more its contribution to the GDP.*

The third dimension, i.e., its role in channeling new capital to public and private companies, as a savings-investment channel refers to its financial intermediation role as illustrated in Figure 1.5. Asset management is one of the two main channels that provide new capital to public and private companies. This makes the industry an important intermediary in the financial system. It is a source of growth within the economy as well as a source of returns to millions of savers, pensioners, and investors.

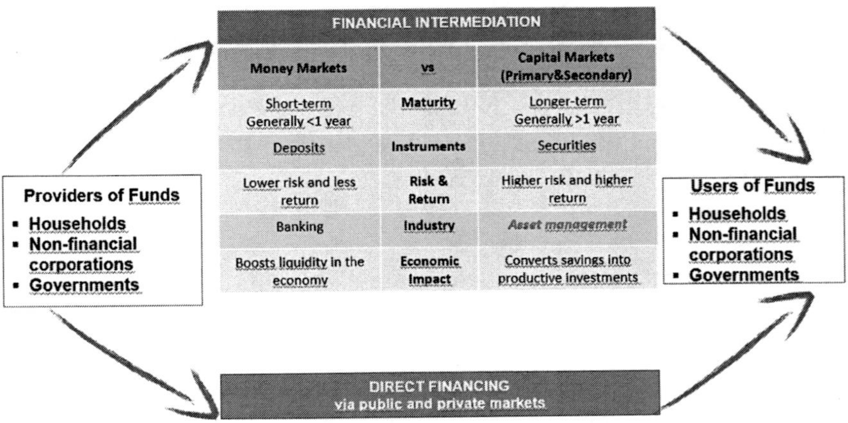

Figure 1.5: Asset management's role within the financial system
Source: Authors' drawing inspired by various text books

The other main financial intermediation industry is banking. As illustrated in Figure 1.5, banking and asset management industries complement each other: while the former mainly provides liquidity to the economy via credit channels to households and corporations, the latter mainly provides longer term capital to corporations and governments, and hence converts savings into productive investments – which further helps grow the economy.

Banking and asset management are almost the same size globally as depicted in the below statistics[4] (Figure 1.6) (Most of the "other financial intermediaries" and "pension funds" are included in the asset management). Furthermore, two trends are noteworthy: the increasing share of central banks (due to quantitative easing after 2008 global financial crisis) and asset management within the global financial institutions. Following the 2008 global financial crisis, the global banking industry was hit by stricter regulation and substantial fines, and was losing influence, so they made fund management a priority area within their businesses. "Asset management has moved center stage for banks," said vice-president of investor services at Moody's and the chief economist of the Bank of England confirmed by saying "*The age of asset management is upon us*" in a Financial Times article in 2015.[5]

As it is detailed in the following Section 1.2: An overview of asset management industry in Turkey below, unlike the global landscape (which is mainly painted by the developed countries), the asset management industry in Turkey is much smaller than the banking system: the total assets under management ("AuM") is 284 billion TL[6] while the banking asset size is 4,491 billion TL[7] as of end of 2019, i.e., the asset management is one sixteenth of the banking industry in Turkey.

4 Global Financial Institutions' Assets. 2020. https://www.statista.com/statistics/421221/global-financial-institutions-assets-by-institution-type/ statistics released December 2020.

5 Marriage, Madison. Banks Embrace "the Age of Asset Management", Financial Times. 2015. https://www.ft.com/content/40c39d3e-9440-11e5-b190-291e94b77c8f.

6 *SPK Monthly Statistics*, April 2020.

7 *BDDK News Bulletin*, April 2020.

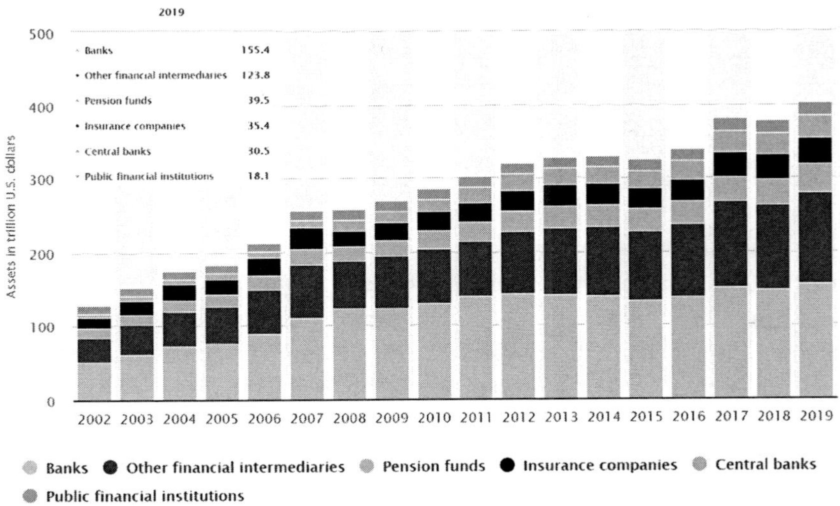

Figure 1.6: Total assets of financial institutions worldwide by institution type
Source: www.Statista.com

1.2 An overview of the asset management industry in Turkey

Asset management is a relatively newly flourishing industry in Turkey. Capital markets regulations substantially changed between 2012 and 2015 thanks to the harmonization process of primary and secondary legislations of Turkey with those of the European Union ("EU") as part of Turkey's quest for accession to the EU. A new Capital Markets Law (No: 6062) was enacted on 30.12.2012 followed by a series of secondary legislation during the next three years. The critical results for asset management have been the following:

(i) Introduction of TEFAS, the Turkish Electronic Funds Trading Platform (2015),
(ii) Segregation of buy-side and sell-side institutions in the market (2015),
(iii) Licensing requirements for employment in asset management (2014),
(iv) New regulations allowing the creation of alternative investment funds (2014).

Though not directly relevant to the abovementioned harmonization process

(v) Inauguration of state support for private pensions (2013), and
(vi) Commencement of auto-enrolment in company retirement plans (2017)

also contributed a lot to the growth of the industry.

Before the segregation of buy- and sell-sides in the capital markets in 2015, besides the asset management companies, banks and brokerage houses could also establish, manage and sell investment funds – in fact, banks were the largest of investment funds providers in the market. There was a conflict of interest in place both for banks and brokerage houses managing investment funds. Banking business is in direct competition with fund management via its deposits for fund providers and via its loans for fund users. Brokerage business is in direct conflict via its intermediation function (i) in issuing securities which, in turn, will be purchased by fund portfolios as well as (ii) in trading securities, i.e., the more trade, the more revenues for the brokerage house, but the more cost to the funds. After the enforcement of the regulation, banks and brokerage houses mostly transferred their investment funds to their affiliated asset managers. The funds with the same investment strategies were merged and the market consolidated.

The introduction of TEFAS allowed investors to gain access to all investment funds in the market through their investment accounts at any bank. This was a revolutionary practice which provided the comparably much smaller independent[8] asset managers to market their funds to all investors without any extra cost. These regulatory developments helped grow the asset management industry both in terms of number of asset managers (from 35 to 50s) and AuM (from 50 billion TL to 284 billion TL) – as shown in Figure 1.7.

The above-stated amendments in the private pension system have been a big catalyst in the growth of the industry. Figure 1.8 illustrates that the pension funds, starting from 2013, stimulated the growth of the industry: the share percentage of pension funds started to increase from a level of 30 % to more than 50 % in just six years following the inauguration of the state support in 2013.

8 Independent asset managers are those without any affiliation to a banking group in Turkey. There are a total of 51 asset managers of which 14 are bank-affiliated as of 30 April 2020. However, these 14 asset managers manage 91 % of the total AuM.

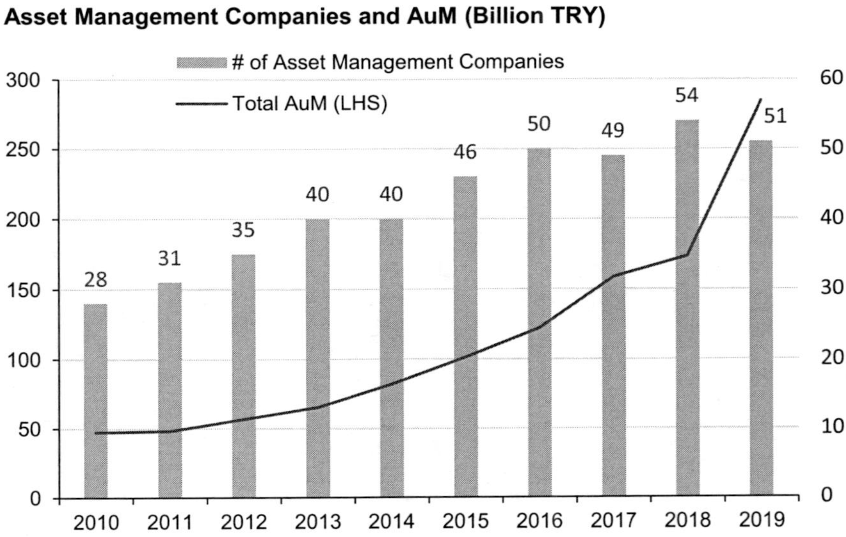

Figure 1.7: Asset Management Industry Development
Source: CMB

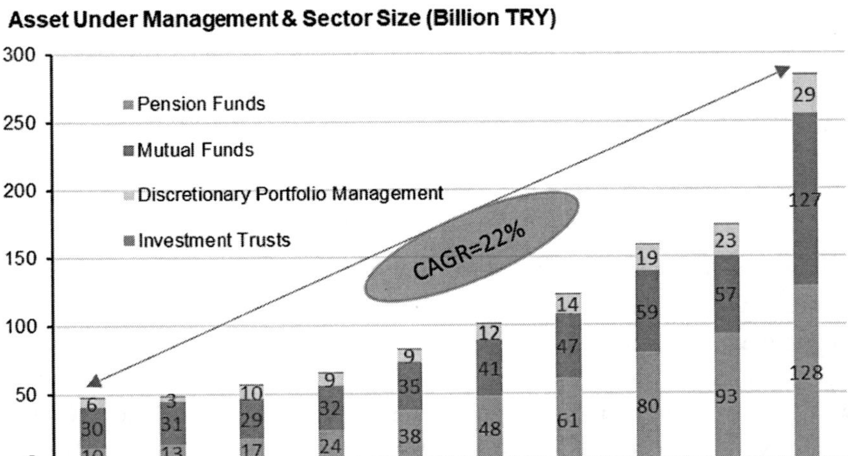

Figure 1.8: Asset Management Growth by Portfolio Type
Source: CMB

In 2019, as observed in Figure 1.9, investment funds increased substantially and levelled out with pension funds.

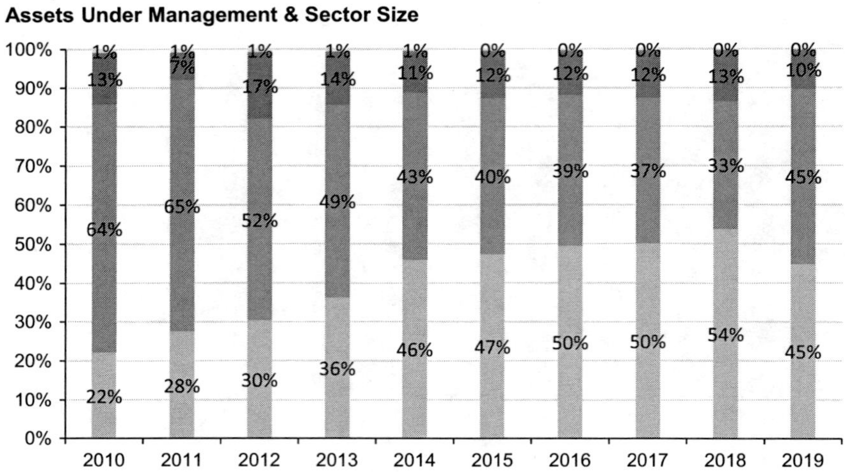

Figure 1.9: Change of Portfolio Composition in the Sector
Source: CMB

Turkey's savings and capital accumulation is insufficient to grow its economy. Hence it requires a substantial amount of foreign capital which renders it susceptible to economic crises both in terms of debt crises as experienced in years 1958, 1970, 2000 (Bilici 2016) and currency crises as experienced in years 1994, 1998–1999, 2001, 2008–2009, and very recently in 2018–2020 (Boratav 2019). Commingling small savings via fund management is an effective policy to overcome the insufficient savings problem. The creation of private pension system (private pension funds) has been remarkably successful in Turkey. Besides growing the savings pool, it is also of significant importance to achieve sustainability and efficiency of the sector. When the fund management industry generates acceptable, i.e., above-market returns in a sustainable manner, then investors continue to grow the pool and will be willing to pay higher fees to the portfolio managers. This will in return create longer term and cost-efficient (with less cost of intermediation) domestic financial resources for the economy to help it grow. As is the case in London, Dublin, and Luxembourg being international fund management centers, the asset management industry may attract foreign capital to be managed in Turkey and be channeled into the Turkish economy's growth.

As we deem generating acceptable, sustainable returns is the initial step to the desired growth of the asset management industry and hence its contribution to economy, we, hereby, in this book analyze whether the industry generates such returns. This is an empirical study covering the last 10 years of Turkish fund management industry including both mutual and pension funds.

2. Data and methodology

2.1 The big picture

Asset management business comprises three main management services: (1) Fund management, (2) Discretionary portfolio management ("DPM"), and (3) Management of investment trusts. Figure 2.1 illustrates the asset management industry breakdown in Turkey by product types. As observed, 90 % of the asset management business is comprised of fund management services including pension funds (47 %) and mutual funds (35 %) management.

The illustration in Figure 2.1 provides the latest available assets-under-management ("AuM") data.

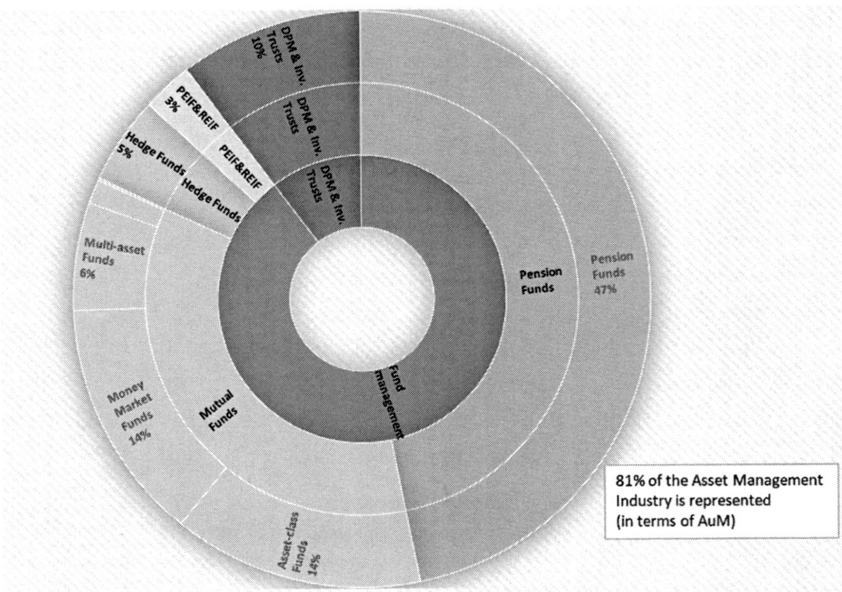

Figure 2.1: Asset management industry breakdown by management services
Source: CMB and TCMA

For the purposes of this analysis, only the fund categories depicted in red are included which, in total, cover 81 % of the asset management industry, and 90 % of the fund management industry which might be considered a sub-category of asset management – as of the end of 2019. The coverage rate would even be higher for earlier years, because the sizes of the excluded categories were much smaller back then.

2.2 Performance analysis methodology in fund management

Performance measurement is quite a well-studied aspect of asset management in financial economics literature. There are two main approaches to performance measurement: (1) single-factor performance measures (or single-index models), and (2) multi-index models. Single-index models evaluate the performance based on a risk factor only. Detailed information about the development and usage of the single-index models is given below as it is our choice of model in our analysis. The latter, as the name suggests, takes two or more factors into account in order to analyze and explain the performance of funds. A well-known one is Fama-French three-factor model, which, built on the CAPM, focuses on the market risk factor by incorporating size and value factors (Fama & French 1992). Another one is Carhart four-factor model, in which the momentum factor is added to the Fama-French three-factor model (Carhart 1997). Then the Nobel laureates Eugene Fama and Kenneth French have developed a five-factor model by adding profitability and investment factors (Fama & French 2015) to their original three-factor model.

Although "the academic profession has moved beyond evaluating performance on the basis of a single measure for risk, the investment community, however, has not" (Elton & Gruber, 2020, p. 2). Also, as Elton & Gruber (2020, p. 2) reveal in their comprehensive literature review:

> *"Although most authors agree that more than one measure of risk is necessary to capture management performance, several argue that performance relative to the single-index model best captures investor behavior. Barber, Huang, and Odean (2016) and* ***Berk and van Binsbergen (2015)*** *showed that the single-index model based on the market portfolio explains investor decisions better than the multi-factor models. Berk and van Binsbergen claimed that this finding is proof that the CAPM is the best model for estimating fund performance. Cremers, Fulkerson, and Riley (2020) provided some support for the use of the prospectus benchmark*

because investors tend to use that benchmark when making investment decisions, even when the benchmark is a poor fit to what the fund is doing."

Hence, we preferred to use single-factor performance measures in our analysis.

The studies of single-index models date back to the 1960s pioneered by Jack L. Treynor (1965), William F. Sharpe (1966), and Michael C. Jensen (1968, 1969). Following the development of the modern portfolio theory in the 1950s which asserts that risk is an inherent part of higher return, these pioneers have established the quantitative link between risk and return (Elton et al. 2010). The Capital Asset Pricing Model ("CAPM") forms the basis for risk-adjusted return analysis, and they are in the form of risk-adjusted ratios (e.g., the Sharpe ratio, Information ratio) or differential returns[9] compared to benchmarks (e.g., Jensen's alpha) (Le Sourd 2007).

Le Sourd (2007) classifies the risk-adjusted single-index models into three broad categories:

(i) Absolute risk-adjusted performance measures (e.g., the Sharpe ratio, the Treynor ratio, Measure based on VaR),
(ii) Relative risk-adjusted performance measures (e.g., Information ratio, Jensen's alpha, Modigliani and Modigliani (or simply M^2) ratio, Market risk-adjusted performance, Style risk-adjusted performance, M3 (risk-adjusted performance measure in multi-management), SHARAD (Style, History and Risk-Adjusted), AP Index, Graham-Harvey measures, Efficiency ratio),
(iii) Measures based on downside risk and higher moments (e.g., Sortino ratio, Actuarial approach, Fouse index, Upside potential ratio, Omega measure).

We perform our analysis utilizing two common measures of each category above.

9 "Differential return," "excess return," "residual return," "abnormal rate of return" or "active return" are terms often used interchangeably in various sources to address the rate of return which is above the benchmark rate of return (which may be the market rate of return, the risk-free rate of return, or any other rate of return that is deemed appropriate to compare against). In asset management, "alpha" (the Greek letter α) represents all these definitions.

2.2.1 Absolute risk-adjusted performance measures

Absolute risk-adjusted performance measures evaluate portfolio returns without any reference to a benchmark. The risk-free rate of return is the only reference against which the portfolio's return is evaluated. In other words, excess return is calculated as the difference between the portfolio return and the risk-free rate of return. Then risk adjustment is made via dividing the excess return either by the standard deviation of the portfolio returns (as in the Sharpe ratio) or by the beta of the portfolio returns (as in the Treynor ratio). We selected the most used ones, i.e., the Sharpe and Treynor ratios.

The Sharpe ratio was initially called the reward-to-variability ratio (Sharpe 1966). Then the creator of the ratio, W. Sharpe opted to use the standard deviation of the *excess returns* instead of the *portfolio returns* as the risk measure in a later article he wrote about 30 years later in 1994 titled *The Sharpe Ratio*. This ratio measures the return of a portfolio in excess of the risk-free rate (what is often called the *risk premium*) compared to the risk in terms of volatility of excess returns (Sharpe 1994).

The Treynor ratio compares the risk premium to the portfolio's systematic risk (i.e., its beta) instead of its total risk (measured by the standard deviation).

2.2.2 Relative risk-adjusted performance measures

Relative risk-adjusted performance measures evaluate portfolio returns in reference to a benchmark. We selected the most used ones, i.e., the Information ratio and Jensen's alpha.

Information ratio, which is sometimes called the appraisal ratio, compares the residual (or excess) return (i.e., the difference between the portfolio returns and its benchmark's returns) to the residual risk (i.e., the standard deviation of the excess returns); in other words, by dividing the residual return to the residual risk.

Jensen's alpha is defined as the differential between the return on the portfolio in excess of the risk-free rate and the return explained by the market model (Jensen 1968). In other words, the benchmark used in Jensen's alpha is the rate of return calculated by the CAPM given the portfolio's market.

2.2.3 Measures based on downside risk and higher moments

Risk is calculated as the total volatility of returns around the mean return. A higher return than the mean return, i.e., a positive return, is also a part of the total volatility; and when the total volatility is used to measure the risk-adjusted return of a portfolio, then these positive returns are also penalized.

While the measures such as Sharpe and the Information ratios consider risk as the total volatility around the mean return, i.e., without any distinction to positive or negative returns, being a measure based on downside risk, Sortino ratio makes this distinction by utilizing the concept of semi-variance in the analysis (Sortino & van der Meer 1991). In Sortino ratio, the excess return is divided by the standard deviation of the negative returns only, and the portfolio is not penalized due to the volatility generating positive excess returns.

Another measure which is also related with downside risk, namely Omega ratio, considers not only the first two moments, i.e., mean and variance, of a distribution of returns, but also higher moments such as skewness and kurtosis. It is defined as the probability weighted ratio of gains versus losses for some thresholds return target (Keating &Shadwick 2002).

The prominent value added of the FMI would be providing the investors with a higher net[10] return than the investors themselves could generate on their own. As it is stated in Le Sourd (2007, p. 5), "*Portfolio alpha is at the core of portfolio managers' concerns.*" Hence the main analysis is whether MF and PF in Turkey sustainably achieve higher performance (i.e., create alpha). We ran an analysis of fund category performance vs the defined category benchmark and the risk-free rate of return in pursuit of the answer. We performed (i) annual, (ii) three-yearly, (iii) five-yearly, and (iv) decade-long analyses between January 1st, 2010 and December 31st, 2019, i.e., analyzing a period of ten years.

As the contemporary performance measurement standards stipulate, the analysis is based on risk-adjusted returns. We utilized commonly referred risk-adjusted performance measures, i.e., (i) the Sharpe ratio, (ii) the

10 Net return is the return net of fund management fees and expenses which are already reflected in the fund unit prices. Investors receive the *net* return, hence the choice of net returns in the analysis.

information ratio, (iii) the Treynor ratio, (iv) Jensen's alpha, (v) Sortino ratio and even a not-so-common one called (vi) Omega ratio within the analysis.

2.3 Data

All the data are obtained right from their original sources, i.e., from the regulatory authorities and exchanges where the data is created and stored as explained below for each data. We identified 8 mutual fund categories and 13 pension fund categories.

2.3.1 Returns data

The fund returns data are calculated based on the daily fund prices obtained from Takas İstanbul,[11] the settlement and custody bank. Takas İstanbul is the central settlement and clearing institution for investment and pension funds, and hence stores all the fund prices, i.e., returns data. The daily fund prices of all funds between 02.01.2010 to 31.12.2019 are obtained. We preferred to use the weekly returns as an optimum compared to

- the daily returns which would contain much noise, and
- the monthly returns which may miss some information.

The weekly returns would dampen the noise and contain the most relevant information required for our performance analysis. Weekly returns of the funds are calculated as follows:

$$\text{Fund Return} = r_i = \frac{P_t - P_{t-7}}{P_{t-7}} \tag{2.1}$$

where

r_i = Weekly return of fund i
P_t = Price of the fund at the tth day
P_{t-7} = Price of the fund 7 days before the tth day

11 Takas İstanbul is short for İstanbul Settlement and Custody Bank Inc., part of Borsa İstanbul Group. Takas İstanbul provides clearing, settlement, and custody services within the framework of capital market and related exchange regulations.

A week is defined as a calendar week, i.e., Monday to Monday. Normally the prices announced on Mondays are Friday's closing prices. If the relevant Monday is a holiday, then Tuesday's prices are used. If the relevant Friday is a holiday, then the price announced on Monday would be Thursday's closing price. Once the single fund returns are calculated, we then calculate two different fund category returns: (i) equally weighted fund category returns, and (ii) AuM-weighted fund category returns.

Equally weighted returns are calculated as the arithmetic average of weekly returns of funds within a category. The fund sizes do not affect the aggregate return of the fund category. Equally weighted weekly returns are calculated as follows:

$$\text{Equally weighted return} = \sum_{i}^{n} \frac{r_i}{n} \tag{2.2}$$

where

r_i = Weekly return of fund i

n = Number of funds within category

AuM-weighted returns are calculated by multiplying the weekly returns of funds with their weekly average AuMs and then dividing it by the total weekly average AuMs of all funds within that fund category. The weekly average AuM of each fund is calculated simply by summing up the daily AuMs and diving them with 7 (in case of missing days in a week due to holidays, then the number of days within that short week). Hence the fund sizes affect the aggregate return of the fund category. In other words, the fund category's return performance reflects more of the big size (high AuM) funds in this analysis.

$$\text{AuM weighted return} = \sum_{i}^{n} \frac{r_i * v_i}{\sum_{i}^{n} v_i} \tag{2.3}$$

where

r_i = Weekly return of fund i

n = Number of funds within category

v_i = Weekly average AuM (value) of fund i

In our analysis, we are interested in the return the investors receive in a mutual or pension fund which is after the management fees are deducted, i.e., already reflected in the fund prices, hence the returns. Therefore, we need not sterilize the fund returns from the management fees.

We re-classified the funds in some specific categories in line with the international terminology – slightly different than the regulatory classification. Tables 2.2 and 2.3 show the process of reclassification. The red rows are omitted, and the same-color rows are combined. The categorization is merely a plausible grouping of different investment strategies. We ended up with 8 mutual and 13 pension fund categories. A total of 279 different mutual and 277 different pension funds are covered within the analysis in the 10-year period between 2010–2019. Table 2.1 illustrates that majority of returns data fall in Region III, which is the "low risk, low return" field in the diagram. The second concentration area is Region II, which is the "low risk, high return" field in the diagram.

Table 2.1: Percentage heatmap of weekly return scatter diagrams

(%)	Equally Weighted Returns					AuM-Weighted Returns			
Region	I	II	III	IV		I	II	III	IV
Mutual Funds									
Gold Fund	23	25	36	16		23	25	36	16
Fixed Income Fund	13	36	33	18		18	32	32	18
Equity Fund	16	38	23	23		16	38	24	22
Multi Asset Fund	16	38	24	22		15	39	24	22
Participation Fund	15	36	33	16		20	33	30	17
Short-term Fixed Income Fund	22	21	44	13		27	11	57	5
Short-term Lease Certificates Fund	39	4	51	6		40	3	50	7
Money Market Fund	29	11	55	5		31	12	54	3
Pension Funds									
Gold Funds	21	26	36	17		22	25	36	17
Initiation Funds	31	8	51	10		31	9	50	10
Initiation Participation Funds	36	5	51	8		36	5	51	8
Fixed Income Funds	16	32	31	21		18	32	29	21
Government Contribution Funds	14	35	33	18		14	35	33	18
Equity Funds	17	37	24	22		16	37	23	24
Government Bonds Funds	15	34	32	19		16	33	30	21
FC Denominated Government Bonds Funds	18	28	38	16		18	30	35	17
Government Contribution Participation Funds	18	30	36	16		17	29	39	15
Standard Participation Funds	16	31	35	18		18	34	28	20
Private Sector Fixed Income Funds	21	32	35	12		17	39	29	15
Money Market Funds	28	8	60	4		28	7	61	4
Standard Funds	19	31	28	22		18	31	29	22

Source: Authors' calculations based on CMB data

Table 2.2: Reclassification of fund categories and refinement for category analysis for mutual funds

Years	2010		2011		2012		2013		2014		2015		2016		2017		2018		2019	
Regulatory List of All Fund Categories	#	AuM (TL)	#	AuM (TL)	#	AuM (TL)	#	AuM (TL)	#	AuM (TL)	#	AuM (TL)	#	AuM (TL)	#	AuM (TL)	#	AuM (TL)	#	AuM (TL)
Gold Fund	7	26,62,00,833	9	83,95,27,493	11	94,99,05,489	11	58,81,20,490	11	39,33,94,843	12	28,70,83,737	12	28,03,22,498	12	38,45,45,421	11	49,55,33,481	13	88,34,25,716
Gold and Other Precious Metals Fund	2	78,53,623	2	1,20,93,932	1	26,24,026	0	0	0	0	0	0	0	0	0	0	1	13,03,196	0	0
Debt Securities Fund	31	2,19,16,66,686	36	1,62,16,04,145	52	1,61,04,73,055	56	2,54,73,80,832	58	2,96,78,42,309	61	3,97,35,94,149	61	4,23,23,12,192	58	4,26,92,69,926	53	3,86,28,71,893	36	3,53,59,64,467
Equity Fund	41	57,71,88,492	44	92,72,96,873	54	79,18,96,068	57	1,14,52,13,538	61	1,06,27,07,894	66	1,15,60,15,208	68	1,21,18,29,984	67	1,54,59,77,899	66	1,73,01,60,574	49	1,42,25,46,949
Index Fund	3	1,72,19,058	3	1,02,64,406	3	1,00,88,223	3	1,12,37,222	3	58,61,743	3	58,71,368	1	0	1	0	1	0	0	0
Equity Concentrated Fund	7	98,09,006	6	99,74,541	4	12,57,877	2	7,63,378	2	8,77,243	2	7,68,708	1	0	1	1,09,648	2	11,84,958	4	14,26,61,722
Multi Asset Fund	8	24,58,33,152	8	29,15,65,591	9	33,58,09,289	9	41,05,17,217	9	40,91,16,146	8	43,48,54,263	7	43,77,74,068	6	49,51,62,193	6	52,23,65,713	6	50,44,08,343
Participation Fund	4	7,83,96,450	7	16,46,45,980	7	14,19,17,179	10	14,26,09,817	11	7,65,62,885	15	6,59,08,588	19	8,70,42,534	20	13,95,40,031	20	31,84,61,531	14	52,67,59,433
Short-term Debt Securities Fund	3	2,22,06,672	11	1,61,04,12,520	21	7,92,95,12,871	23	10,004,725,123	23	12,079,921,234	24	13,533,791,523	23	15,551,215,411	24	17,112,441,722	26	15,953,863,516	25	14,219,505,676
Short-term Bond and Debentures Fund	3	5,17,65,105	4	4,74,66,626	4	3,11,87,666	4	3,42,59,494	4	3,39,83,217	3	2,61,42,317	1	0	0	0	0	0	0	0
Lease Certificates Fund	0	0	0	0	0	0	0	0	0	0	0	0	0	0	0	0	1	6,86,259	0	0
Short-term Lease Certificates Fund	0	0	0	0	0	0	0	0	0	0	0	0	0	0	4	17,82,19,456	6	54,50,03,973	8	2,55,41,40,271
Liquid Fund	28	9,13,11,94,150	22	7,94,49,95,877	14	2,63,68,01,457	14	2,33,44,05,291	12	8,73,47,234	9	2,19,88,499	2	5,11,227	1	0	1	0	0	0
Money Market Fund	4	7,05,41,37,435	10	8,32,66,68,718	22	11,859,070,068	24	11,011,797,171	24	11,693,553,947	26	13,505,100,865	26	12,494,355,596	25	13,344,015,25	26	14,239,040,525	25	31,927,801,454
Bond and Debenture Fund	13	10,58,86,458	11	6,62,52,696	8	4,08,23,036	6	3,46,15,027	5	2,42,99,469	5	2,15,03,089	1	0	0	0	0	0	0	0
Capital Guaranteed Fund	25	11,32,43,967	41	22,66,85,286	35	7,50,57,192	35	1,84,46,830	20	1,15,01,179	20	13,33,952	0	0	0	0	0	0	0	0
Variable Fund	108	2,51,66,32,886	117	2,32,34,04,434	120	1,82,00,54,330	126	3,16,48,76,301	125	2,36,03,48,329	124	3,35,94,37,207	103	3,31,28,30,960	90	4,20,83,80,068	92	5,18,78,98,263	60	5,14,62,71,398
Private Fund	8	1,68,79,473	7	2,04,73,472	3	14,30,662	3	14,07,267	1	0	1	0	1	0	1	0	1	0	0	0
Hedge Fund	8	15,42,81,650	22	17,19,75,152	24	16,51,61,127	34	26,08,44,629	39	32,44,35,072	54	65,64,06,800	80	1,09,93,48,738	100	1,88,84,17,451	155	3,12,49,39,055	223	15,216,449,286
Fund of Funds	5	1,77,78,058	6	1,49,32,585	6	1,31,88,045	8	2,07,16,153	8	3,89,03,680	11	15,40,91,104	16	27,38,58,430	17	1,01,88,80,134	19	1,73,35,59,857	17	1,84,34,52,955
Capital Protective Fund	127	68,50,90,109	213	1,14,38,44,001	249	65,38,89,660	195	17,26,15,523	78	5,78,86,826	39	3,41,43,492	31	5,42,15,753	25	5,07,82,010	12	9,50,05,671	0	0
Foreign Securities Fund	3	1,02,03,845	4	1,79,05,338	3	1,50,77,334	2	1,42,04,476	1	86,80,040	1	78,33,895	1	25,49,408	0	0	0	0	60	5,14,62,71,398
FX Denominated Fixed Income Fund	10	3,07,61,385	9	4,52,75,242	10	5,15,22,916	11	11,51,03,853	11	14,58,49,363	0	0	0	0	0	0	0	0	14	2,46,51,51,796
FX Denominated Equity Fund	3	7,55,08,466	7	13,27,54,406	8	7,45,28,521	8	10,58,32,374	8	12,31,57,697	0	0	0	0	0	0	0	0	8	98,02,53,517
FX Denominated Participation Fund	0	0	0	0	0	0	1	0	1	8,28,324	0	0	0	0	0	0	0	0	6	6,10,78,129
Total	**451**	**23,379,737,459**	**599**	**25,970,019,313**	**668**	**29,211,276,092**	**642**	**32,139,692,008**	**515**	**31,907,058,63**	**484**	**37,245,868,765**	**454**	**39,038,166,799**	**452**	**44,635,741,185**	**499**	**47,811,878,465**	**568**	**86,576,142,511**

Omitted Funds (#, TL)	**297**	**3,62,03,80,338**	**426**	**4,09,72,49,915**	**458**	**2,86,99,09,788**	**423**	**3,87,40,47,406**	**292**	**3,07,15,90,510**	**250**	**4,21,32,46,449**	**232**	**4,74,28,03,288**	**233**	**7,16,64,59,664**	**279**	**10,141,402,845**	**388**	**30,858,928,480**
Omitted Funds %	**66%**	**15%**	**71%**	**16%**	**69%**	**10%**	**66%**	**12%**	**57%**	**10%**	**52%**	**11%**	**51%**	**12%**	**52%**	**16%**	**56%**	**21%**	**68%**	**36%**

Fund Categories Subject to Analysis

Gold Fund	9	27,40,54,456	11	85,16,21,425	12	95,25,29,515	11	58,81,20,490	11	39,33,94,843	12	28,70,83,737	12	28,03,22,498	12	38,45,45,421	12	49,68,36,677	13	88,34,25,716
Fixed Income Fund	44	2,29,75,53,144	47	1,68,78,56,840	60	1,65,12,96,091	62	2,58,19,95,860	63	2,99,21,41,777	66	3,99,50,97,238	62	4,23,23,12,192	58	4,26,92,69,926	53	3,86,28,71,893	36	3,53,59,64,467
Equity Fund	51	60,42,16,557	53	94,75,35,820	61	80,32,42,168	62	1,15,72,14,138	66	1,06,94,46,880	71	1,16,26,55,284	70	1,21,18,29,984	69	1,54,60,87,547	69	1,73,13,45,532	53	1,56,52,08,670
Multi Asset Fund	8	24,58,33,152	8	29,15,65,591	9	33,58,09,289	9	41,05,17,217	9	40,91,16,146	8	43,48,54,263	7	43,77,74,068	6	49,51,62,193	6	52,23,65,713	6	50,44,08,343
Participation Fund	4	7,83,96,450	7	16,46,45,980	7	14,19,17,179	10	14,26,09,817	11	7,65,62,885	15	6,59,08,588	19	8,70,42,534	20	13,95,40,031	21	31,91,47,790	14	52,67,59,433
Short-term Fixed Income Fund	6	7,39,71,778	15	1,65,78,79,146	25	7,96,07,00,537	27	10,038,984,617	27	12,113,904,451	27	13,559,933,840	24	15,551,215,411	24	17,112,441,722	26	15,953,863,516	25	14,219,505,676
Short-term Lease Certificates Fund	0	0	0	0	0	0	0	0	0	0	0	0	0	0	4	17,82,19,456	6	54,50,03,973	8	2,55,41,40,271
Money Market Fund	32	16,185,331,585	32	16,271,664,595	36	14,495,871,525	38	13,346,202,461	36	11,780,901,181	35	13,527,089,365	28	12,494,866,823	26	13,344,01,225	27	14,239,040,525	25	31,927,801,454
Total	**154**	**19,759,357,121**	**173**	**21,872,769,398**	**210**	**26,341,366,305**	**219**	**28,265,644,602**	**223**	**28,835,468,163**	**234**	**33,032,622,316**	**222**	**34,295,363,511**	**219**	**37,469,281,522**	**220**	**37,670,475,620**	**180**	**55,717,214,032**

Source: CMB

Table 2.3: Reclassification of fund categories and refinement for category analysis for pension funds

Years	2010		2011		2012		2013		2014		2015		2016		2017		2018		2019	
Regulatory List of All Fund Categories	#	AuM (TL)	#	AuM (TL)	#	AuM (TL)	#	AuM (TL)	#	AuM (TL)	#	AuM (TL)	#	AuM (TL)	#	AuM (TL)	#	AuM (TL)	#	AuM (TL)
Gold Fund	0	0	0	0	0	0	11	3,50,98,905	12	18,82,17,780	11	42,52,49,631	11	89,34,60,560	13	2,31,57,05,179	13	5,17,17,51,388	16	11,51,86,98,024
Initiation Fund	0	0	0	0	0	0	0	0	0	0	0	0	8	0	14	27,34,72,469	14	47,24,74,899	14	42,74,56,489
Initiation Participation Fund	0	0	0	0	0	0	0	0	0	0	0	0	10	0	16	44,75,96,899	16	76,15,62,229	17	65,50,28,291
Fixed Income Fund	14	4,08,58,32,515	15	4,78,94,03,177	17	7,11,74,10,454	17	8,52,18,79,323	17	9,45,42,90,219	17	10,90,28,01,290	17	11,45,67,45,588	17	11,82,07,14,224	23	14,98,58,68,904	22	11,62,41,11,836
Government Contribution Fund	0	0	0	0	0	0	18	60,31,21,475	18	1,92,27,97,556	18	3,74,63,86,708	18	5,95,55,08,153	18	8,34,38,89,899	17	9,75,47,69,935	17	12,58,93,85,028
Index Fund	1	1,05,41,509	3	1,14,19,727	3	1,79,23,738	3	4,33,77,015	3	5,88,40,667	3	13,47,28,345	3	30,70,45,169	3	47,97,39,204	3	54,24,76,540	0	0
Equity Fund	16	48,24,51,046	20	77,71,70,665	24	1,16,97,41,557	25	1,74,11,18,193	26	2,14,53,82,840	26	2,63,73,29,636	26	3,17,25,38,932	26	3,85,52,50,158	28	4,42,08,70,729	33	4,66,71,90,024
Equity Concentrated Fund	3	10,30,88,435	3	16,53,03,465	0	0	0	0	0	0	0	0	0	0	0	0	0	0	0	0
Government Debantures Fund	12	1,24,13,97,449	13	1,47,26,75,738	9	87,65,24,841	10	1,27,99,04,890	10	1,50,46,47,368	10	1,79,85,53,105	10	2,06,57,02,905	10	2,28,60,57,753	11	2,85,24,95,781	10	3,10,01,68,250
Government FX-denominated Debantures Fund	20	42,51,37,223	22	54,13,75,462	22	70,84,75,665	22	79,54,22,196	22	1,21,97,98,786	22	2,39,31,26,321	22	3,77,54,25,750	22	5,98,09,63,485	22	8,84,48,57,340	24	12,67,96,61,991
Private Sector and Government Debantures Fund	0	0	0	0	0	0	0	0	0	0	0	0	0	0	0	0	0	0	0	0
Government Contribution Participation Fund	0	0	0	0	0	0	7	1,80,62,580	8	7,96,22,802	8	17,66,13,567	10	29,29,99,806	13	39,74,57,101	13	54,81,89,665	15	99,79,68,439
Standard Participation Fund	1	1,15,969	2	1,22,15,571	3	5,59,90,849	6	12,74,11,936	8	27,51,11,590	8	54,92,41,541	8	90,40,22,699	9	1,25,19,73,672	10	1,57,59,00,059	28	5,21,73,86,300
Precious Metals Fund	0	0	0	0	0	0	1	2,15,416	1	43,19,426	1	1,46,48,859	1	3,80,68,389	1	9,62,31,925	1	22,04,08,097	0	0
Liquid Fund-Government	5	31,08,09,876	5	32,69,33,936	1	1,51,74,530	1	1,38,49,187	1	1,35,30,941	1	1,33,56,868	1	1,44,19,362	1	1,32,05,346	0	0	0	0
Compulsary Standard Participation Fund	0	0	0	0	0	0	0	0	0	0	0	0	0	0	16	6,250	16	1,21,17,77,228	0	0
Compulsary Standard Fund	0	0	0	0	0	0	0	0	0	0	0	0	0	0	14	6,250	14	66,69,97,986	0	0
Private Sector Debantures Fund	0	0	1	9,57,931	2	33,64,993	3	4,51,80,859	3	9,35,57,888	3	17,77,31,174	3	26,46,55,291	3	37,57,48,838	3	53,98,12,389	4	60,08,07,706
Money Market Fund	12	86,19,41,280	14	85,93,81,736	20	1,56,22,47,593	22	1,73,37,04,199	22	2,95,61,25,937	22	4,02,33,63,266	22	5,83,12,70,284	22	7,03,67,99,028	22	8,36,21,50,772	18	10,66,81,98,195
Standard Fund	5	35,10,07,365	7	46,01,76,213	8	67,21,20,555	17	1,09,93,63,842	17	1,75,00,11,071	17	2,85,91,90,784	17	3,87,33,13,123	17	5,01,45,86,637	17	5,46,87,66,762	29	5,99,74,61,627
Balanced Fund	4	19,98,84,011	4	23,38,63,797	7	28,20,75,792	7	36,86,38,985	7	44,71,49,884	7	61,81,17,170	7	80,00,08,450	7	1,14,28,50,844	7	1,70,80,73,972	0	0
Variable Fund	44	2,39,03,98,202	56	3,64,51,68,475	60	4,78,98,62,764	66	7,33,00,45,293	71	9,34,21,19,025	76	12,13,28,40,750	82	14,91,25,92,520	181	19,01,23,46,526	178	22,83,23,61,489	162	23,62,62,99,014
Fund of Funds	0	0	0	0	0	0	0	0	1	0	1	6,03,635	1	64,55,945	2	1,41,29,853	2	1,90,67,798	2	2,07,54,908
Participation Fund	0	0	0	0	0	0	0	0	0	0	0	0	0	0	1	0	1	0	0	0
Liquid Fund-Balanced	1	77,52,051	1	76,31,271	0	0	0	0	0	0	0	0	0	0	0	0	0	0	0	0
International Balanced Fund	2	34,17,028	1	19,04,539	0	0	0	0	0	0	0	0	0	0	0	0	0	0	0	0
Participation Variable Fund	0	0	0	0	0	0	0	0	0	0	0	0	0	0	0	0	0	0	9	1,09,30,91,808
Total	140	10,473,773,960	167	13,305,581,701	176	17,270,913,331	236	23,756,394,296	247	31,455,523,779	251	42,603,882,649	277	54,564,232,925	426	70,158,731,538	431	90,960,633,963	420	105,483,667,929

Omitted Funds (#, TL)	51	2,60,14,51,292	62	3,88,85,68,081	67	5,07,19,38,556	73	7,69,86,84,278	79	9,78,92,68,909	84	12,75,15,61,554	90	15,71,90,56,915	191	20,16,93,27,222	188	24,55,95,03,259	173	24,74,01,45,730
Omitted Funds %	36%	25%	37%	29%	38%	29%	31%	32%	32%	31%	33%	30%	32%	29%	45%	29%	44%	27%	41%	23%

Fund Categories Subject to Analysis																				
Gold Fund	0	0	0	0	0	0	12	3,53,14,322	13	19,25,37,206	12	43,98,98,490	12	93,15,28,949	14	2,41,19,37,104	14	5,39,21,59,485	16	11,51,86,98,024
Initiation Fund	0	0	0	0	0	0	0	0	0	0	0	0	8	0	14	27,34,72,469	14	47,24,74,899	14	42,74,56,489
Initiation Participation Fund	0	0	0	0	0	0	0	0	0	0	0	0	10	0	16	44,75,96,899	16	76,15,62,229	17	65,50,28,291
Fixed Income Fund	14	4,08,58,32,515	15	4,78,94,03,177	17	7,11,74,10,454	17	8,52,18,79,323	17	9,45,42,90,219	17	10,90,28,01,290	17	11,45,67,45,588	17	11,82,07,14,224	23	14,98,58,68,904	22	11,62,41,11,836
Government Contribution Fund	0	0	0	0	0	0	18	60,31,21,475	18	1,92,27,97,556	18	3,74,63,86,708	18	5,95,55,08,153	18	8,34,38,89,899	17	9,75,47,69,935	17	12,58,93,85,028
Equity Fund	20	59,60,80,991	26	95,38,93,857	27	1,18,76,65,294	28	1,78,44,95,208	29	2,20,42,23,507	29	2,77,20,57,981	29	3,47,95,84,101	29	4,33,49,89,362	31	4,96,33,47,269	33	4,66,71,90,024
Government Bonds Fund	12	1,24,13,97,449	13	1,47,26,75,738	9	87,65,24,841	10	1,27,99,04,890	10	1,50,46,47,368	10	1,79,85,53,105	10	2,06,57,02,905	10	2,28,60,57,753	11	2,85,24,95,781	10	3,10,01,68,250
FC Denominated Government Bonds Fund	20	42,51,37,223	22	54,13,75,462	22	70,84,75,665	22	79,54,22,196	22	1,21,97,98,786	22	2,39,31,26,321	22	3,77,54,25,750	22	5,98,09,63,485	22	8,84,48,57,340	24	12,67,96,61,991
Government Contribution Participation Fund	0	0	0	0	0	0	7	1,80,62,580	8	7,96,22,802	8	17,66,13,567	10	29,29,99,806	13	39,74,57,101	13	54,81,89,665	15	99,79,68,439
Standard Participation Fund	1	1,15,969	2	1,22,15,571	3	5,59,90,849	6	12,74,11,936	8	27,51,11,590	8	54,92,41,541	8	90,40,22,699	25	1,25,19,79,922	26	2,78,76,77,288	28	5,21,73,86,300
Private Sector Fixed Income Fund	0	0	1	9,57,931	2	33,64,993	3	4,51,80,859	3	9,35,57,888	3	17,77,31,174	3	26,46,55,291	3	37,57,48,838	3	53,98,12,389	4	60,08,07,706
Money Market Fund	17	1,17,27,51,156	19	1,18,63,15,672	21	1,57,74,22,123	23	1,74,75,53,386	23	2,96,96,56,877	23	4,03,67,20,134	23	5,84,56,89,645	23	7,05,00,04,374	22	8,36,21,50,772	18	10,66,81,98,195
Standard Fund	5	35,10,07,365	7	46,01,76,213	8	67,21,20,555	17	1,09,93,63,842	17	1,75,00,11,071	17	2,85,91,90,784	17	3,87,33,13,123	31	5,01,45,92,887	31	6,13,57,64,748	29	5,99,74,61,627
Total	89	7,87,23,22,668	105	9,41,70,13,620	109	12,19,89,74,775	163	16,05,77,10,017	168	21,66,62,54,870	167	29,85,23,21,095	187	38,84,51,76,010	235	49,98,94,04,316	243	66,40,11,30,704	247	80,74,35,22,199

Source: CMB

2.3.2 Benchmark data

We defined a benchmark for each fund category as shown in Tables 2.4 and 2.5 for mutual and pension funds, respectively. The category benchmarks are formed based on the commonly determined specific benchmarks for funds within that category and crosschecked with the overall asset allocation of each category for the whole analysis period. A heatmap of the asset allocations in each mutual and pension fund category over the analyzed 10-year period is presented in Tables 2.6 and 2.7, respectively.

Table 2.4: Benchmarks for mutual fund categories

Mutual Fund Categories	Category Benchmarks
Gold Fund	BIST-KYD Gold Price Index (calculated over averages)
Fixed Income Fund	%50 TDTUMT1: BIST-KYD Government All T1 + %30 OSABTT1[a]: BIST-KYD Private Sector Fixed T1 + %20 ODEGST1[b] BIST-KYD Private Sector Floating T1
Equity Fund	BIST All Total Return Index
Multi Asset Fund	%10 TD91G: BIST-KYD Government 91 Days + %25 BIST All Total Return Index+ %65 TDTUMT1: BIST-KYD Government All T1
Participation Fund	%50 KDEVLT1[c]: BIST-KYD Government Lease Certificates T1 +%50 KOZELT1[d]: BIST-KYD Private Sector Lease Certificates T1
Short-term Fixed Income Fund	TD91G: BIST-KYD Government 91 GUN
Short-term Lease Certificates Fund	%50 KDEVLT1: BIST-KYD Government Lease Certificates T1 +%50 KOZELT1: BIST-KYD Private Sector Lease Certificates T1
Money Market Fund	TD91G: BIST-KYD Government 91 GUN

Source: Authors defined benchmarks utilizing indices announced and calculated by Borsa İstanbul

[a] This index is started to be calculated beginning from 31 December 2010. Hence the aggregate benchmark and the analysis is performed starting from this date.

[b] This index is started to be calculated beginning from 31 December 2010. Hence the aggregate benchmark and the analysis is performed starting from this date.

[c] This index is started to be calculated beginning from 28 June 2013. Hence the aggregate benchmark and the analysis is performed starting from this date.

[d] This index is started to be calculated beginning from 28 June 2013. Hence the aggregate benchmark and the analysis is performed starting from this date.

Moreover, for pension funds, we also used the corresponding category benchmarks cited by Kuzubaş et al. (2019).

The data for indices which comprise the benchmarks are obtained from Borsa İstanbul. Borsa İstanbul, in association with the Turkish Institutional Investment Managers' Association, calculates and publishes all the indices which are singularly or in some combination utilized as benchmarks in

Table 2.5: Benchmarks for pension fund categories

Pension Fund Categories	Category Benchmarks
Gold Fund	BIST-KYD Gold Price Index (calculated over averages)
Initiation Fund	BIST-KYD 1 Month Time Deposit Index
Initiation Participation Fund	BIST-KYD 1 Month Time Participation Account Index
Fixed Income Fund	%50 TDTUMT1: BIST-KYD Government All T1 + %30 OSABTT1: BIST-KYD Private Sector Fixed T1 + %20 ODEGST1 BIST-KYD Private Sector Floating T1
Government Contribution Fund	BIST-KYD Government All T1
Equity Fund	BIST All Total Return Index
Government Bonds Fund	BIST-KYD Government All T1
Foreign Currency Denominated Government Bonds Fund	%50 EBUSD: BIST-KYD Government EUROBOND USD + %50 EBEUR BIST-KYD Government EUROBOND EUR
Government Contribution Participation Fund	KDEVLT1: BIST-KYD Government Lease Certificates T1
Standard Participation Fund	%50 KDEVLT1 BIST-KYD Government Lease Certificates T1 + %20 BIST-KYD Gold Price Index + %30 BIST-KYD 1 Month Time Participation Account Index
Private Sector Fixed Income Fund	%60 OSABTT1: BIST-KYD Private Sector Fixed T1 + %40 ODEGST1 BIST-KYD Private Sector Floating T1
Money Market Fund	TD91G: BIST-KYD Government 91 Days
Standard Fund	%50 TDTUMT1: BIST-KYD Government All T1 + %30 BIST-KYD 1 Month Time Deposit Index +%10 BIST All Total Return Index + %10 BIST-KYD Gold Price Index

Source: Authors defined benchmarks utilizing indices announced and calculated by Borsa İstanbul

the fund management industry in Turkey.[12] Some indices are started to be calculated after 02.01.2010, therefore the analysis involving those indices within the benchmarks are also performed thence forward.

The indices are also published daily as values (like prices). We followed the same methodology to calculate the weekly returns out of the index values, i.e., Monday to Monday.

$$\text{Index Return} = r_B = \frac{V_t - V_{t-7}}{V_{t-7}} \tag{2.4}$$

where

r_B = Index weekly return

V_t = Value of the index at the tth day

V_{t-7} = Value of the index 7 days before the tth day

Then we calculated the benchmark returns which are comprised of either one single index or a combination of indices with different percentages within the benchmark.

$$\text{Benchmark return} = \sum_i^n r_B * w_i \tag{2.5}$$

where

r_B = Index weekly return

n = Number of indices within the benchmark

w_i = Percentage of index i within the benchmark

2.3.3 Data for asset allocations of fund portfolios

The daily percentage data for asset allocation within the portfolios of each funds are obtained from Central Securities Depository of the Turkish capital markets ("CSD"). There are 12 asset types defined: (1) Government debentures in local currency, (2) Treasury bills, (3) Reverse Repo,[13] (4) Stocks, (5) Private sector debentures, (6) Foreign securities,

12 *BIST-KYD Indexes Main Rules*. https://www.borsaistanbul.com/files/bist-kyd-endeksleri-temel-kurallari_14082017.pdf.

13 Repo: Repurchasing agreements, i.e., sale of securities with an obligation to buy back at a predefined date which is generally shorter than a month, and hence providing short-term liquidity and paying interest for that liquidity. For the party on the other end of a repo agreement (who buys the security and agrees to sell it at the predefined date), it is a "reverse repo" transaction.

Table 2.6: Heatmap of asset allocations for mutual fund categories

Mutual Funds	T-bills	Govern ment Bonds	Reverse Repo	Equities	Private Sector Bonds	Foreign Currency Securities	Money Market	Govern ment Foreign Bonds	Govern ment Lease Certifi-cates	Private Sector Lease Certifi-cates	Precious Metals	Other
Gold Fund	0%	0%	2%	0%	0%	0%	1%	0%	0%	0%	96%	0%
Fixed income Fund	42%	1%	8%	3%	28%	3%	3%	10%	0%	0%	0%	3%
Short-term Fixed Income Fund	24%	1%	21%	0%	39%	0%	7%	3%	0%	0%	0%	5%
Equity Fund	3%	0%	8%	76%	1%	8%	2%	0%	0%	0%	0%	3%
Multi Asset Fund	32%	1%	18%	35%	6%	6%	1%	0%	0%	0%	0%	1%
Participation Fund	0%	0%	3%	8%	0%	6%	0%	1%	51%	29%	2%	0%
Money Market Fund	11%	3%	64%	1%	10%	0%	8%	0%	0%	0%	0%	3%
Short-term Lease Certificates Fund	0%	0%	0%	0%	0%	0%	0%	0%	13%	78%	0%	10%

Source: Authors' visualization based on CSD data

Table 2.7: Heatmap of asset allocations for pension fund categories

Pension Funds	T-bills	Govern ment Bonds	Reverse Repo	Equities	Private Sector Bonds	Foreign Currency Securities	Money Market	Govern ment Foreign Bonds	Govern ment Lease Certifi-cates	Private Sector Lease Certifi-cates	Precious Metals	Other
Gold Fund	1%	0%	0%	1%	0%	0%	1%	0%	0%	0%	96%	0%
Initiation Fund	91%	1%	3%	0%	0%	0%	5%	0%	0%	0%	0%	0%
Initiation Participation Fund	0%	0%	0%	0%	1%	0%	0%	0%	78%	21%	0%	0%
Fixed Income Fund	73%	0%	5%	1%	6%	0%	1%	4%	0%	0%	0%	9%
Government Conttribution Fund	83%	0%	0%	4%	1%	0%	0%	0%	3%	0%	0%	9%
Equity Fund	3%	0%	6%	86%	1%	0%	2%	0%	0%	0%	0%	2%
Government Bonds Fund	82%	1%	8%	1%	3%	0%	0%	0%	0%	0%	0%	6%
FX Government Bonds Fund	6%	0%	6%	0%	0%	3%	1%	81%	0%	0%	0%	3%
Gov. Contribution Participation Fund	0%	0%	0%	1%	0%	0%	0%	0%	94%	1%	0%	3%
Standard Participation Fund	0%	0%	0%	12%	3%	0%	0%	0%	70%	7%	8%	0%
Private Sector Fixed Income Fund	27%	0%	4%	0%	65%	0%	2%	0%	0%	0%	0%	3%
Money Market Fund	17%	2%	60%	0%	9%	0%	2%	0%	0%	0%	0%	11%
Standard Fund	75%	0%	3%	3%	4%	0%	0%	0%	1%	0%	12%	0%

Source: Authors' visualization based on CSD data

(7) Money market at Takas İstanbul, (8) Government debentures in hard currency, (9) Government lease certificates (sukuk), (10) Private sector lease certificates (sukuk), (11) Precious metals, (12) Other.

2.3.4 Risk-free rate data

We utilized the two-year government bond yield as the risk-free rate (which is a market consensus) in Turkey.[14] The data is obtained from Finnet, a private data provider company, one of a few in the Turkish capital markets. We gathered the daily closing value of the two-year government bond yield for the analyzed period. Then we calculated the average of the last one year for every day – a smoothing process required to isolate the excess volatility of the daily rates. As the interest rate is an annual figure, we divided that average into 52 to reach the weekly interest rate for that specific day. Hence, we created the weekly risk-free rate which was compatible to be utilized vis-à-vis the weekly returns data.

$$\text{Weekly risk free rate} = R_f = \frac{1}{52}\sum_{i}^{252}\frac{r_{t-i}}{252} \tag{2.6}$$

where

r_{t-i} = Risk-free rate on t^{th} day calculated on a moving average basis starting from day i which is 252 days (i.e., a year) earlier than the tth day

We could have also used the Weighted Average Cost of Funding (WACF) by the CBRT as the risk-free rate. WACF is the weighted average of interest rates of funding made by the Central Bank for various instruments (repo etc.) at different maturities (overnight, weekly, etc.) to meet the market liquidity needs. Figure 2.2 shows the trend of this interest rate together with the CBRT Total Funding, which is the sum of the amount of funding made by the Central Bank with these instruments to meet the liquidity needs in the market.[15]

14 Turkish Institutional Investment Managers' Association publishes an annual performance report on pension funds in Turkey since 2016 and they use the two-year government bond yield as the risk-free rate of return. http://www.tkyd.org.tr/assets/raporlar/EYF_Performans_2018_Aralik-9a85f5af46e7a0be5591aefad0dc3890.pdf.

15 *Weighted Average Cost of Funding*. 2020. CBRT. https://evds2.tcmb.gov.tr/index.php?/evds/dashboard/1441.

The two-year government bond yield has most of the time between 2011–2019 been higher than the weighted average cost of funding of the CBRT as depicted in Figure 2.3. Thus, we have subjected the funds to a harder test in terms of the Sharpe and Treynor ratios. On the other hand, government's crowding-out effect may sometimes distort the CBRT WACF. Using the 2-year government bond yield as the risk-free rate of return (R_f) is more of a market-based approach.

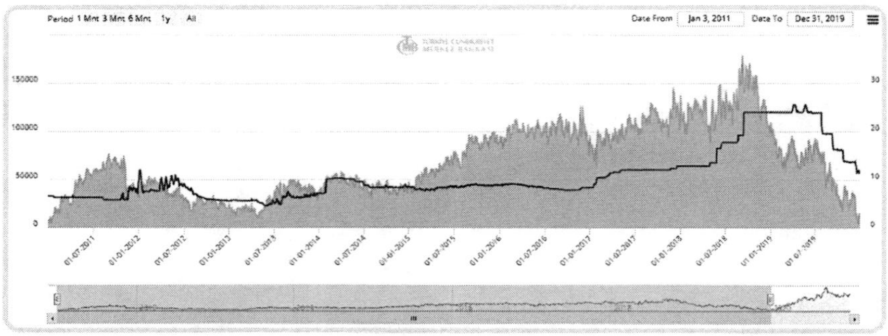

Figure 2.2: Weighted average cost (line) and amount (area) of the CBRT funding
Source: CBRT

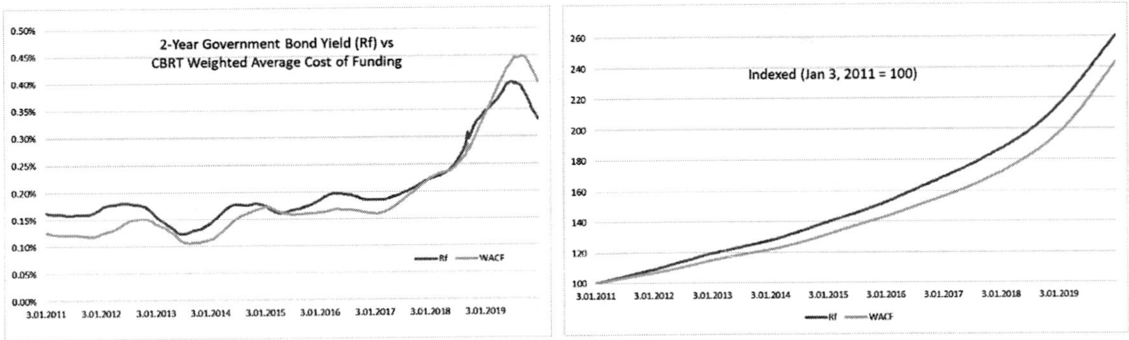

Figure 2.3: 2-Year government bond yield vs CBRT weighted average cost of funding
Source: CBRT, converted to weekly rates and indexed by the author

2.3.5 Risk-adjusted performance measures data

We calculated six different risk-adjusted performance measures for four different time periods: annual, 3 years, 5 years, and 10 years. If either the fund category or the benchmark data was not available for 10 years, then we used the entire period of the existing data instead of the 10-year analysis (e.g., 2.5 years or 6.5 years, etc.).

We calculated each of the six risk-adjusted performance measures based on weekly returns using the number of weeks within each analyzed period, i.e., n=52 for annual analysis, n=156 for 3-yearly analysis, n=260 for 5-yearly analysis, and n=520 for a decade-long analysis (and n would be equal to the number of weeks contained in shorter existence periods than 10 years). We used both equally and AuM-weighted weekly returns data. We calculated the risk-adjusted performance measures as follows:

$$\text{Sharpe ratio} = \frac{\overline{R_p} - \overline{R_f}}{\sigma\left(R_p - R_f\right)} \tag{2.7}$$

$$\text{Treynor ratio} = \frac{\overline{R_p} - \overline{R_f}}{\beta_p} \tag{2.8}$$

$$\text{Information ratio} = \frac{\overline{R_p} - \overline{R_B}}{\sigma\left(R_p - R_B\right)} \tag{2.9}$$

$$\text{Jensen's Alpha} = a_p = \left[\overline{R_p} - \left\{\overline{R_f} + \beta_p * \left(\overline{R_B} - \overline{R_f}\right)\right\}\right] \tag{2.10}$$

$$\text{Sortino ratio} = \frac{\overline{R_p} - \overline{R_B}}{DR} \tag{2.11}$$

$$\text{Omega ratio} = \frac{\sum_{i=1}^{n}\left(R_p^i - R_B^i\right)f(x)}{\sum_{i=1}^{n}\left(R_B^i - R_p^i\right)f(y)} \tag{2.12}$$

$$f(x) = 1 \text{ if } R_p \geq R_B, f(x) = 0 \text{ if } R_p < R_B$$

$$f(y) = 1 \text{ if } R_B \geq R_p, f(y) = 0 \text{ if } R_B < R_p$$

where

n = number of weeks (data points) within the analysed period

Average returns are calculated as follows:

$$\overline{R_p} = \text{Average portfolio (fund category) return for the period} = \frac{\sum_i^n R_p}{n} \quad (2.13)$$

$$\overline{R_f} = \text{Average risk-free rate of return for the period} = \frac{\sum_i^n R_f}{n} \quad (2.14)$$

$$\overline{R_B} = \text{Average benchmark return for the period} = \frac{\sum_i^n R_B}{n} \quad (2.15)$$

Risk measures are calculated as follows:

$$\sigma_p = \text{Standard deviation of portfolio (fund category) returns} = \sqrt{\frac{\sum_i^n \left(R_p^i - \frac{\sum_i^n R_p^i}{n} \right)^2}{n-1}} \quad (2.16)$$

$$\beta_p = \frac{\sum_{i=1}^n (R_p^i - \overline{R_p}) * (R_B^i - \overline{R_B})}{\sum_{i=1}^n (R_B^i - \overline{R_B})^2} \quad (2.17)$$

$$\sigma_{(R_p - R_f)} = \text{St. deviation of excess returns} = \sqrt{\frac{1}{n-1} \sum_i^n \left((R_p^i - R_f^i) - \frac{\sum_i^n (R_p^i - R_f^i)}{n} \right)^2} \quad (2.18)$$

$$\sigma_{(R_p - R_B)} = \text{St. deviation of excess returns} = \sqrt{\frac{1}{n-1} \sum_i^n \left((R_p^i - R_B^i) - \frac{\sum_i^n (R_p^i - R_B^i)}{n} \right)^2} \quad (2.19)$$

$$DR = \text{Downside Risk} = \sqrt{\frac{1}{n} \sum_{i=1}^n \left(R_p - R_B \right)^2 f(t)} \quad (2.20)$$

where

$$f(t) = 1 \text{ if } R_p < R_B \upsilon$$

$$f(t) = 0 \text{ if } R_p \geq R_B$$

We need to note that one should be wary of interpretation of the Treynor ratios and Jensen's alphas in our analysis.

Beta (β_p), the risk measure used in Treynor ratio calculation (Formula 2.8 above), is the sensitivity or correlation of the portfolio returns (the fund category returns in our study) to the overall market returns (the category benchmark returns in our study). In short, beta is described as the excess return (in excess of the overall market rate) per unit of market risk. As the market of each fund category is different (the category benchmarks are different), it is not appropriate to compare the Treynor ratios across different fund categories.

The above caution is valid for Jensen's alpha, too. In addition, as per the Formula 2.10 above, when $R_B < R_f$ and $\beta_p > 1$, then Jensen's alpha will be as much higher as $\beta_p{}^*\left(\overline{R_B} - \overline{R_f}\right)$. This can be the case especially for fixed income type of funds because the benchmarks defined can be lower than the 2-year government bond yield (the risk-free rate of return) while following the same trend, i.e., having a positive beta. Hence, one should be cautious in interpreting the Jensen's alpha ratio in such cases.

2.3.6 Management fee data

The management fees of each fund in year 2019 are collected from the Public Disclosure Platform (PDP). Then we summed up the management fees of each fund in a fund category in 2019 and divided the sum by the number of funds in the category (in other words we calculated the simple arithmetic average) to reach the fund category's management fee. We tried to bring the correspondent mutual and pension funds on the same line in

Table 2.8: Management fees (average by fund category)

Mutual Funds	2019
Gold Fund	1.69%
Short-term Fixed Income Fund	1.96%
Short-term Lease Certificates Fund	1.48%
Fixed Income Fund	1.55%
Equity Fund	2.40%
Participation Fund	1.56%
Money Market Fund	1.18%
Multi Asset Fund	2.50%

Pension Funds	2019
Gold Fund	1.02%
Initiation Fund	0.85%
Initiation Participation Fund	0.83%
Fixed Income Fund	1.58%
Government Contribution Fund	0.33%
Equity Fund	1.83%
Government Bonds Fund	1.60%
FC Denominated Government Bonds Fund	1.52%
Government Contribution Participation Fund	0.35%
Standard Participation Fund	1.44%
Private Sector Fixed Income Fund	1.88%
Money Market Fund	0.99%
Standard Fund	1.35%

Source: PDP

order to compare their management fees. As would be expected, management fees of pension funds are lower than those of the mutual funds.

We just gathered and calculated the 2019 management fees, because we did not perform any analysis using the management fees, but rather utilized this data to explain the below-the-benchmark returns of some fund categories where the funds closely follow up the benchmark and narrow positive margin of the funds' returns are eradicated by the high management fees.

In our analysis, we are interested in the return the investors receive in a mutual or pension fund which is after the management fees are deducted, i.e., already reflected in the fund prices, hence the returns. Therefore, we need not sterilize the fund returns from the management fees.

3. Fund category performance analysis

The analysis aims to answer the question whether the fund management industry, i.e., the professional portfolio managers, has been able to create excess return, i.e., alpha for investors in a predefined investment strategy. In other words, given an investment strategy, which is basically the fund category itself, would investors earn a statistically significant excess return by entrusting their funds to professional asset managers rather than investing in a benchmark representing that investment strategy?

3.1 Mutual fund categories vs defined benchmarks

We analyzed the statistical significance of the excess returns for each fund category, i.e., "the aggregate return – the category benchmark return" via one-sample t-test analysis at 95 % confidence interval. The null and alternative hypotheses are as follows

$$H_0 = \mu = 0 \tag{3.1}$$

$$H_a = \mu > 0 \tag{3.2}$$

We ran this analysis for four different time periods: (1) Annual analysis for 10 years (Table 3.1), (2) Three-yearly analysis for 8 periods between 2010–2019 (Table 3.3), (3) Five-yearly analysis for 6 periods between 2010–2019 (Table 3.5), and (4) Ten-yearly analysis (Table 3.7).

According to annual analysis, there are statistically significant positive returns over the benchmark only for "equity," "multi-asset," and "money market" funds and only for the year 2017 both with equally weighted and AuM-weighted returns analysis (Table 3.1).

However, we should note that estimation of expected values from daily or higher frequency financial data may be problematic. The use of weekly data in our analysis may also suffer from this problem. Due to non-stationarity of time series, using the sample mean as an estimator is not robust. Therefore, although we provide the t-test results based on means, we approach the results with caution. As a matter of fact, there are many more positive excess returns in the annual analysis as observed in Table 3.2 (yellow cells). They are just not statistically significant as per t-test.

Table 3.1: Annual excess returns' t-test analysis

Excess Return Equally Returns	2010		2011		2012		2013		2014		2015		2016		2017		2018		2019	
	P-Value	t-test	P-Value	t-test	P-Value	t-test	P-Value	t-test	P-Value	t-test	P-Value	t-test	P-Value	t-test	P-Value	t-test	P-Value	t-test	P-Value	t-test
Gold Fund	1.0000	-9.3159	0.9993	-3.3799	1.0000	-5.6800	0.9938	-2.5956	1.0000	-4.3277	0.9985	-3.1213	0.9999	-3.9803	0.9904	-2.4188	0.6854	-0.4859	0.9215	-1.4361
Fixed Income Fund	*n.a*	*n.a*	1.0000	-4.4021	0.9761	-2.0286	0.8555	-1.0713	0.8399	-1.0037	0.1223	1.1772	0.2625	0.6400	0.4128	0.2215	0.3743	0.3222	0.6657	-0.4305
Equity Fund	0.2472	0.6883	0.8503	-1.0483	0.0904	1.3571	0.5061	-0.0154	0.3250	0.4566	0.5354	-0.0893	0.4682	0.0802	0.0084	2.4703	0.7255	-0.6033	0.3233	0.4612
Multi Asset Fund	0.4789	0.0531	0.9034	-1.3188	0.1773	0.9344	0.7208	-0.5891	0.8291	-0.9595	0.5117	-0.0295	0.6844	-0.4831	0.0181	2.1505	0.5753	-0.1908	0.5129	-0.0325
Participation Fund	*n.a*	*n.a*	*n.a*	*n.a*	*n.a*	*n.a*	*n.a*	*n.a*	0.5939	-0.2387	0.6818	-0.4755	0.2705	0.6154	0.5168	-0.0423	0.2908	0.5547	0.7328	-0.6255
Short-term Fixed Income Fund	1.0000	-14.7283	1.0000	-5.0155	1.0000	-4.2824	0.9999	-4.1889	0.9727	-1.9667	0.9650	-1.8510	0.9218	-1.4384	0.0731	1.4756	0.3051	0.5129	0.8546	-1.0674
Short-term Lease Certificates Fund	*n.a*	*n.a*	*n.a*	*n.a*	*n.a*	*n.a*	*n.a*	*n.a*	*n.a*	*n.a*	*n.a*	*n.a*	*n.a*	*n.a*	*n.a*	*n.a*	0.0689	1.5075	0.9921	-2.4990
Money Market Fund	1.0000	-20.2332	1.0000	-5.1718	1.0000	-4.6101	0.9407	-1.5876	0.7647	-0.7269	0.5995	-0.2533	0.8533	-1.0615	0.0051	2.6646	0.1027	1.2829	0.7936	-0.8257

Excess Return Weighted Average	2010		2011		2012		2013		2014		2015		2016		2017		2018		2019	
	P-Value	t-test	P-Value	t-test	P-Value	t-test	P-Value	t-test	P-Value	t-test	P-Value	t-test	P-Value	t-test	P-Value	t-test	P-Value	t-test	P-Value	t-test
Gold Fund	1.0000	-10.7564	1.0000	-4.4815	1.0000	-9.0440	0.9967	-2.8337	1.0000	-4.8596	0.9989	-3.2321	1.0000	-6.3336	0.9912	-2.4550	0.8434	-1.0186	0.8995	-1.2952
Fixed Income Fund	*n.a*	*n.a*	1.0000	-7.7076	1.0000	-4.8098	0.5022	-0.0056	0.8873	-1.2274	0.1142	1.2192	0.3101	0.4985	0.2789	0.5900	0.2227	0.7689	0.6971	-0.5193
Equity Fund	0.2032	0.8373	0.8397	-1.0030	0.0694	1.5036	0.5275	-0.0693	0.2813	0.5829	0.4767	0.0588	0.4231	0.1950	0.0127	2.3023	0.5410	-0.1034	0.2581	0.6536
Multi Asset Fund	0.4306	0.1757	0.8939	-1.2632	0.1361	1.1100	0.6338	-0.3437	0.5851	-0.2162	0.6580	-0.4092	0.7017	-0.5327	0.0154	2.2217	0.4600	0.1009	0.6846	-0.4835
Participation Fund	*n.a*	*n.a*	*n.a*	*n.a*	*n.a*	*n.a*	*n.a*	*n.a*	0.6051	-0.2679	0.2576	0.6554	0.0874	1.3763	0.4849	0.0379	0.1808	0.9205	0.9048	-1.3273
Short-term Fixed Income Fund	1.0000	-18.0068	1.0000	-4.3817	1.0000	-4.3267	0.9978	-2.9781	0.9896	-2.3859	0.9881	-2.3298	0.9920	-2.4920	0.1924	0.8768	0.4067	0.2371	0.9110	-1.3655
Short-term Lease Certificates Fund	*n.a*	*n.a*	*n.a*	*n.a*	*n.a*	*n.a*	*n.a*	*n.a*	*n.a*	*n.a*	*n.a*	*n.a*	*n.a*	*n.a*	*n.a*	*n.a*	0.0640	1.5474	0.9894	-2.3794
Money Market Fund	1.0000	-22.6360	1.0000	-4.7511	0.9998	-3.8446	0.9576	-1.7571	0.8128	-0.8963	0.6187	-0.3038	0.8085	-0.8799	0.0044	2.7226	0.5556	-0.1406	0.7883	-0.8070

Source: Authors' calculations

Table 3.2: Annual excess returns

Excess Return (Equally weighted)	2010	2011	2012	2013	2014	2015	2016	2017	2018	2019
Gold Fund	-0.000739	-0.000836	-0.000604	-0.000295	-0.000492	-0.000479	-0.000515	-0.000545	-0.000278	-0.000837
Fixed Income Fund	n.a	-0.000832	-0.000380	-0.000155	-0.000405	**0.000620**	**0.000446**	**0.000137**	**0.000555**	-0.000441
Equity Fund	**0.001873**	-0.003694	**0.003120**	-0.000052	**0.001012**	-0.000277	**0.000184**	**0.005797**	-0.002284	**0.001316**
Multi Asset Fund	**0.000072**	-0.002779	**0.001115**	-0.000961	-0.000964	-0.000037	-0.000527	**0.002770**	-0.000560	-0.000065
Participation Fund	n.a	n.a	n.a	n.a	-0.000171	-0.000291	**0.000242**	-0.000027	**0.000988**	-0.000373
Short-term Fixed Income Fund	-0.000735	-0.000615	-0.000332	-0.000397	-0.000192	-0.000161	-0.000119	**0.000160**	**0.000122**	-0.000252
Short-term Lease Certificates Fund	n.a	n.a	n.a	n.a	n.a	n.a	n.a	n.a	**0.000394**	-0.00085
Money Market Fund	-0.00091	-0.00059	-0.00046	-0.00024	-0.00011	-0.000026	-0.000099	**0.000312**	**0.000324**	-0.00024

Excess Return (AuM-weighted)	2010	2011	2012	2013	2014	2015	2016	2017	2018	2019
Gold Fund	-0.000621	-0.000740	-0.000519	-0.000302	-0.000431	-0.000452	-0.000472	-0.000497	-0.000443	-0.000735
Fixed Income Fund	n.a	-0.000665	-0.000460	-0.000001	-0.000560	**0.000889**	**0.000303**	**0.000485**	**0.001914**	-0.000661
Equity Fund	**0.002505**	-0.003861	**0.003886**	-0.000266	**0.001411**	**0.000184**	**0.000448**	**0.005247**	-0.000568	**0.001712**
Multi Asset Fund	**0.000261**	-0.003061	**0.001502**	-0.000654	-0.000284	-0.000651	-0.000592	**0.002863**	**0.000269**	-0.000788
Participation Fund	n.a	n.a	n.a	n.a	-0.000584	**0.000955**	**0.001130**	**0.000039**	**0.001953**	-0.000599
Short-term Fixed Income Fund	-0.000838	-0.000503	-0.000398	-0.000359	-0.000250	-0.000207	-0.000201	**0.000098**	**0.000049**	-0.000298
Short-term Lease Certificates Fund	n.a	n.a	n.a	n.a	n.a	n.a	n.a	n.a	**0.000421**	-0.0008
Money Market Fund	-0.00105	-0.00056	-0.00038	-0.00025	-0.00011	-0.000032	-0.000083	**0.00032**	-3.6E-05	-0.00024

Source: Authors' calculations

Table 3.3: 3-Yearly excess returns' t-test analysis

Excess Return Equally Returns	2010-2012		2011-2013		2012-2014		2013-2015		2014-2016		2015-2017		2016-2018		2017-2019	
	P-Value	t-test	P-Value	t-test	P-Value	t-test	P-Value	t-test	P-Value	t-test	P-Value	t-test	P-Value	t-test	P-Value	t-test
Gold Fund	1.0000	-7.7895	1.0000	-5,8784	1.0000	-7,1723	1.0000	-5,7053	1.0000	-6,4819	1.0000	-5,1325	0.9831	-2,1425	0.9746	-1,9685
Fixed Income Fund	*n.a*	*n.a*	1.0000	-4,4124	0.9774	-2,0186	0.4650	0.0881	0.2466	0.6869	0.1301	1.1301	0.2798	0.5848	0.4522	0.1202
Equity Fund	0.3982	0.2583	0.5461	-0,1161	0.1889	0.8847	0.4462	0.1355	0.4178	0.2079	0.1051	1.2585	0.2323	0.7332	0.1825	0.9085
Multi Asset Fund	0.7158	-0.5715	0.8144	-0,8969	0.6400	-0,3591	0.8050	-0,8621	0.7851	-0,7917	0.1495	1.0419	0.3100	0.4970	0.2849	0.5695
Participation Fund	*n.a*	*n.a*	*n.a*	*n.a*	*n.a*	*n.a*	*n.a*	*n.a*	0.5855	-0,2162	0.5313	-0,0787	0.2660	0.6263	0.3831	0.2978
Short-term Fixed Income Fund	1.0000	-10,6594	1.0000	-7,6959	1.0000	-5,8688	1.0000	-4,6183	0.9987	-3,0671	0.7650	-0,7241	0.2756	0.5972	0.4656	0.0864
Short-term Lease Certificates Fund	*n.a*	*n.a*	*n.a*	*n.a*	*n.a*	*n.a*	*n.a*	*n.a*	*n.a*	*n.a*	*n.a*	*n.a*	*n.a*	*n.a*	*n.a*	*n.a*
Money Market Fund	1.0000	-11,9878	1.0000	-6,0081	0.9996	-3,4135	0.9419	-1,5793	0.8735	-1,1475	0.1588	1.0027	0.0355	1.8177	0.1658	0.9739

Excess Return Weighted Average	2010-2012		2011-2013		2012-2014		2013-2015		2014-2016		2015-2017		2016-2018		2017-2019	
	P-Value	t-test	P-Value	t-test	P-Value	t-test	P-Value	t-test	P-Value	t-test	P-Value	t-test	P-Value	t-test	P-Value	t-test
Gold Fund	1.0000	-10,2039	1.0000	-7,5056	1.0000	-8,3085	1.0000	-6,0358	1.0000	-7,5070	1.0000	-5,5609	0.9980	-2,9258	0.9876	-2,2670
Fixed Income Fund	*n.a*	*n.a*	0.9999	-3,7237	0.9709	-1,9077	0.3587	0.3626	0.2749	0.5992	0.0907	1.3427	0.1574	1.0085	0.2754	0.5980
Equity Fund	0.3244	0.4564	0.5159	-0,0400	0.1674	0.9675	0.4042	0.2428	0.3269	0.4493	0.0970	1.3043	0.2109	0.8056	0.1629	0.9858
Multi Asset Fund	0.6590	-0.4106	0.7436	-0,6560	0.4164	0.2113	0.7152	-0,5698	0.7435	-0,6557	0.2457	0.6898	0.2115	0.8034	0.2444	0.6939
Participation Fund	*n.a*	*n.a*	*n.a*	*n.a*	*n.a*	*n.a*	*n.a*	*n.a*	0.2921	0.5483	0.1390	1.0886	0.1055	1.2561	0.2811	0.5809
Short-term Fixed Income Fund	1.0000	-10,8807	1.0000	-6,6494	1.0000	-5,4818	1.0000	-4,4776	1.0000	-4,1555	0.9682	-1,8686	0.5856	-0,2165	0.6794	-0,4669
Short-term Lease Certificates Fund	*n.a*	*n.a*	*n.a*	*n.a*	*n.a*	*n.a*	*n.a*	*n.a*	*n.a*	*n.a*	*n.a*	*n.a*	*n.a*	*n.a*	*n.a*	*n.a*
Money Market Fund	1.0000	-11,4800	1.0000	-5,6283	0.9997	-3,4863	0.9654	-1,8296	0.8852	-1,2062	0.1375	1.0956	0.2492	0.6786	0.4535	0.1170

Source: Authors' calculations

Table 3.4: 3-Yearly access returns

Excess Return (Equally weighted)	2010-2012	2011-2013	2012-2014	2013-2015	2014-2016	2015-2017	2016-2018	2017-2019
Gold Fund	-0.000726	-0.000578	-0.000464	-0.000422	-0.000495	-0.000513	-0.000446	-0.000553
Fixed Income Fund	n.a	-0.000453	-0.000313	0.000020	0.000220	0.000401	0.000379	0.000084
Equity Fund	0.000433	-0.000208	0.001360	0.000228	0.000306	0.001901	0.001232	0.001610
Multi Asset Fund	-0.000531	-0.000875	-0.000270	-0.000654	-0.000510	0.000735	0.000561	0.000715
Participation Fund	n.a	n.a	n.a	n.a	-0.000073	-0.000025	0.000401	0.000196
Short-term Fixed Income Fund	-0.000561	-0.000448	-0.000307	-0.000250	-0.000157	-0.000040	0.000055	0.000010
Short-term Lease Certificates Fund	n.a	n.a	n.a	n.a	n.a	n.a	n.a	n.a
Money Market Fund	-0.000655	-0.000430	-0.000270	-0.000125	-0.000079	0.000062	0.000179	0.000132

Excess Return (AuM-weighted)	2010-2012	2011-2013	2012-2014	2013-2015	2014-2016	2015-2017	2016-2018	2017-2019
Gold Fund	-0.000627	-0.000520	-0.000417	-0.000395	-0.000451	-0.000474	-0.000471	-0.000558
Fixed Income Fund	n.a	-0.000374	-0.000340	0.000109	0.000211	0.000559	0.000901	0.000579
Equity Fund	0.000843	-0.000080	0.001677	0.000443	0.000681	0.001960	0.001709	0.002130
Multi Asset Fund	-0.000433	-0.000738	0.000188	-0.000530	-0.000509	0.000540	0.000847	0.000781
Participation Fund	n.a	n.a	n.a	n.a	0.000500	0.000708	0.001041	0.000464
Short-term Fixed Income Fund	-0.000580	-0.000420	-0.000336	-0.000272	-0.000219	-0.000104	-0.000018	-0.000050
Short-term Lease Certificates Fund	n.a	n.a	n.a	n.a	n.a	n.a	n.a	n.a
Money Market Fund	-0.000662	-0.000396	-0.000247	-0.000131	-0.000074	0.000068	0.000067	0.000016

Source: Authors' calculations

According to three-yearly analysis, there is a statistically significant positive return over the benchmark only for "money market" fund and only for the period of 2016–2018 with equally weighted returns analysis (Table 3.3). This single statistically significant return disappears when the analysis is run with AuM-weighted returns indicating that the larger funds must have performed worse than the smaller ones. However, as observed in Table 3.4, there are many periods with positive access returns in all funds but the gold funds which fail the t-test.

According to five-yearly (Table 3.5) and ten-yearly (Table 3.7) analyses, there is no statistically significant positive return for any period for any fund category. However, as observed in Tables 3.6 and 3.8, there are many periods with positive access returns in some fund categories, but they fail the t-test.

Table 3.5: Five-yearly excess returns' t-test analysis

Excess Return Equally Returns	2010-2014		2011-2013		2012-2014		2013-2015		2014-2016		2015-2017	
	P-Value	t-test	P-Value	t-test	P-Value	t-test	P-Value	t-test	P-Value	t-test	P-Value	t-test
Gold Fund	1.0000	-9.0911	1.0000	-7.7152	1.0000	-8.5820	1.0000	-6.8340	0.9998	0.0000	0.9988	-3.0673
Fixed Income Fund	*n.a*	*n.a*	0.9379	-1.5420	0.4495	0.1270	0.2883	0.5591	0.2554	0.0000	0.2801	0.5833
Equity Fund	0.3625	0.3522	0.4933	0.0167	0.2531	0.6655	0.1354	1.1036	0.2412	0.0000	0.2351	0.7233
Multi Asset Fund	0.8512	-1.0437	0.8614	-1.0888	0.6885	-0.4923	0.4609	0.0984	0.4278	0.0000	0.3504	0.3847
Participation Fund	*n.a*	*n.a*	*n.a*	*n.a*	*n.a*	*n.a*	*n.a*	*n.a*	0.3643	0.0000	0.3988	0.2568
Short-term Fixed Income Fund	1.0000	-10.6941	1.0000	-7.6699	1.0000	-6.0505	0.9994	-3.2623	0.7307	0.0000	0.7470	-0.6660
Short-term Lease Certificates Fund	*n.a*	*n.a*	*n.a*	*n.a*	*n.a*	*n.a*	*n.a*	*n.a*	*n.a*	*n.a*	*n.a*	*n.a*
Money Market Fund	1.0000	-8.3116	1.0000	-4.9573	0.9996	-3.3830	0.7148	-0.5683	0.1274	0.0000	0.2651	0.6284

Excess Return Weighted Average	2010-2014		2011-2015		2012-2016		2013-2017		2014-2018		2015-2019	
	P-Value	t-test	P-Value	t-test	P-Value	t-test	P-Value	t-test	P-Value	t-test	P-Value	t-test
Gold Fund	1.0000	-11.1901	1.0000	-9.2180	1.0000	-9.9916	1.0000	-7.4107	1.0000	0.0000	0.9997	-3.4435
Fixed Income Fund	*n.a*	*n.a*	0.8031	-0.8542	0.4378	0.1568	0.2062	0.8210	0.1412	0.0000	0.1689	0.9601
Equity Fund	0.3035	0.5151	0.4253	0.1884	0.1911	0.8753	0.1356	1.1029	0.1846	0.0000	0.1762	0.9315
Multi Asset Fund	0.7164	-0.5729	0.7873	-0.7984	0.5816	-0.2061	0.4178	0.2077	0.3353	0.0000	0.3887	0.2830
Participation Fund	*n.a*	*n.a*	*n.a*	*n.a*	*n.a*	*n.a*	*n.a*	*n.a*	0.1666	0.0000	0.1169	1.1933
Short-term Fixed Income Fund	1.0000	-10.2537	1.0000	-7.3043	1.0000	-6.4428	1.0000	-3.9669	0.9621	0.0000	0.9472	-1.6239
Short-term Lease Certificates Fund	*n.a*	*n.a*	*n.a*	*n.a*	*n.a*	*n.a*	*n.a*	*n.a*	*n.a*	*n.a*	*n.a*	*n.a*
Money Market Fund	1.0000	-8.8650	1.0000	-4.9477	0.9995	-3.3426	0.7202	-0.5840	0.4269	0.0000	0.5619	-0.1558

Source: Authors' calculations

Table 3.6: 5-Yearly excess returns

Excess Return (Equally weighted)	2010-2014	2011-2015	2012-2016	2013-2017	2014-2018	2015-2019
Gold Fund	-0.0005932	-0.0005413	-0.0004771	-0.0004652	-0.0004617	-0.0005307
Fixed Income Fund	n.a	-0.0002280	0.0000252	0.0001286	0.0002705	0.0002633
Equity Fund	0.0004519	0.0000220	0.0007974	0.0013328	0.0008864	0.0009471
Multi Asset Fund	-0.0007033	-0.0007251	-0.0002748	0.0000562	0.0001363	0.0003162
Participation Fund	n.a	n.a	n.a	n.a	0.0001485	0.0001079
Short-term Fixed Income Fund	-0.0004540	-0.0003392	-0.0002399	-0.0001414	-0.0000376	-0.0000497
Short-term Lease Certificates Fund	n.a	n.a	n.a	n.a	n.a	n.a
Money Market Fund	-0.0004628	-0.0002855	-0.0001873	-0.0000324	0.0000799	0.0000540
Excess Return (AuM-weighted)	**2010-2014**	**2011-2015**	**2012-2016**	**2013-2017**	**2014-2018**	**2015-2019**
Gold Fund	-0.0005227	-0.0004889	-0.0004351	-0.0004308	-0.0004589	-0.0005197
Fixed Income Fund	n.a	-0.0001573	0.0000343	0.0002233	0.0006065	0.0005862
Equity Fund	0.0007350	0.0002709	0.0011326	0.0014049	0.0013444	0.0014045
Multi Asset Fund	-0.0004472	-0.0006296	-0.0001357	0.0001364	0.0003209	0.0002202
Participation Fund	n.a	n.a	n.a	n.a	0.0006984	0.0006954
Short-term Fixed Income Fund	-0.0004698	-0.0003435	-0.0002831	-0.0001838	-0.0001022	-0.0001118
Short-term Lease Certificates Fund	n.a	n.a	n.a	n.a	n.a	n.a
Money Market Fund	-0.0004693	-0.0002655	-0.0001709	-0.0000312	0.0000124	-0.0000134

Source: Authors' calculations

Table 3.7: Ten-yearly excess returns' t-test analysis

Excess Return Equally Returns	P-Value	t-test
Gold Fund	0.0000	-6.0832
Fixed Income Fund	0.8497	-0.1896
Equity Fund	0.4453	0.7638
Multi Asset Fund	0.7159	-0.3642
Participation Fund	0.9219	0.0981
Short-term Fixed Income Fund	0.0000	-5.7482
Short-term Lease Certificates Fund	0.0000	-0.8892
Money Market Fund	0.3755	-3.9008
Excess Return Weighted Average	**P-Value**	**t-test**
Gold Fund	0.0000	-6.6040
Fixed Income Fund	0.6573	0.4051
Equity Fund	0.8489	1.0315
Multi Asset Fund	0.4184	-0.2061
Participation Fund	0.7995	0.8397
Short-term Fixed Income Fund	0.0000	-6.9166
Short-term Lease Certificates Fund	0.2390	-0.7097
Money Market Fund	0.0000	-4.6960

Source: Authors' calculations

Table 3.8: 10-Yearly excess returns

Excess Return (Equally weighted)	2010-2019
Gold Fund	-0.0005620
Fixed Income Fund	-0.0000489
Equity Fund	**0.0006995**
Multi Asset Fund	-0.0001936
Participation Fund	**0.0000362**
Short-term Fixed Income Fund	-0.0002519
Short-term Lease Certificates Fund	n.a
Money Market Fund	-0.0002044
Excess Return (AuM-weighted)	**2010-2019**
Gold Fund	-0.0005212
Fixed Income Fund	**0.0001401**
Equity Fund	**0.0010698**
Multi Asset Fund	-0.0001135
Participation Fund	**0.0005058**
Short-term Fixed Income Fund	-0.0002908
Short-term Lease Certificates Fund	n.a
Money Market Fund	-0.0002414

Source: Authors' calculations

Then we analyzed each of the eight mutual fund categories based on the single-index performance measures we designated for the same time intervals both with equally weighted and AuM-weighted returns data.

3.1.1 Gold funds

It is clearly observed in Figure 3.1 that the gold funds performed below the defined category benchmark between 2010 and 2019. We shall evaluate via six different single-index performance measures whether this conclusion holds from a risk-adjusted point of view as well in the following tables (Tables 3.9 and 3.10).

Tables 3.9 and 3.10 show the selected single-index performance measures for gold funds with equally weighted and AuM-weighted returns data, respectively. While the "1 Year" section of the table shows annual

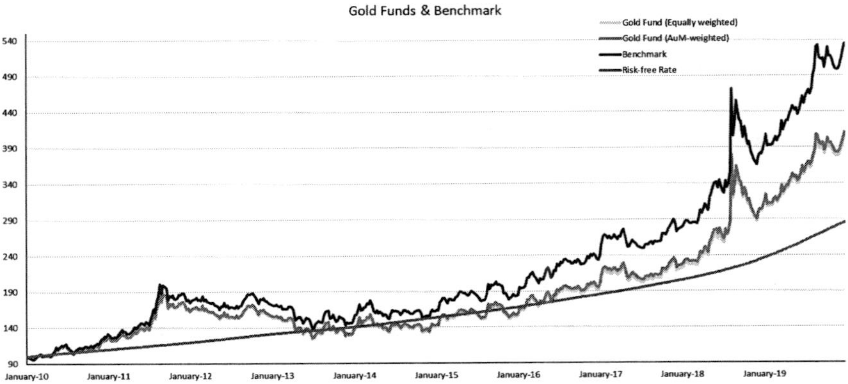

Figure 3.1: Gold funds' performance vs benchmark (2010=100)
Source: Takas İstanbul, Borsa İstanbul, Finnet; indexed by the author

performances, the "3 Year" and "5 Year" sections show performances for 3 years and for 5 years starting, respectively, with that year where the data point is located. The "10 Year" section shows the performance for the entire decade. We highlighted the successful results in the tables.

It is observed that except for the absolute risk-adjusted performance measures, namely the Sharpe and Treynor ratios, both the relative risk-adjusted performance measures (i.e., Information ratio and Jensen's alpha) and the ones based on downside risk and higher moments (i.e., Sortino and Omega ratios) yield negative results (and less than 1 in case of Omega ratio). These results indicate that gold funds could not beat their defined category benchmark which was BIST-KYD Gold Price Index.[16] This is also verified by all negative Sortino ratios which means the investors are not rewarded for taking additional risk with investing in the gold mutual funds rather than simply buying the benchmark. The Omega ratio is not above 1; i.e., the above-benchmark-returns are not more than the below-ones in any period (annual, 3-year, 5-year, the whole decade) in 10 years.

16 Although not part of the analysis, from an empirical point of view, we attribute this result to high fund management fees in gold funds which is on average 1.7 % (Table 2.8).

Table 3.9: Gold funds' performance analysis (equally weighted returns)

Gold Funds (Equally Weighted)	2010	2011	2012	2013	2014	2015	2016	2017	2018	2019
1-Year										
Sharpe Ratio	**0.123882**	**0.147063**	-0.160124	-0.158099	-0.011975	**0.017372**	**0.129970**	**0.051724**	**0.089495**	**0.101062**
Treynor Ratio	**0.002358**	**0.004852**	-0.002985	-0.004197	-0.000299	**0.000371**	**0.002537**	**0.000993**	**0.004984**	**0.002070**
Information Ratio	-1.291887	-0.468706	-0.787677	-0.359948	-0.600139	-0.432840	-0.559614	-0.335422	-0.067380	-0.199155
Jensen's Alpha	-0.000665	-0.000556	-0.000691	-0.000408	-0.000486	-0.000453	-0.000383	-0.000479	-0.000165	-0.000582
Sortino Ratio	-0.798548	-0.491893	-0.636953	-0.414401	-0.546888	-0.467020	-0.535321	-0.383899	-0.099793	-0.234641
Omega Ratio	0.039316	0.232133	0.100420	0.389277	0.189866	0.266254	0.250219	0.265332	0.782110	0.556700
3-Year										
Sharpe Ratio	**0.057252**	-0.030324	-0.105819	-0.056624	**0.038749**	**0.063970**	**0.078860**	**0.073990**		
Treynor Ratio	**0.001405**	-0.000814	-0.002490	-0.001376	**0.000862**	**0.001296**	**0.002824**	**0.002650**		
Information Ratio	-0.623658	-0.470651	-0.574241	-0.456791	-0.518966	-0.410925	-0.170683	-0.157609		
Jensen's Alpha	-0.000637	-0.000587	-0.000526	-0.000450	-0.000449	-0.000444	-0.000357	-0.000455		
Sortino Ratio	-0.583853	-0.483456	-0.539586	-0.474948	-0.508272	-0.441284	-0.235172	-0.202088		
Omega Ratio	0.138511	0.226522	0.210428	0.273747	0.229976	0.254470	0.511777	0.574915		
5-Year										
Sharpe Ratio	-0.002724	-0.018607	-0.040832	-0.005737	**0.054593**	**0.070660**				
Treynor Ratio	-0.000068	-0.000472	-0.000920	-0.000130	**0.001711**	**0.002168**				
Information Ratio	-0.563805	-0.478477	-0.532230	-0.423825	-0.219709	-0.190227				

Gold Funds (Equally Weighted)	2010	2011	2012	2013	2014	2015	2016	2017	2018	2019
Jensen's Alpha	-0.000573	-0.000538	-0.000491	-0.000453	-0.000404	-0.000445				
Sortino Ratio	-0.543366	-0.487797	-0.517081	-0.448853	-0.290824	-0.239694				
Omega Ratio	0.180590	0.227580	0.226703	0.262683	0.414908	0.492260				
10-Year										
Sharpe Ratio	0.037589									
Treynor Ratio	0.001052									
Information Ratio	-0.266767									
Jensen's Alpha	-0.000507									
Sortino Ratio	-0.321933									
Omega Ratio	0.364724									

Source: Authors' calculations

In the annual analysis, the Sharpe and Treynor ratios are positive for the first two years (i.e., 2010 and 2011) and for the last five years (i.e., 2015–2019) which means the gold mutual funds achieved aggregate risk-adjusted returns above the risk-free rate in these years but not in others.

In a 3-yearly analysis, gold funds achieved a higher performance than the risk-free rate for 5 periods out of 8 periods between 2010–2019 (figures marked in bold in the Sharpe and Treynor ratios in 3-Year section in Tables 3.9 and 3.10).

The results table does not change almost at all when the analysis is made with AuM-weighted data other than the first 5-year period between 2010–2014. In a 5-yearly analysis, gold funds achieved a higher performance than the risk-free rate for the last 2 periods (2014–2018 and 2015–2019) out of 6 periods between 2010–2019 in equally weighted and for 3 periods (2010–2014 in addition to the above two) in AuM-weighted calculations (figures marked in bold in the Sharpe and Treynor ratios in 5-Year section in Tables 3.9 and 3.10). This means in 2010–2014 period the larger gold funds had higher returns than the smaller ones and hence dragged the aggregate return above the risk-free rate.

Table 3.10: Gold funds' performance analysis (AuM-weighted returns)

Gold Funds (AuM-Weighted) Gold Funds (AuM-Weighted)	2010	2011	2012	2013	2014	2015	2016	2017	2018	2019
1-Year										
Sharpe Ratio	**0.129599**	**0.147481**	-0.152653	-0.158067	-0.009391	**0.018477**	**0.129169**	**0.053150**	**0.084641**	**0.104209**
Treynor Ratio	**0.002466**	**0.004866**	-0.002845	-0.004196	-0.000234	**0.000394**	**0.002527**	**0.001021**	**0.004709**	**0.002134**
Information Ratio	-1.491639	-0.621474	-1.254180	-0.392960	-0.673912	-0.448218	-0.923497	-0.340447	-0.141258	-0.179608
Jensen's Alpha	-0.000562	-0.000553	-0.000567	-0.000408	-0.000426	-0.000435	-0.000401	-0.000463	-0.000444	-0.000536
Sortino Ratio	-0.834989	-0.568068	-0.786853	-0.443741	-0.594007	-0.498700	-0.711394	-0.407516	-0.194031	-0.215922
Omega Ratio	0.023627	0.138791	0.023520	0.351711	0.176562	0.246698	0.082526	0.218334	0.616470	0.590787
3-Year										
Sharpe Ratio	**0.060598**	-0.027727	-0.103065	-0.055141	**0.040297**	**0.064820**	**0.076500**	**0.072290**		
Treynor Ratio	**0.001487**	-0.000744	-0.002425	-0.001340	**0.000896**	**0.001313**	**0.002738**	**0.002587**		
Information Ratio	-0.816963	-0.600929	-0.665214	-0.483252	-0.601038	-0.445229	-0.233091	-0.181505		
Jensen's Alpha	-0.000567	-0.000527	-0.000467	-0.000418	-0.000421	-0.000435	-0.000451	-0.000528		
Sortino Ratio	-0.662302	-0.559379	-0.605497	-0.508352	-0.576655	-0.490113	-0.303342	-0.226163		
Omega Ratio	0.072439	0.159299	0.176827	0.254435	0.170764	0.186353	0.394021	0.533031		
5-Year										
Sharpe Ratio	**0.000203**	-0.016276	-0.038513	-0.004116	**0.053686**	**0.069603**				
Treynor Ratio	**0.000005**	-0.000413	-0.000868	-0.000093	**0.001681**	**0.002134**				
Information Ratio	-0.693981	-0.571676	-0.619653	-0.459590	-0.279473	-0.213557				
Jensen's Alpha	-0.000508	-0.000486	-0.000445	-0.000423	-0.000441	-0.000488				

(*Continued*)

Table 3.10: Continued

Gold Funds (AuM-Weighted) Gold Funds (AuM-Weighted)	**2010**	**2011**	**2012**	**2013**	**2014**	**2015**	**2016**	**2017**	**2018**	**2019**
Sortino Ratio	-0.609514	-0.550362	-0.588001	-0.494707	-0.351056	-0.262515				
Omega Ratio	0.133685	0.179923	0.173116	0.212679	0.329998	0.446771				
10-Year										
Sharpe Ratio	0.038466									
Treynor Ratio	0.001076									
Information Ratio	-0.289607									
Jensen's Alpha	-0.000492									
Sortino Ratio	-0.341629									
Omega Ratio	0.324336									

Source: Authors' calculations

In the decade-long analysis, gold funds achieved a higher performance than the risk-free rate both in equally weighted and AuM-weighted calculations (figures marked in bold in the Sharpe and Treynor ratios in 10-Year section in Tables 3.9 and 3.10).

The Treynor ratio scatter diagrams (Figure 3.2) depict the strong relationship between the gold funds' aggregate returns and the category benchmark. This demonstrates that the fund managers prefer to include gold and gold denominated securities in their portfolios that closely follow the gold prices (which is basically the benchmark) although they have a 20 % room in their portfolios to deviate from gold and gold denominated securities. In fact, the heatmap of asset allocations (Table 2.7) shows that 96 % of gold funds are allocated to gold.

The Jensen's alpha graphics (Figure 3.3) show that the gold funds could not generate above-market returns during the analyzed 10-year period. Given the finding in Figure 3.2 that the gold funds closely follow the benchmark, we can say that the aggregate return is decreased by the fund management fee which is observed to be as high as 1.7 % on average for gold funds in the market, and hence the aggregate return is dragged below the benchmark.

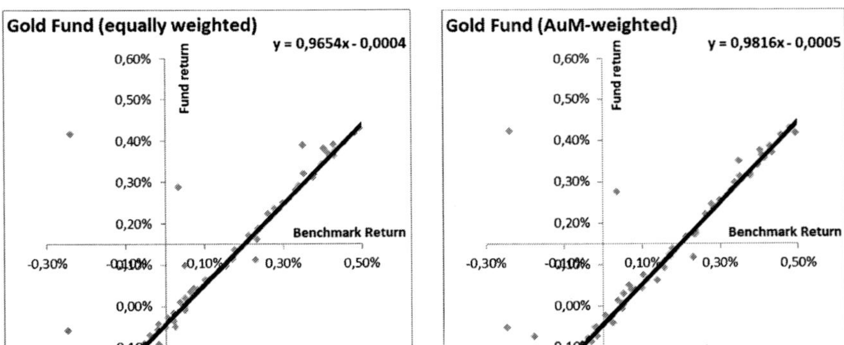

Figure 3.2: Gold funds' Treynor ratio graphics
Source: Authors' calculations

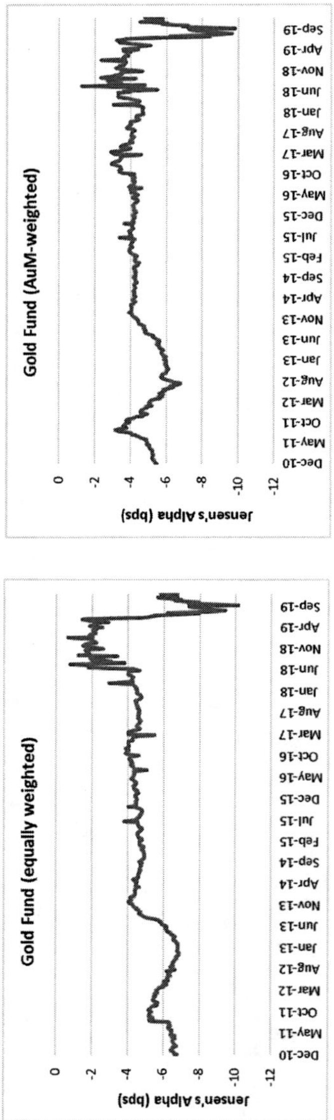

Figure 3.3: Gold funds' Jensen's alpha graphics
Source: Authors' calculations

It is interesting that this fact is also acknowledged by the portfolio managers in the market: When they are asked whether the asset-class mutual funds yield more than the specific asset itself, the portfolio managers responded in the affirmative but for gold funds (Figure 3.4).

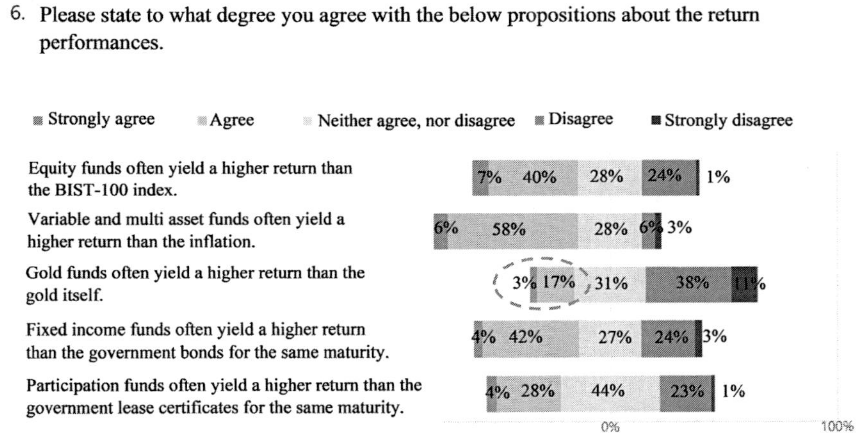

Figure 3.4: Portfolio managers' response about fund performances
Source: Survey on the portfolio managers' perception about the fund management market conducted by the authors

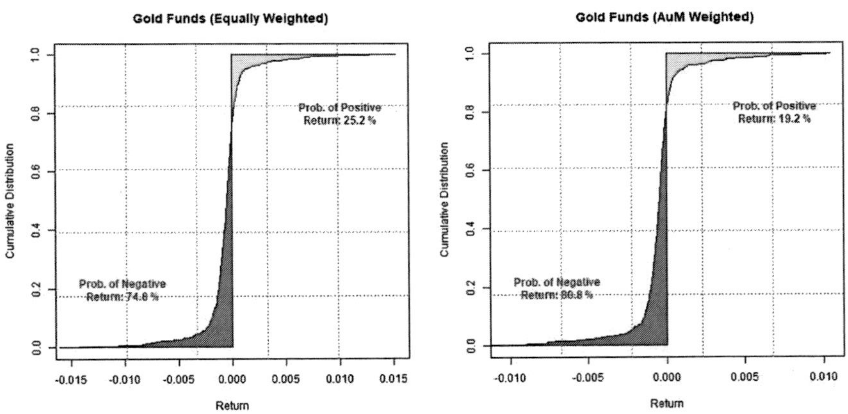

Figure 3.5: Gold funds' Omega ratio graphics
Source: Authors' calculations

The Omega ratio is basically the green area (the returns above the benchmark) divided by the red area (the returns below the benchmark) in Figure 3.5. The small Omega ratios (which are all below 1 and mostly less than 0.5 in Tables 3.9 and 3.10) show, in consistency with the Treynor ratio, that gold funds generated seldom above-benchmark returns.

3.1.2 Fixed income funds

It is observed in Figure 3.6 that the fixed income funds performed below the defined category benchmark between 2010–2017 and above the benchmark between 2018–2019.

Tables 3.11 and 3.12 show the selected single-index performance measures for fixed income funds with equally weighted and AuM-weighted returns data, respectively. The year 2010 data is not available (n.a.) as the two of three indices that form the category benchmark are only available starting from 2011.

In 2011, fixed income funds yielded negative (and below 1 in case of Omega) risk-adjusted returns as per both equally and AuM-weighted data. In 2012, only the absolute return measures became positive as per both equally and AuM-weighted data. 2013 results are the same as 2011, i.e., all negative (and Omega below 1) ratios. In 2014, the results are the same as those in 2012 as per both equally and AuM-weighted data. In 2015,

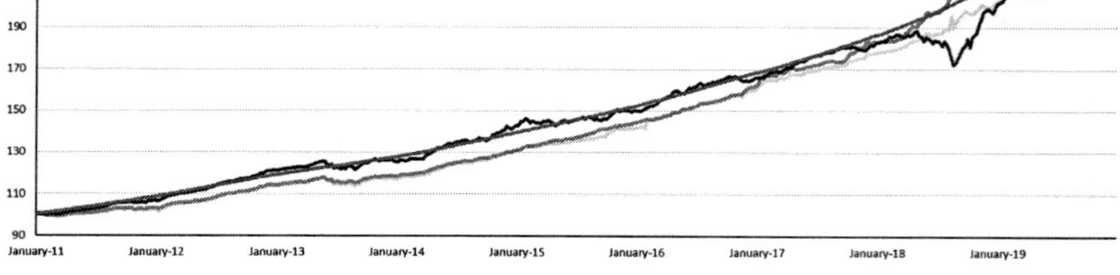

Figure 3.6: Fixed income funds' performance vs benchmark (2010=100)
Source: Takas İstanbul, Borsa İstanbul, Finnet; indexed by the authors

the Sharpe and Treynor ratios are negative as per both equally and AuM-weighted data while the other risk-adjusted performance measures are all positive and the Omegas are above 1. In 2016, all measures yield negative results as per both equally and AuM-weighted data. There is a significant size effect in years 2017 and 2018: while all results are negative (and Omega ratios are below 1) as per equally weighted data, it is vice versa as per AuM-weighted data, i.e., the larger funds must have performed better than the smaller fixed income funds. In 2019, as per both equally and AuM-weighted data, only the Sharpe and Treynor ratios are positive, indicating that the fund category could achieve returns above the risk-free rate, but not above its benchmark.

In 3-yearly analysis, the fund category yielded negative (and below 1 Omega) ratios for all the seven periods as per equally weighted data. While it has been the same situation for the first four periods as per AuM-weighted data, in the fifth period (namely 2015–2017 period), the fund category achieved positive ratios in relative performance measures and measures based on downside risk and higher moments but failed to return positive absolute risk-adjusted returns. In the following last two periods, as per AuM-weighted data, the fund category returned all positive ratios (and above 1 Omega ratios).

Table 3.11: Fixed income funds' performance analysis (equally weighted returns)

Fixed Income Funds (Equally Weighted)	2010	2011	2012	2013	2014	2015	2016	2017	2018	2019
1-Year										
Sharpe Ratio	n.a	-0.496162	**0.082314**	-0.225474	**0.090335**	-0.108931	-0.102318	-0.121218	-0.141633	**0.102389**
Treynor Ratio	n.a	-0.001011	**0.000176**	-0.001087	**0.000402**	-0.000608	-0.000421	-0.000377	-0.001522	**0.000919**
Information Ratio	n.a	-0.830171	-0.408885	-0.285436	-0.275708	**0.133366**	-0.184388	-0.045941	-0.003922	-0.130285
Jensen's Alpha	n.a	-0.000899	-0.000560	-0.000356	-0.000209	**0.000071**	-0.000287	-0.000130	-0.000391	-0.000061
Sortino Ratio	n.a	-0.658041	-0.446149	-0.337410	-0.310639	**0.251715**	-0.228239	-0.065162	-0.005508	-0.172671
Omega Ratio	n.a	0.106668	0.362435	0.456242	0.484702	**1.449663**	0.642726	0.893091	0.989788	0.695590
3-Year										
Sharpe Ratio	n.a	-0.212063	-0.054230	-0.106881	-0.050427	-0.105920	-0.115124	-0.045211		
Treynor Ratio	n.a	-0.000714	-0.000226	-0.000538	-0.000243	-0.000464	-0.000795	-0.000369		
Information Ratio	n.a	-0.509364	-0.293426	-0.084445	-0.085309	-0.005717	-0.037242	-0.055778		
Jensen's Alpha	n.a	-0.000572	-0.000365	-0.000231	-0.000166	-0.000117	-0.000265	-0.000210		
Sortino Ratio	n.a	-0.497328	-0.329687	-0.120204	-0.119697	-0.008992	-0.051523	-0.076076		
Omega Ratio	n.a	0.257078	0.441443	0.785453	0.798836	0.985080	0.892741	0.850342		
5-Year										
Sharpe Ratio	n.a	-0.141216	-0.074599	-0.105106	-0.083464	-0.065573				
Treynor Ratio	n.a	-0.000595	-0.000334	-0.000474	-0.000524	-0.000464				
Information Ratio	n.a	-0.226240	-0.141711	-0.095819	-0.041391	-0.038355				

Table 3.11: **Continued**

Fixed Income Funds (Equally Weighted)	2010	2011	2012	2013	2014	2015	2016	2017	2018	2019
Jensen's Alpha	n.a	-0.000402	-0.000245	-0.000222	-0.000197	-0.000187				
Sortino Ratio	n.a	-0.288539	-0.191980	-0.133038	-0.057812	-0.053331				
Omega Ratio	n.a	0.531325	0.677956	0.771726	0.884717	0.892087				
10-Year										
Sharpe Ratio	-0.099770									
Treynor Ratio	-0.000599									
Information Ratio	-0.114960									
Jensen's Alpha	-0.000334									
Sortino Ratio	-0.153859									
Omega Ratio	0.698773									

Source: Authors' calculations

Table 3.12: Fixed income funds' performance analysis (AuM-weighted returns)

Fixed Income Funds (AuM-Weighted)	2010	2011	2012	2013	2014	2015	2016	2017	2018	2019
					1-Year					
Sharpe Ratio	n.a	-0.501487	**0.097509**	-0.231251	**0.100716**	-0.107472	-0.089822	**0.082619**	**0.125784**	**0.071656**
Treynor Ratio	n.a	-0.000995	**0.000202**	-0.001124	**0.000469**	-0.000530	-0.000419	**0.000369**	**0.001644**	**0.000699**
Information Ratio	n.a	-1.144486	-0.704060	-0.010905	-0.208457	**0.160331**	-0.039967	**0.083406**	**0.105754**	-0.127792
Jensen's Alpha	n.a	-0.000681	-0.000410	-0.000279	-0.000090	**0.000045**	-0.000099	**0.000086**	**0.000344**	-0.000060
Sortino Ratio	n.a	-0.763723	-0.653640	-0.017531	-0.251549	**0.266546**	-0.055558	**0.130837**	**0.174571**	-0.169381
Omega Ratio	n.a	0.038903	0.158917	0.969425	0.587649	**1.471326**	0.905152	**1.235664**	**1.316411**	0.704926
					3-Year					
Sharpe Ratio	n.a	-0.211986	-0.057826	-0.113812	-0.024364	-0.051185	**0.054493**	**0.092858**		
Treynor Ratio	n.a	-0.000714	-0.000250	-0.000597	-0.000116	-0.000229	**0.000461**	**0.000850**		
Information Ratio	n.a	-0.311352	-0.176304	-0.009936	-0.019529	**0.070598**	**0.059813**	**0.010347**		
Jensen's Alpha	n.a	-0.000425	-0.000258	-0.000153	-0.000037	**0.000009**	**0.000107**	**0.000129**		
Sortino Ratio	n.a	-0.406749	-0.223586	-0.014387	-0.027741	**0.108832**	**0.096146**	**0.015492**		
Omega Ratio	n.a	0.402139	0.595547	0.974400	0.953008	**1.192058**	**1.196215**	**1.030217**		
					5-Year					
Sharpe Ratio	n.a	-0.149837	-0.065076	-0.086075	**0.034468**	**0.030739**				
Treynor Ratio	n.a	-0.000675	-0.000315	-0.000422	**0.000244**	**0.000228**				
Information Ratio	n.a	-0.102796	-0.049824	-0.001403	**0.038774**	**0.023682**				

Fixed Income Funds (AuM-Weighted)	2010	2011	2012	2013	2014	2015	2016	2017	2018	2019
Jensen's Alpha	n.a	-0.000277	-0.000126	-0.000096	**0.000070**	**0.000059**				
Sortino Ratio	n.a	-0.144775	-0.070963	-0.002032	**0.060727**	**0.035550**				
Omega Ratio	n.a	0.743253	0.873573	0.996399	**1.117777**	**1.070305**				
10-Year										
Sharpe Ratio	-0.073527									
Treynor Ratio	-0.000520									
Information Ratio	-0.028811									
Jensen's Alpha	-0.000128									
Sortino Ratio	-0.042461									
Omega Ratio	0.912515									

Source: Authors' calculations

In a 5-yearly analysis, fixed income funds yielded all negative ratios (and less than 1 Omega) in all the five periods as per equally weighted data. While it has been the same situation for the first three periods as per AuM-weighted data, in the last two periods, the AuM-weighted data yielded all positive (and Omega above 1) results, indicating that the larger funds returned better than the smaller ones and dragged the risk-adjusted returns to positive (and above 1 in case of Omega).

In the decade (9 years to be precise) long analysis, all the measures are negative (and the Omega ratio is lower than 1) as per both equally and AuM-weighted returns data (10-Year section in Tables 3.11 and 3.12).

The Treynor ratio scatter diagrams (Figure 3.7) illustrate that there is a strong positive relationship between the fixed income funds' aggregate returns and the category benchmark as per equally weighted data. However, while still positive, the strength of the relationship decreases a lot as per the AuM-weighted data.

The Jensen's alpha graphics (Figure 3.8) also depict the differentiation between the equally weighted returns' and AuM-weighted returns' results. While the alpha is mostly negative as per equally weighted data (other than for short periods and less than 2 bps), it is positive for longer periods and with higher (above 5 bps) ratios as per AuM-weighted data. This pattern indicates that the larger funds have performed better than the smaller ones.

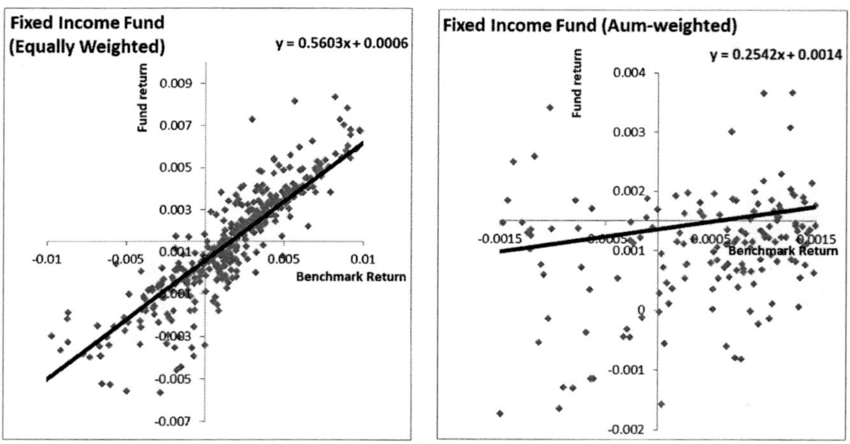

Figure 3.7: Fixed income funds' Treynor ratio graphics
Source: Authors' calculations

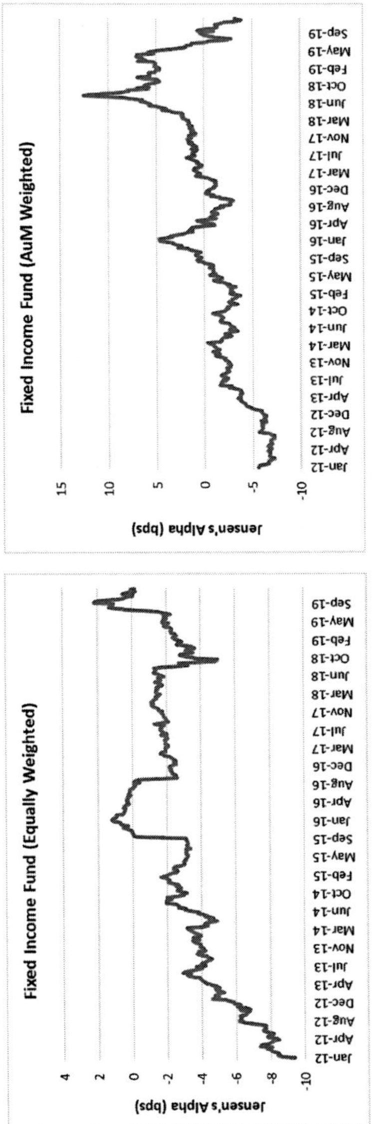

Figure 3.8: Fixed funds' Jensen's alpha graphics
Source: Authors' calculations

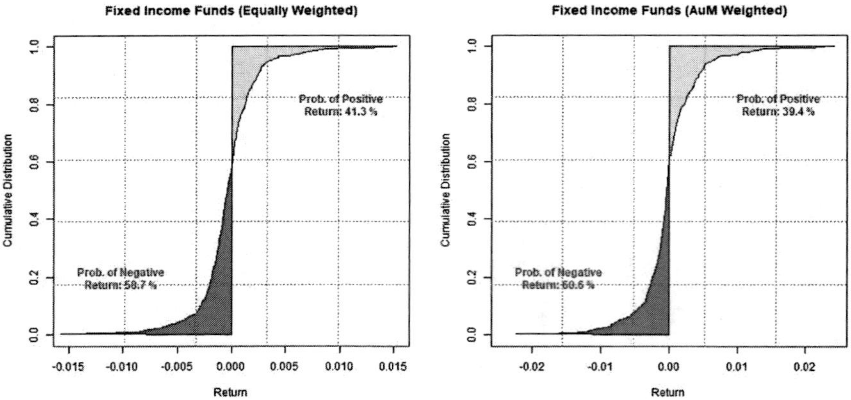

Figure 3.9: Fixed funds' omega graphics
Source: Authors' calculations

The Omega ratio is basically the green area (the returns above the benchmark) divided by the red area (the returns below the benchmark) in Figure 3.9. The probability of positive returns is around 40 % both in equally weighted returns (41 %) and in AuM-weighted returns (39 %). This finding is consistent with the portfolio managers' expectation where only 46 % agreed with the statement that fixed income funds generally yield more than the government bonds.

3.1.3 Equity funds

It is observed in Figure 3.10 that except for the August 2011–August 2012 period, the equity funds performed above the defined category benchmark almost for the entire 10 years. This result is compatible with the portfolio managers' perception where 47 % of the respondents stated that equity funds generally yield more than the BIST-100 index itself as opposed to 25 % who stated otherwise – and a 28 % were indifferent.

Tables 3.13 and 3.14 show the selected single-index performance measures for equity funds with equally weighted and AuM-weighted returns data, respectively. It is observed that the two tables are almost alike in terms of bold (i.e., positive ratios or greater than 1 in case of Omega ratio) and non-bold ones (i.e., negative ratios or less than 1 in case of Omega ratio). This is an indication that there is less of a size effect in equity funds. There

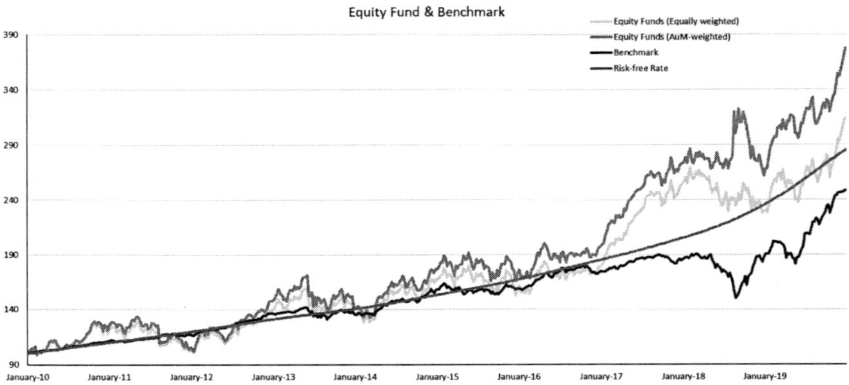

Figure 3.10: Equity funds' performance vs benchmark (2010=100)
Source: Takas İstanbul, Borsa İstanbul, Finnet; indexed by the authors

are a few different ratios in annual analysis in 2015, in 3-yearly analysis for the period of 2016–2018, and in 5-yearly analysis for the period of 2011–2015 – all of which will be explained below in the respective paragraphs.

Equity funds achieved a higher annual risk-adjusted performance than the risk-free rate for 6 years in 10 years based on the Sharpe and Treynor[17] ratios with both equally- and AuM-weighted returns data (Tables 3.13 and 3.14). It is interesting to observe that on an annual basis, based on all performance measures, there is a "successful" year (bold figures) followed by an "unsuccessful" (non-bold) one: 2010 has been successful, 2011 unsuccessful, 2012 successful, 2013 unsuccessful, 2014 successful, 2015 unsuccessful, 2016 and 2017 successful (the exception in the pattern), then 2018 unsuccessful, and 2019 successful again. As mentioned in the above paragraph, the year 2015 is different with AuM-weighted data: while only Jensen's alpha, though negligible, gives a positive ratio as per equally weighted data; Information and Sortino ratios also yield positive and Omega ratio yields greater than 1 results as per AuM-weighted data. This means that larger funds have performed better than the smaller ones to achieve above-benchmark return in 2015 and dragged the risk-adjusted performance measures to positive (and above 1 in case of Omega ratio).

17 With the addition of 2018, it is 7 out of 10 years based on the Treynor ratio with AuM-weighted data.

Table 3.13: Equity funds' performance analysis (equally weighted returns)

Equity Funds (Equally Weighted)	2010	2011	2012	2013	2014	2015	2016	2017	2018	2019
1-Year										
Sharpe Ratio	0.104991	-0.164793	0.235520	-0.048859	0.118898	-0.068540	0.008431	0.305177	-0.164926	0.118363
Treynor Ratio	0.000453	-0.002291	0.001865	-0.000657	0.001605	-0.001102	0.000111	0.019135	-0.009871	0.003470
Information Ratio	0.095453	-0.145367	0.188201	-0.002135	0.063314	-0.012385	0.011627	0.342569	-0.083657	0.063962
Jensen's Alpha	0.000982	-0.003171	0.001758	0.001658	0.000344	0.000776	0.000194	0.005236	-0.003441	0.001537
Sortino Ratio	0.130027	-0.169364	0.339002	-0.002884	0.090091	-0.018382	0.018049	0.671202	-0.107127	0.096608
Omega Ratio	1.269321	0.649833	1.631106	0.994354	1.175038	0.969429	1.157849	2.394850	0.808421	1.162865
3-Year										
Sharpe Ratio	0.031042	-0.020440	0.073974	-0.011790	0.010501	0.051817	0.013125	0.052593		
Treynor Ratio	0.000274	-0.000235	0.000901	-0.000170	0.000151	0.000811	0.000500	0.001999		
Information Ratio	0.020682	-0.009292	0.070830	0.010846	0.016647	0.100759	0.059075	0.072739		
Jensen's Alpha	0.000076	0.000156	0.001044	0.000651	0.000346	0.002198	0.000806	0.001465		
Sortino Ratio	0.027068	-0.012162	0.102176	0.015203	0.024163	0.158727	0.084577	0.104293		
Omega Ratio	1.057876	0.974622	1.205332	1.028498	1.042709	1.286785	1.202180	1.199900		
5-Year										
Sharpe Ratio	0.025468	-0.008143	0.029669	0.037066	0.012390	0.017210				
Treynor Ratio	0.000303	-0.000109	0.000393	0.000534	0.000337	0.000512				
Information Ratio	0.021844	0.001036	0.041275	0.068444	0.043627	0.044857				

Table 3.13: Continued

Equity Funds (Equally Weighted)	2010	2011	2012	2013	2014	2015	2016	2017	2018	2019
Jensen's Alpha	0.000319	0.000206	0.000878	0.001620	0.000779	0.000832				
Sortino Ratio	0.028993	0.001400	0.059858	0.100617	0.062331	0.064732				
Omega Ratio	1.060456	1.002785	1.111986	1.191402	1.117896	1.118722				
10-Year										
Sharpe Ratio	0.021339									
Treynor Ratio	0.000501									
Information Ratio	0.033496									
Jensen's Alpha	0.000698									
Sortino Ratio	0.046275									
Omega Ratio	1.090537									

Source: Authors' calculations

In a 3-yearly analysis, equity funds achieved a higher performance in all performance measures almost during all 8 periods; the only exception is the period of 2011–2013 when all measures yield negative results (below 1 for Omega ratio) other than the Jensen's alpha both based on equally- and AuM-based data (3-Year section in Tables 3.13 and 3.14). The Sharpe and Treynor ratios are negative for the period of 2013–2015 (both based on equally- and AuM-based data) which shows that the equity funds performed below the risk-free rate for this period. The Treynor ratio is negative for the 2016–2018 period as well based on AuM-weighted data, because the beta is negative for this specific period.

In a 5-yearly analysis, equity funds achieved a higher performance in almost all performance measures during all 6 periods both based on equally- and AuM-based data (5-Year section in Tables 3.13 and 3.14). The only exception is the period of 2011–2015 when the Sharpe and Treynor ratios yield negative results based on equally weighted data – which means the smaller funds performed worse than the larger ones dragging the aggregate return below the risk-free rate.

Table 3.14: Equity funds' performance analysis (AuM-weighted returns)

Equity Funds (AuM-Weighted)	2010	2011	2012	2013	2014	2015	2016	2017	2018	2019
1-Year										
Sharpe Ratio	0.124281	-0.157636	0.249556	-0.050046	0.128158	-0.050650	0.021940	0.289250	-0.084929	0.180259
Treynor Ratio	0.000538	-0.002556	0.002008	-0.000673	0.001717	-0.000797	0.000293	0.335979	0.011382	0.006819
Information Ratio	0.116119	-0.139088	0.208507	-0.009607	0.080830	0.008147	0.028034	0.319266	-0.014341	0.090643
Jensen's Alpha	0.001508	-0.003416	0.002284	0.001814	0.000556	0.001335	0.000458	0.004496	-0.003120	0.002562
Sortino Ratio	0.161578	-0.161262	0.379713	-0.012827	0.116973	0.012148	0.044529	0.637428	-0.023425	0.130774
Omega Ratio	1.338417	0.657860	1.728757	0.974707	1.227840	1.020834	1.204890	2.328108	0.958078	1.276710
3-Year										
Sharpe Ratio	0.045470	-0.013859	0.078956	-0.003205	0.026429	0.054877	0.032842	0.076528		
Treynor Ratio	0.000421	-0.000160	0.000963	-0.000046	0.000377	0.000864	-0.176292	0.018953		
Information Ratio	0.036540	-0.003200	0.077459	0.019441	0.035970	0.104428	0.064538	0.078927		
Jensen's Alpha	0.000459	0.000352	0.001288	0.000947	0.000725	0.002243	0.000749	0.001788		
Sortino Ratio	0.048189	-0.004180	0.111503	0.027087	0.052892	0.165728	0.107149	0.128269		
Omega Ratio	1.105307	0.991118	1.228465	1.052106	1.095874	1.308366	1.252199	1.269760		
5-Year										
Sharpe Ratio	0.034156	0.001844	0.041175	0.038265	0.031024	0.037056				
Treynor Ratio	0.000408	0.000025	0.000545	0.000549	0.001732	0.002380				
Information Ratio	0.031947	0.011686	0.054285	0.068397	0.055782	0.057770				

(*Continued*)

Table 3.14: Continued

Equity Funds (AuM-Weighted)	2010	2011	2012	2013	2014	2015	2016	2017	2018	2019
Jensen's Alpha	0.000575	0.000487	0.001226	0.001734	0.000994	0.001058				
Sortino Ratio	0.042545	0.015737	0.078897	0.099669	0.088516	0.091458				
Omega Ratio	1.090275	1.032142	1.152493	1.196462	1.173190	1.180970				
10-Year										
Sharpe Ratio	0.035528									
Treynor Ratio	0.001287									
Information Ratio	0.045236									
Jensen's Alpha	0.000896									
Sortino Ratio	0.065450									
Omega Ratio	1.134537									

Source: Authors' calculations

In the decade-long analysis, equity funds achieved a higher performance in all performance measures based on both equally and AuM-based data (10-Year section in Tables 3.13 and 3.14). As stated earlier, this means that the portfolio managers' perception about equity funds yielding more than the BIST-100 itself holds in the long term.

The Treynor ratio scatter diagrams (Figure 3.11) illustrate that there is a strong relationship between the equity funds' aggregate returns and the category benchmark. The heatmap in Table 2.6 shows that 76 % of assets are invested in stocks trading at Borsa İstanbul; hence the strong relationship with the category benchmark which is nothing but the BIST-100 itself.

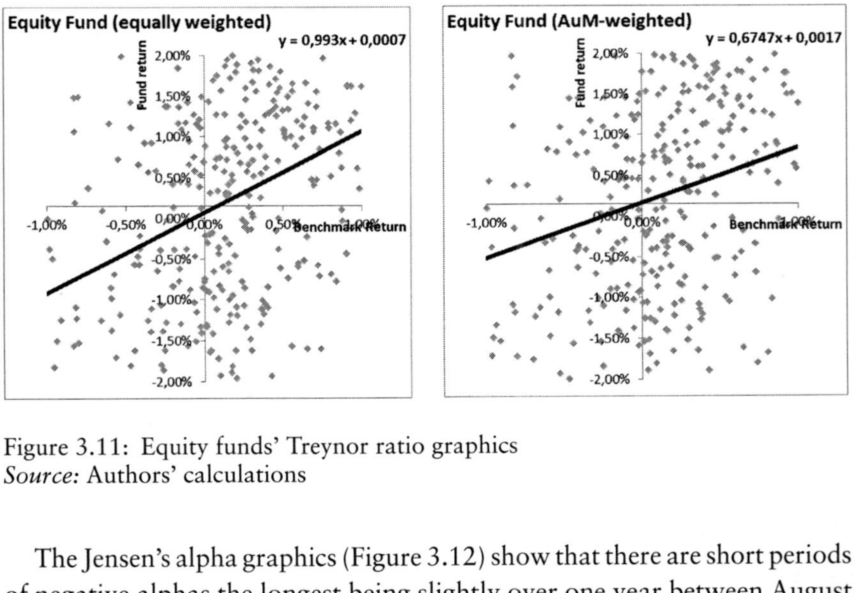

Figure 3.11: Equity funds' Treynor ratio graphics
Source: Authors' calculations

The Jensen's alpha graphics (Figure 3.12) show that there are short periods of negative alphas the longest being slightly over one year between August 2011–October 2012, and the others being shorter such as 7 months between May-November 2016, 3 months between December 2018–February 2019, and 5 months between July-December 2019. This is an indication that the portfolio managers often generate higher risk-adjusted returns than the CAPM-deducted ones in equity funds.

The Omega ratios of equity funds, both with equally- and AuM-weighted returns, indicate that the probability of positive returns (57 %) is higher than the negative ones (Figure 3.13). Hence, we can say that the investors can entrust their investments in equities to the portfolio managers.

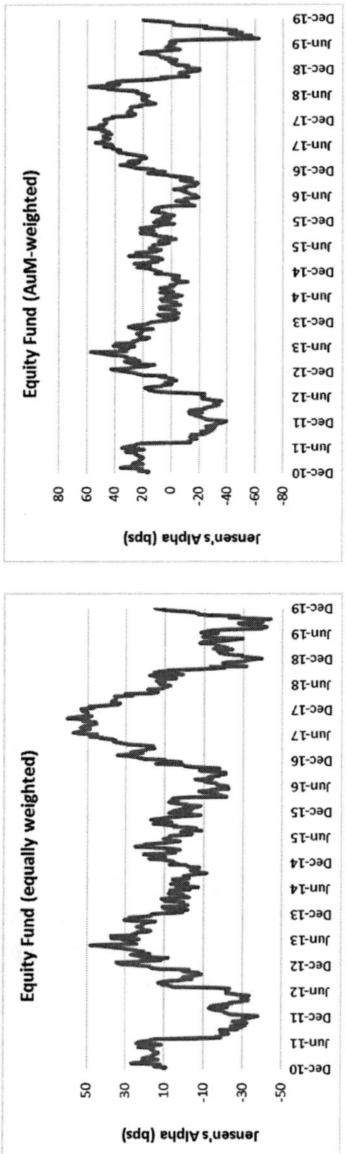

Figure 3.12: Equity funds' Jensen's alpha graphics
Source: Authors' calculations

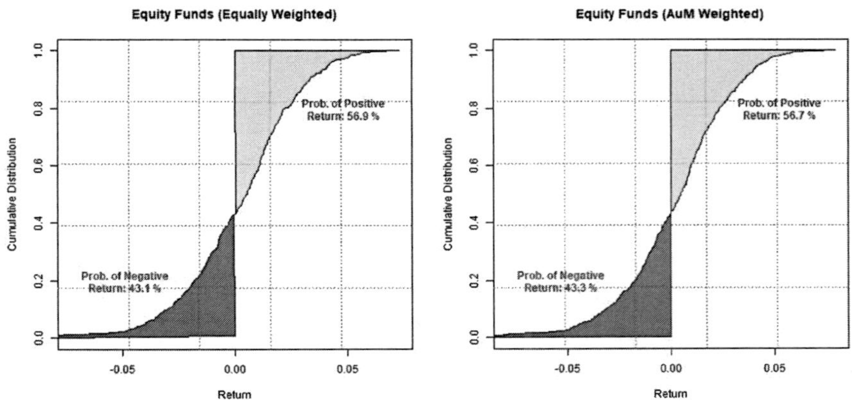

Figure 3.13: Equity funds' Omega graphics
Source: Authors' calculations

3.1.4 Multi asset funds

As observed in Figure 3.14, multi asset funds almost always performed below the category benchmark other than about 3 months between August-October 2018.

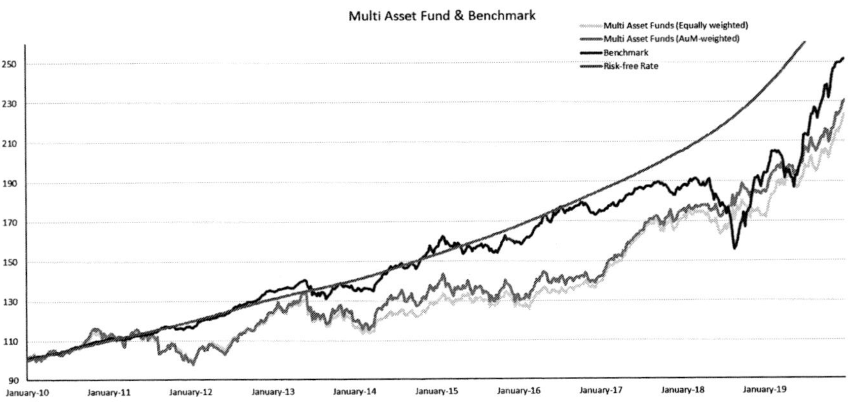

Figure 3.14: Multi asset funds' performance vs benchmark (2010=100)
Source: Takas İstanbul, Borsa İstanbul, Finnet; indexed by the authors

This result may be due to inappropriate benchmark selection. As the name suggests, it is difficult to represent the multi asset fund category with a benchmark. Compared to the realized asset allocations of 10 years in multi asset funds (Figure 3.2), we seem to have underrated BIST-100 index (25 % in benchmark vs 35 % in real allocations) and overrated government bond index (65 % in benchmark vs 32 % in real allocations).

Tables 3.15 and 3.16 show the selected single-index performance measures for equity funds with equally weighted and AuM-weighted returns data, respectively.

The annual analysis sections are almost alike in terms of bold (i.e., positive ratios or greater than 1 in case of Omega ratio) figures in equally- and AuM-weighted data other than 2018 and 2019. All measures indicate positive risk-adjusted returns (and above 1 Omega) in 2010, except the Jensen's alpha. In 2011, they all become negative and less than 1 in Omega. In 2012, all become positive again and vice versa in 2013. In 2014, the negative results prevail other than the absolute risk-adjusted return measures which means the fund category return has been above the risk-free rate. The negative results, this time as per all measures, continue to be negative in 2015 and 2016. In 2017, they are all positive (and Omega above 1). While all measures are negative as per equally weighted data in 2018, as per AuM-weighted data, Information and Sortino ratios become positive and Omega ratio becomes greater than 1. The larger multi asset funds must have performed better in 2018 than the smaller ones. In 2019, Sharpe, Treynor, and Jens's alpha ratios are positive while other measures are negative (and Omega less than 1). This time indicating that the smaller ones must have performed better than the larger funds.

Table 3.15: Multi asset funds' performance analysis (equally weighted returns)

Multi Asset Funds (Equally Weighted)	2010	2011	2012	2013	2014	2015	2016	2017	2018	2019
1-Year										
Sharpe Ratio	**0.024740**	-0.209824	**0.212881**	-0.134569	**0.028656**	-0.124980	-0.061166	**0.228816**	-0.174660	**0.123001**
Treynor Ratio	**0.000094**	-0.002019	**0.001322**	-0.001544	**0.000339**	-0.001733	-0.000735	**0.005154**	-0.020502	**0.003940**
Information Ratio	**0.007368**	-0.182878	**0.129576**	-0.081697	-0.133059	-0.004087	-0.070513	**0.298219**	-0.026454	-0.004505
Jensen's Alpha	-0.000231	-0.002408	**0.000543**	-0.000384	-0.000713	-0.000272	-0.000535	**0.002351**	-0.002190	**0.000900**
Sortino Ratio	**0.009307**	-0.205215	**0.218397**	-0.104651	-0.163717	-0.006343	-0.097501	**0.561271**	-0.040747	-0.006303
Omega Ratio	**1.019196**	0.566943	**1.405210**	0.804294	0.721085	0.989140	0.948998	**2.140364**	0.925487	0.988162
3-Year										
Sharpe Ratio	-0.026700	-0.079864	**0.003326**	-0.088486	-0.056914	**0.002290**	-0.027131	**0.032077**		
Treynor Ratio	-0.000183	-0.000773	**0.000035**	-0.001104	-0.000723	**0.000031**	-0.001387	**0.001553**		
Information Ratio	-0.045756	-0.071808	-0.028754	-0.069021	-0.063385	**0.083420**	**0.039821**	**0.045594**		
Jensen's Alpha	-0.000692	-0.000729	-0.000329	-0.000639	-0.000523	**0.000550**	-0.000114	**0.000463**		
Sortino Ratio	-0.056008	-0.088405	-0.038819	-0.091636	-0.086472	**0.131494**	**0.062125**	**0.069375**		
Omega Ratio	0.876780	0.813598	0.927170	0.833214	0.848996	**1.242575**	**1.160725**	**1.139185**		

(Continued)

Multi Asset Funds (Equally Weighted)	2010	2011	2012	2013	2014	2015	2016	2017	2018	2019
5-Year										
Sharpe Ratio	-0.046129	-0.071308	-0.032046	-0.032837	-0.038225	-0.015125				
Treynor Ratio	-0.000476	-0.000853	-0.000372	-0.000409	-0.001125	-0.000496				
Information Ratio	-0.064727	-0.067524	-0.030532	**0.006101**	**0.011294**	**0.023856**				
Jensen's Alpha	-0.000731	-0.000706	-0.000274	**0.000025**	-0.000211	-0.000003				
Sortino Ratio	-0.079827	-0.085188	-0.041954	**0.008611**	**0.017108**	**0.035888**				
Omega Ratio	0.834767	0.826804	0.922739	**1.016087**	**1.033964**	**1.071615**				
10-Year										
Sharpe Ratio	-0.031568									
Treynor Ratio	-0.000757									
Information Ratio	-0.015970									
Jensen's Alpha	-0.000287									
Sortino Ratio	-0.021966									
Omega Ratio	0.955364									

Source: Authors' calculations

In 3-yearly analysis, the first two periods have negative risk-adjusted returns in all measures both as per equally and AuM-weighted data. In the third period (2012–2014), all measures continue to be negative based on equally weighted data while it is vice versa based on AuM-weighted data. We can state that in this period the larger funds must have shown better risk-adjusted performance than the smaller ones. In the following two periods based on both equally and AuM-weighted data, all measures yield negative results again. In period 2015–2017, all measures are successful as per equally weighted data while the Sharpe and Treynor ratios are negative as per AuM-weighted data which means the larger funds failed to generate risk-adjusted returns above the risk-free rate. In the period 2016–2018, the Sharpe and Treynor ratios are negative as per both equally and AuM-weighted data while all other measures indicate successful results as per both data structure.[18] In the last 3-yearly period, all measures yielded successful results as per both equally and AuM-weighted data.

In 5-yearly analysis, all periods yield the same results as per both equally and AuM-weighted data.[19] In the first three periods, all measures show unsuccessful results. In the last three periods, the Sharpe and Treynor ratios are negative while all others yield successful results. In a decade-long analysis all measures show unsuccessful results both as per equally and AuM-weighted data which indicates that the multi asset fund category could not beat the defined category benchmark as was illustrated in Figure 3.14.

18 Jensen's alpha is negative as per equally weighted data but it is negligible.
19 Jensen's alphas are negligible, hence not included in the explanations.

Table 3.16: Multi asset funds' performance analysis (AuM-weighted returns)

Multi Asset Funds (AuM-Weighted)	2010	2011	2012	2013	2014	2015	2016	2017	2018	2019
1-Year										
Sharpe Ratio	**0.039544**	-0.198263	**0.224471**	-0.103356	**0.069407**	-0.126708	-0.056406	**0.240147**	-0.145710	**0.064632**
Treynor Ratio	**0.000152**	-0.001849	**0.001388**	-0.001202	**0.000733**	-0.001529	-0.000565	**0.005581**	-0.012422	**0.001522**
Information Ratio	**0.024359**	-0.175176	**0.153926**	-0.047664	-0.029975	-0.056752	-0.078472	**0.308098**	**0.013991**	-0.067055
Jensen's Alpha	-0.000084	-0.002518	**0.000732**	**0.000123**	-0.000650	-0.000164	-0.000588	**0.002433**	-0.001343	-0.000011
Sortino Ratio	**0.031178**	-0.202128	**0.253992**	-0.063358	-0.040656	-0.083423	-0.113153	**0.656095**	**0.022417**	-0.093628
Omega Ratio	**1.065295**	0.586596	**1.484033**	0.881752	0.926167	0.865597	0.937991	**2.263774**	**1.040410**	0.836300
3-Year										
Sharpe Ratio	-0.016674	-0.062206	**0.033660**	-0.062209	-0.041648	-0.013707	-0.001146	**0.042114**		
Treynor Ratio	-0.000113	-0.000611	**0.000336**	-0.000716	-0.000457	-0.000155	-0.000045	**0.001526**		
Information Ratio	-0.032874	-0.052520	**0.016921**	-0.045622	-0.052494	**0.055226**	**0.064536**	**0.055557**		
Jensen's Alpha	-0.000646	-0.000542	**0.000037**	-0.000329	-0.000492	**0.000618**	**0.000296**	**0.000545**		
Sortino Ratio	-0.040991	-0.066340	**0.023630**	-0.062394	-0.073397	**0.087388**	**0.105912**	**0.088506**		
Omega Ratio	0.910488	0.862027	**1.045238**	0.888263	0.875051	**1.152237**	**1.243769**	**1.170675**		
5-Year										
Sharpe Ratio	-0.022482	-0.052674	-0.016299	-0.021144	-0.018365	-0.022208				
Treynor Ratio	-0.000218	-0.000571	-0.000171	-0.000236	-0.000429	-0.000579				
Information Ratio	-0.035528	-0.049517	-0.012781	**0.012879**	**0.026402**	**0.017549**				

Multi Asset Funds (AuM-Weighted)	**2010**	**2011**	**2012**	**2013**	**2014**	**2015**	**2016**	**2017**	**2018**	**2019**
Jensen's Alpha	-0.000507	-0.000533	-0.000098	**0.000255**	**0.000064**	-0.000042				
Sortino Ratio	-0.045191	-0.064221	-0.017952	**0.018570**	**0.040936**	**0.027132**				
Omega Ratio	0.906362	0.872706	0.967462	**1.034075**	**1.075893**	**1.049796**				
					10-Year					
Sharpe Ratio	-0.022249									
Treynor Ratio	-0.000463									
Information Ratio	-0.009038									
Jensen's Alpha	-0.000191									
Sortino Ratio	-0.012543									
Omega Ratio	0.975318									

Source: Authors' calculations

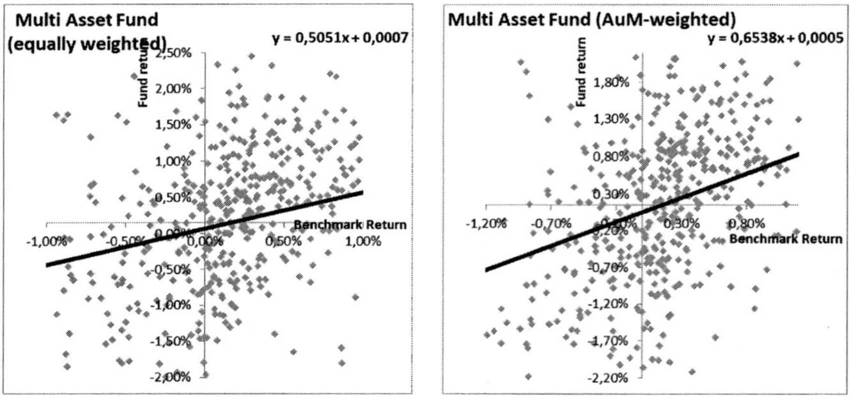

Figure 3.15: Multi asset funds' Treynor ratio graphics
Source: Authors' calculations

The Treynor ratio scatter diagrams above (Figure 3.15) illustrate that there is a strong relationship between the multi asset funds' aggregate returns and the category benchmark although we mentioned that the benchmark might be missing some weight on BIST-100 index as evidenced by the heatmap in Table 2.7.

The Jensen's alpha graphics (Figure 3.16) demonstrate that the multi asset funds could create positive alphas only for two short periods: 2013 and 2017–June 2018. This finding follows the general picture painted above where we observe that the multi asset funds could not beat the market, i.e., the defined category benchmark.

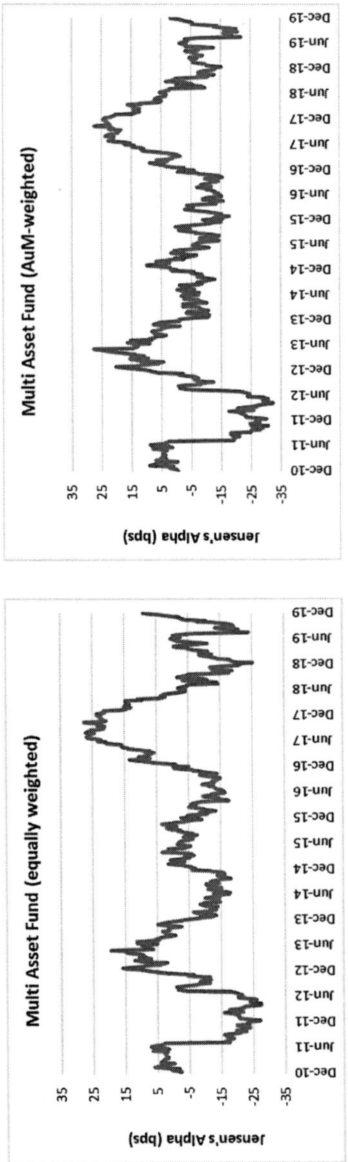

Figure 3.16: Multi asset funds' Jensen's alpha graphics
Source: Authors' calculations

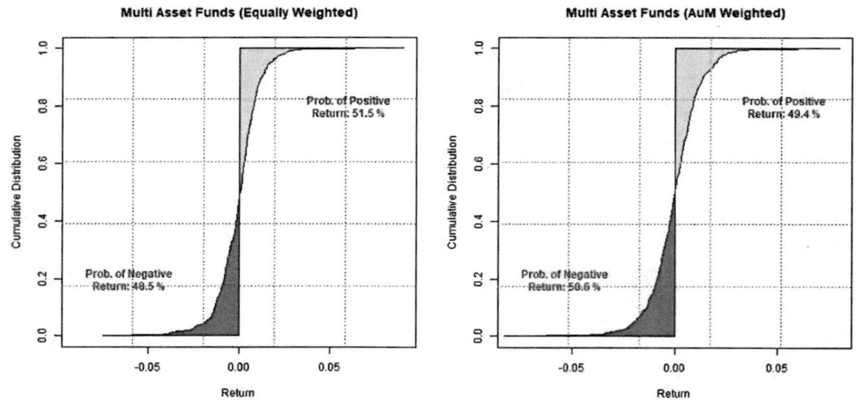

Figure 3.17: Multi asset funds' Omega graphics
Source: Authors' calculations

The Omega ratios of multi asset funds, both with equally and AuM-weighted returns, (51 and 49 %, respectively) indicate that the probability of positive returns is almost the same with the negative ones (Figure 3.17).

3.1.5 Participation funds

Participation (a.k.a. Islamic or non-interest bearing) funds are relatively new to the investors and still have a small share in the market: their market share within our analyzed universe starts at 0.2 % in 2010, increases to 0.5 % in 2013 and ends at 0.9 % (not even 1 %) in 2019. There are two distinguishing features in the below graphic of this fund category's returns compared to the risk-free rate and the defined category benchmark (Figure 3.18): (i) the return performance of the funds calculated based on *equally weighted* data has always been below the return performance of the funds calculated based on *AuM-weighted* data, (ii) the return performance of the funds calculated based on equally weighted data has even been below the risk-free rate for most of the observed period until August 2018.

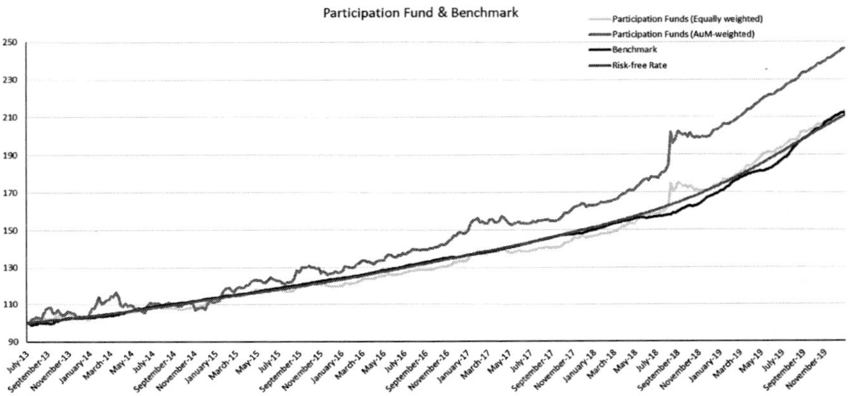

Figure 3.18: Participation funds' performance vs benchmark (July 2013=100)
Source: Takas İstanbul, Borsa İstanbul, Finnet; indexed by the authors

These results indicate that while larger funds yield above risk-free and benchmark returns, the smaller funds cannot. In other words, smaller participation funds cannot generate as high returns as larger ones. This is due to the nature of the participation asset market which is dominated by the participation banks and the government as issuers and again by the participation banks as owners of participation asset management companies who are the managers of larger participation funds in the market. In short, the assets in the market are scarce and the larger funds crowd out the market for high yielding assets. The second feature observed can also partially be attributed to the explained crowding out effect. But also, to the very definition of the participation funds should be playing a role: the risk-free rate is the 2-year government bond return, i.e., the interest rate as per the yield generated in the market on the government bonds; however, participation funds, by definition, cannot invest in interest-bearing assets. Although the funding market is the same for the participation assets as well, i.e., the profit rates generated by the participation accounts do follow the interest rates on commercial bank accounts, the timing may differ such that in rising interest rate environment, participation asset returns follow the interest rates from behind while in decreasing interest rate environment, participation asset returns stay above the interest rates for some more time before levelling out when the high yielding financial assets are exhausted.

Table 3.17: Participation funds' performance analysis (equally weighted returns)

Participation Funds (Equally Weighted)	2010	2011	2012	2013	2014	2015	2016	2017	2018	2019
1-Year										
Sharpe Ratio	n.a	n.a	n.a	n.a	**0.012042**	-0.057036	**0.044398**	-0.045808	**0.063066**	**0.048525**
Treynor Ratio	n.a	n.a	n.a	n.a	**0.000162**	-0.000162	-0.000438	**0.000140**	-0.000774	-0.000747
Information Ratio	n.a	n.a	n.a	n.a	-0.033104	-0.065943	**0.090327**	-0.005865	**0.076917**	-0.086743
Jensen's Alpha	n.a	n.a	n.a	n.a	-0.000027	-0.000310	**0.000074**	-0.000431	**0.000565**	**0.000262**
Sortino Ratio	n.a	n.a	n.a	n.a	-0.045509	-0.094517	**0.150149**	-0.008966	**0.158003**	-0.115368
Omega Ratio	n.a	n.a	n.a	n.a	0.907180	0.850258	**1.285094**	0.984935	**1.331554**	0.809415
3-Year										
Sharpe Ratio	n.a	n.a	n.a	n.a	-0.006862	-0.029563	**0.030035**	**0.031797**		
Treynor Ratio	n.a	n.a	n.a	n.a	-0.000072	**0.000443**	-0.000288	-0.000781		
Information Ratio	n.a	n.a	n.a	n.a	-0.017313	-0.006304	**0.049958**	**0.023846**		
Jensen's Alpha	n.a	n.a	n.a	n.a	-0.000047	-0.000138	**0.000088**	**0.000260**		
Sortino Ratio	n.a	n.a	n.a	n.a	-0.024810	-0.009534	**0.097111**	**0.044398**		
Omega Ratio	n.a	n.a	n.a	n.a	0.953843	0.983901	**1.215834**	**1.087576**		
5-Year										
Sharpe Ratio	n.a	n.a	n.a	n.a	**0.014899**	**0.018339**				
Treynor Ratio	n.a	n.a	n.a	n.a	-0.000229	-0.000861				

Participation Funds (Equally Weighted)	2010	2011	2012	2013	2014	2015	2016	2017	2018	2019
Information Ratio	n.a	n.a	n.a	n.a	0.021549	0.015924				
Jensen's Alpha	n.a	n.a	n.a	n.a	0.000078	0.000119				
Sortino Ratio	n.a	n.a	n.a	n.a	0.038567	0.028733				
Omega Ratio	n.a	n.a	n.a	n.a	1.078059	1.056021				
6.5-Year										
Sharpe Ratio	0.008908				0.008834					
Treynor Ratio	-0.001361				-0.001361					
Information Ratio	0.005336				0.005336					
Jensen's Alpha	0.000058				0.000058					
Sortino Ratio	0.009059				0.009059					
Omega Ratio	1.017750				1.017750					

Source: Author's calculations

Our analysis begins with the year 2014, because the indices forming the benchmark started to be calculated by the index provider on 28 June 2013.

The annual analysis results are quite different based on equally and AuM-weighted returns data as observed in Figure 3.18 (Tables 3.17 and 3.18). In 2014, the Sharpe and Treynor ratios are positive, and the rest are negative (and the Omega ratio is less than 1) as per equally weighted data. As per AuM-weighted data, Sharpe ratio is positive, but the Treynor ratio is positive thanks to negative beta. We shall observe this somewhat contradicting result between Sharpe and Treynor ratios in participation funds because the beta is negative as per both equally and AuM-weighted data – as observed in Figure 3.19. In 2015, while all ratios are negative (and the Omega ratio is less than 1) as per equally weighted data, it is vice versa as per AuM-weighted data since the larger funds raise the risk-adjusted aggregate return above the risk-free rate and the defined category benchmark. This pattern of contradicting results between equally and AuM-weighted data is the outcome of the market dynamics explained in the second paragraph of this sub-section above. In 2016, both the equally and AuM-weighted data yield positive results (and Omega above 1) in terms of all the measures but the Treynor ratio – again negative betas at work. The 2017 results are like 2015 results: all measures yield negative (and Omega less than 1) results (except for a negligible positive Treynor) as per equally weighted data and other than a positive Sharpe ratio, it is vice versa as per AuM-weighted data (except for a negligible Jensen's alpha). 2018 results are the same with those of 2016. In 2019, except for a positive Sharpe ratio (and a negligible Jensen's alpha) as per equally weighted data, all measures yield negative results both as per equally and AuM-weighted data.

In 3-yearly analysis, the first two periods, namely 2014–2016 and 2015–2017 periods, have unsuccessful results as per equally weighted data (other than a negligible positive Treynor ratio in the second period). However, as per AuM-weighted data both periods have successful results (other than negative negligible Treynor ratios in both periods). Again, the market dynamics mentioned in the second paragraph of this sub-section are at work. The remaining two periods (namely 2016–2018 and 2017–2019) in the 3-yearly analysis yield the same successful results as per both equally and AuM-weighted data: all measures other than the Treynor ratios are positive, and the Omega ratios are greater than 1. The Treynor ratios being negative suggest that the participation funds' correlation with the risk-free rate is negative during these periods, i.e., the funds' returns are increasing while the risk-free rate, which is basically the 2-year government bond yield, is decreasing – a phenomenon we explained in the second paragraph of this sub-section.

There are only two 5-yearly periods both of which produced successful results in terms of all measures (again other than negative negligible Treynor ratios) as per borh equally and AuM-weighted data.

As the oldest benchmark data starts in July 2013, the longest period lasts for 6.5 years in which all measures result in positive (and in case of Omega greater than 1) ratios as per both equally and AuM-weighted returns (again except the negative negligible Treynor ratio as per equally weighted data).

Table 3.18: Participation funds' performance analysis (AuM-weighted returns)

Participation Funds (AuM-Weighted)	2010	2011	2012	2013	2014	2015	2016	2017	2018	2019
1-Year										
Sharpe Ratio	n.a	n.a	n.a	n.a	-0.022432	0.093851	0.190930	-0.018188	0.117590	-0.036282
Treynor Ratio	n.a	n.a	n.a	n.a	0.003876	0.001028	-0.000480	0.000068	-0.001532	0.001547
Information Ratio	n.a	n.a	n.a	n.a	-0.037152	0.090893	0.202847	0.005259	0.127656	-0.184062
Jensen's Alpha	n.a	n.a	n.a	n.a	-0.000331	0.000956	0.000714	-0.000450	0.001501	-0.000048
Sortino Ratio	n.a	n.a	n.a	n.a	-0.050835	0.164105	0.367358	0.007886	0.318666	-0.222308
Omega Ratio	n.a	n.a	n.a	n.a	0.904944	1.282104	1.645408	1.014220	1.702240	0.628646
3-Year										
Sharpe Ratio	n.a	n.a	n.a	n.a	0.048083	0.077387	0.087202	0.053774		
Treynor Ratio	n.a	n.a	n.a	n.a	-0.001047	-0.000462	-0.000773	-0.001401		
Information Ratio	n.a	n.a	n.a	n.a	0.043900	0.087156	0.100731	0.046507		
Jensen's Alpha	n.a	n.a	n.a	n.a	0.000567	0.000499	0.000669	0.000531		
Sortino Ratio	n.a	n.a	n.a	n.a	0.065481	0.149642	0.212765	0.096760		
Omega Ratio	n.a	n.a	n.a	n.a	1.133004	1.270091	1.430050	1.195474		
5-Year										
Sharpe Ratio	n.a	n.a	n.a	n.a	0.056850	0.077585				
Treynor Ratio	n.a	n.a	n.a	n.a	-0.000801	-0.002103				
Information Ratio	n.a	n.a	n.a	n.a	0.060134	0.074003				

Participation Funds (AuM-Weighted)	2010	2011	2012	2013	2014	2015	2016	2017	2018	2019
Jensen's Alpha	n.a	n.a	n.a	n.a	0.000609	0.000708				
Sortino Ratio	n.a	n.a	n.a	n.a	0.101496	0.146959				
Omega Ratio	n.a	n.a	n.a	n.a	1.207997	1.283661				
6.5-Year										
Sharpe Ratio	0.049289				0.049229					
Treynor Ratio	-0.001142				0.000766					
Information Ratio	0.045673				0.045673					
Jensen's Alpha	0.000512				0.000512					
Sortino Ratio	0.074482				0.074482					
Omega Ratio	1.156082				1.156082					

Source: Authors' calculations

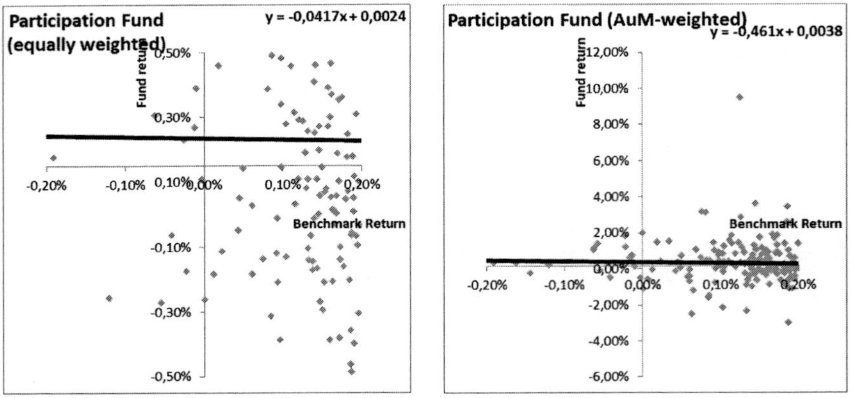

Figure 3.19: Participation funds' Treynor ratio graphics
Source: Authors' calculations

The Treynor ratio scatter diagrams (Figure 3.19) are the only set of graphs that illustrate two different results as per equally and AuM-weighted data: while the equally weighted data draws no relationship between the participation funds' aggregate returns and the category benchmark, the AuM-weighted data draws a negative relationship.

The Jensen's alpha graphics (Figure 3.20) also support our general conclusion about the participation funds that the larger funds have dragged up the aggregate return, because the AuM-weighted graphic shows longer periods of above zero-line returns while the equally weighted one shows much shorter ones.

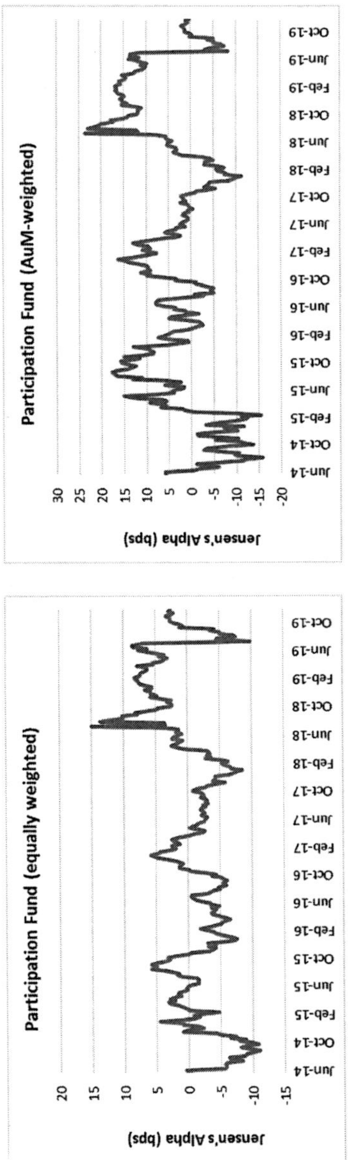

Figure 3.20: Participation funds' Jensen's alpha ratio graphics
Source: Authors' calculations

The Omega ratios of participation funds, both with equally and AuM-weighted returns, (46 and 51 %, respectively) indicate that the probability of positive returns is less than 50 % (Figure 3.21).

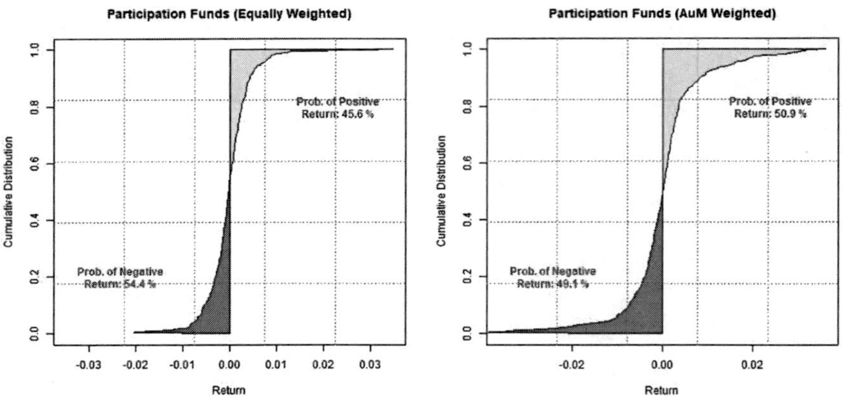

Figure 3.21: Participation funds' Omega ratio graphics
Source: Authors' calculations

3.1.6 Short-term fixed income funds

Short-term fixed income fund category is one of the three categories[20] which has one of the highest market shares in the fund management industry. As observed in Figure 3.22, the short-term fixed income funds have performed below the risk-free rate and the defined category benchmark (which is basically short-term government bonds) for the entire decade. The reason would mainly be the high management fees averaging 1.96 % as per equally weighted data in 2019

20 The other two categories are the fixed income and money market funds categories. The three categories together comprise more than 90 % of the analyzed total AuM each year reflecting the fixed income and short-term nature (or preferences) of the market.

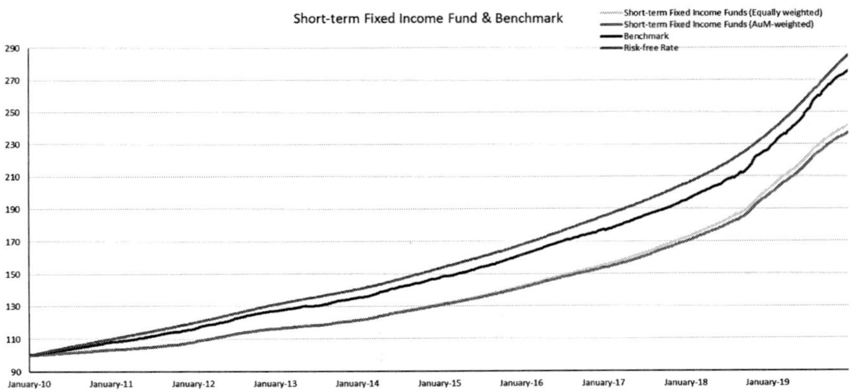

Figure 3.22: Short-term fixed income funds' performance vs benchmark (2010= 100)
Source: Takas İstanbul, Borsa İstanbul, Finnet; indexed by the authors

In the annual analysis, we observe that before the year 2017, the short-term fixed income fund category resulted in negative figures (and less than 1 for Omega) as per all risk-adjusted performance measures based on both equally and AuM-weighted data (Tables 3.19 and 3.20). In 2017, based on equally weighted data, all performance ratios are positive, and the Omega is greater than 1 demonstrating that the category achieved superior results compared to the risk-free rate and the defined benchmark. However, the absolute risk measures (Sharpe and Treynor) are negative as per the AuM-weighted data in 2017 indicating that the larger funds must have performed worse than the smaller ones dragging the returns to negative (Jensen's alpha is also negative in 2017 but it is negligible). In 2018 all measures are positive (and the Omega is greater than 1) and it is vice versa in 2019 as per both equally and AuM-weighted data.

Table 3.19: Short-term fixed income funds' performance (equally weighted returns)

Short-term Fixed Income Funds (Equally Weighted)	2010	2011	2012	2013	2014	2015	2016	2017	2018	2019
1-Year										
Sharpe Ratio	-3.282292	-0.910113	-0.573524	-0.692482	-0.597121	-0.695221	-0.722710	**0.003954**	**0.343237**	-0.142586
Treynor Ratio	-0.003756	-0.001424	-0.000621	-0.000966	-0.000779	-0.000592	-0.001255	**0.000008**	**0.001072**	-0.000454
Information Ratio	-2.042446	-0.695527	-0.593868	-0.580896	-0.272735	-0.256687	-0.195541	**0.204634**	**0.071123**	-0.148028
Jensen's Alpha	-0.001000	-0.000717	-0.000320	-0.000461	-0.000210	-0.000141	-0.000208	**0.000025**	**0.000254**	-0.000168
Sortino Ratio	-0.900125	-0.599348	-0.568566	-0.551165	-0.342945	-0.307939	-0.243112	**0.388242**	**0.112113**	-0.191678
Omega Ratio	0.005037	0.168652	0.225288	0.251943	0.467884	0.485353	0.584848	**1.736608**	**1.238762**	0.666009
3-Year										
Sharpe Ratio	-1.027449	-0.709834	-0.593438	-0.554188	-0.645973	-0.423124	**0.045490**	**0.074722**		
Treynor Ratio	-0.001235	-0.000952	-0.000696	-0.000649	-0.000781	-0.000610	**0.000075**	**0.000156**		
Information Ratio	-0.853435	-0.616166	-0.469876	-0.369757	-0.245563	-0.057977	**0.047513**	**0.006919**		
Jensen's Alpha	-0.000639	-0.000499	-0.000331	-0.000276	-0.000183	-0.000104	**0.000033**	**0.000040**		
Sortino Ratio	-0.676414	-0.560999	-0.490933	-0.411832	-0.301331	-0.083748	**0.074603**	**0.010030**		
Omega Ratio	0.118001	0.208928	0.302296	0.377224	0.504771	0.852869	**1.168508**	**1.020571**		
5-Year										
Sharpe Ratio	-0.842870	-0.608336	-0.571359	-0.474773	-0.103946	-0.057820				
Treynor Ratio	-0.001121	-0.000806	-0.000632	-0.000539	-0.000137	-0.000083				

Short-term Fixed Income Funds (Equally Weighted)	2010	2011	2012	2013	2014	2015	2016	2017	2018	2019
Information Ratio	-0.663221	-0.475670	-0.375236	-0.202322	-0.038190	-0.041306				
Jensen's Alpha	-0.000526	-0.000377	-0.000265	-0.000190	-0.000047	-0.000043				
Sortino Ratio	-0.597094	-0.480008	-0.414723	-0.258022	-0.057015	-0.058634				
Omega Ratio	0.188456	0.284674	0.371901	0.583699	0.888106	0.880245				
10-Year										
Sharpe Ratio	-0.438144									
Treynor Ratio	-0.000568									
Information Ratio	-0.252073									
Jensen's Alpha	-0.000283									
Sortino Ratio	-0.312679									
Omega Ratio	0.483221									

Source: Authors' calculations

Table 3.20: Short-term fixed income funds' performance (AuM-weighted returns)

Short-term Fixed Income Funds (AuM-Weighted)	2010	2011	2012	2013	2014	2015	2016	2017	2018	2019
1-Year										
Sharpe Ratio	-5.019985	-2.418070	-1.060443	-1.421128	-0.937601	-1.021492	-1.079724	-0.201826	**0.273525**	-0.182610
Treynor Ratio	-0.015012	-0.008709	-0.001364	-0.002139	-0.001353	-0.000875	-0.001722	-0.000454	**0.000634**	-0.000510
Information Ratio	-2.497096	-0.607633	-0.600002	-0.412988	-0.330861	-0.323083	-0.338843	**0.121588**	**0.032885**	-0.189360
Jensen's Alpha	-0.001184	-0.000750	-0.000382	-0.000471	-0.000269	-0.000187	-0.000290	-0.000040	**0.000166**	-0.000220
Sortino Ratio	-0.929564	-0.599949	-0.566620	-0.432700	-0.390364	-0.371639	-0.381823	**0.212088**	**0.048822**	-0.234745
Omega Ratio	0.000000	0.223175	0.220928	0.345054	0.412845	0.403080	0.397323	**1.395385**	**1.103226**	0.591743
3-Year										
Sharpe Ratio	-1.709556	-1.452475	-1.111426	-1.018768	-0.979737	-0.660531	-0.075783	-0.002442		
Treynor Ratio	-0.003056	-0.002111	-0.001325	-0.001129	-0.001243	-0.001009	-0.000106	-0.000004		
Information Ratio	-0.871151	-0.532378	-0.438899	-0.358498	-0.332704	-0.149608	-0.017229	-0.037384		
Jensen's Alpha	-0.000734	-0.000517	-0.000371	-0.000307	-0.000247	-0.000169	-0.000035	-0.000023		
Sortino Ratio	-0.708344	-0.529966	-0.460872	-0.396931	-0.381973	-0.201579	-0.025330	-0.051506		
Omega Ratio	0.128935	0.261612	0.321715	0.382144	0.401712	0.662823	0.957200	0.896570		
5-Year										
Sharpe Ratio	-1.364265	-1.146642	-1.039817	-0.826631	-0.241168	-0.155126				
Treynor Ratio	-0.002384	-0.001553	-0.001151	-0.000934	-0.000281	-0.000204				
Information Ratio	-0.635909	-0.452992	-0.399567	-0.246016	-0.110578	-0.100709				

Short-term Fixed Income Funds (AuM-Weighted)	2010	2011	2012	2013	2014	2015	2016	2017	2018	2019
Jensen's Alpha	-0.000587	-0.000401	-0.000316	-0.000243	-0.000111	-0.000105				
Sortino Ratio	-0.595744	-0.475799	-0.429533	-0.299132	-0.153053	-0.134991				
Omega Ratio	0.209435	0.307343	0.344509	0.514805	0.720223	0.737641				
10-Year										
Sharpe Ratio	-0.590918									
Treynor Ratio	-0.000671									
Information Ratio	-0.303313									
Jensen's Alpha	-0.000338									
Sortino Ratio	-0.359655									
Omega Ratio	0.429980									

Source: Authors' calculations

In 3-yearly analysis, all periods other than the last two yielded negative (and in case of Omegas less than 1) results in terms of all risk-adjusted measures as per equally weighted data, and it is vice versa for the last two periods, namely 2016–2018 and 2017–2019. However, as per AuM-weighted data, all periods returned negative (and in case of Omegas less than 1) results in terms of all risk-adjusted measures. This means in the last two periods, the larger funds must have performed worse than the smaller ones dragging the aggregate risk-adjusted returns to negative.

In 5-yearly analysis, all periods have unsuccessful results in terms of all risk-adjusted measures as per both equally and AUM-weighted data.

The decade-long analysis shows all negative results as well in terms of all risk-adjusted measures as per both equally and AUM-weighted data. We attribute these unsuccessful results to high management fees.

The Treynor ratio scatter diagrams (Figure 3.23) illustrate that there is a strong relationship between the funds' aggregate returns and the category benchmark as per both equally and AuM-weighted data.

The Jensen's alpha graphics (Figure 3.24) visualizes the unsuccessful results stated in the Tables 3.19 and the 3.20: the short-term fixed income fund category could not generate alpha up until 2017 and decreased below the zero line again in 2019.

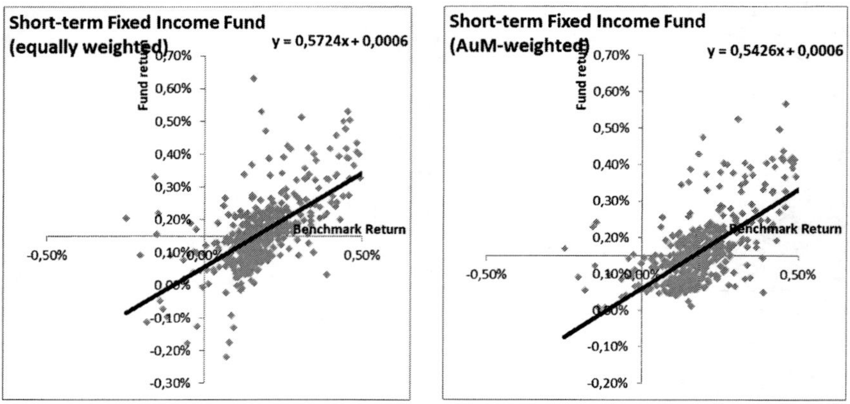

Figure 3.23: Short-term fixed income funds' Treynor ratio graphics
Source: Authors' calculations

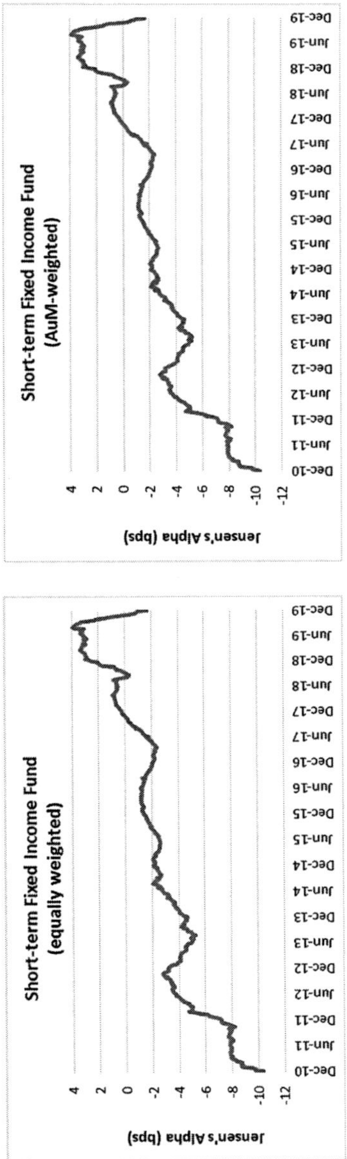

Figure 3.24: Short-term fixed income funds' Jensen's alpha ratio graphics
Source: Authors' calculations

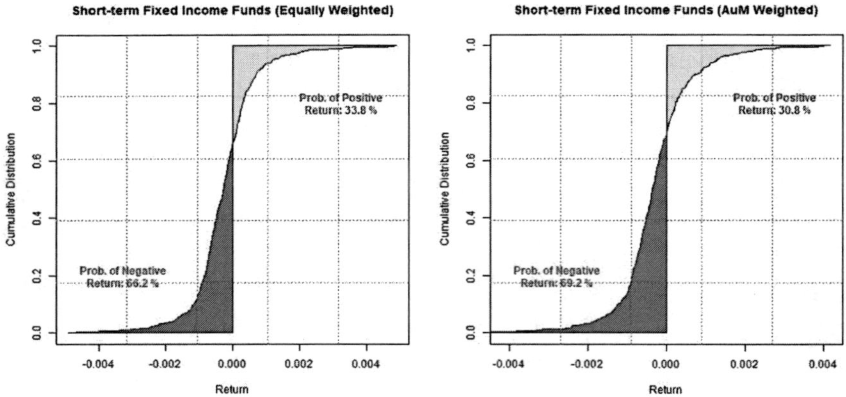

Figure 3.25: Short-term fixed income funds' Omega ratio graphics
Source: Authors' calculations

The Omega graphs of short-term fixed income funds, both with equally and AuM-weighted returns, indicate that the probability of negative returns is 66 and 69 %, respectively, again confirming the unsuccessful results of this fund category compared to its benchmark (Figure 3.25).

3.1.7 Short-term lease certificates funds

Inaugurated in May 2017, short-term lease certificate funds are the newest fund product added to the market. These funds are the "participation way" alternative to short-term fixed income funds and to money market funds combined. Although new, this fund category proved to be addressing a need in the market as evidenced by the fact that the AuM increased sharply in 2.5 years and the market share of this category reached to 4 % in 2019.

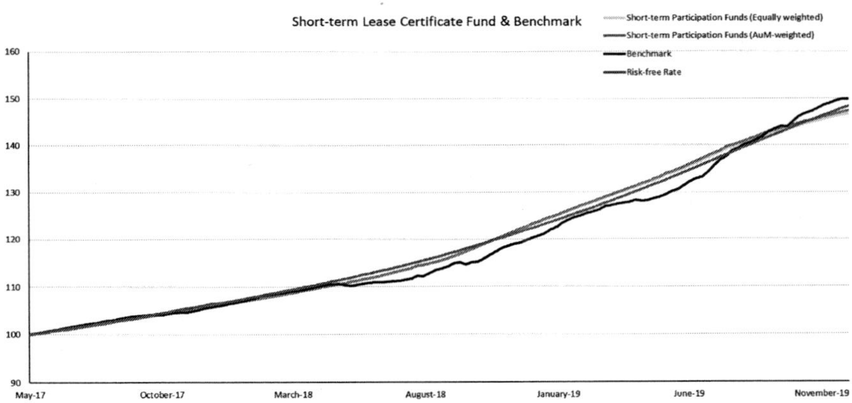

Figure 3.26: Short-term lease certificate funds' performance vs benchmark (5/2017=100)
Source: Takas İstanbul, Borsa İstanbul, Finnet; indexed by the authors

We used the same category benchmark as we used for the participation funds: 50 % government lease certificates and 50 % that of private sector; simply because there is no index specific to a short term for lease certificates – the market is not large and liquid enough to allow term specific indices to be created. As observed in Figure 3.26, short-term lease certificates funds' returns closely followed the benchmark and the risk-free rate.

We just have two annual analysis and a 2.5-years analysis for this fund category and both the equally and AuM-weighted data result in the same conclusion which means the fund sizes do not significantly affect the aggregate return.

Table 3.21: Short-term lease certificate funds' performance (equally weighted returns)

Short-term Lease Certificates Funds (Equally Weighted)	2010	2011	2012	2013	2014	2015	2016	2017	2018	2019
1-Year										
Sharpe Ratio	n.a	n.a	n.a	n.a	n.a	n.a	n.a	n.a	0.235017	-0.414574
Treynor Ratio	n.a	n.a	n.a	n.a	n.a	n.a	n.a	n.a	0.000754	-0.005192
Information Ratio	n.a	n.a	n.a	n.a	n.a	n.a	n.a	n.a	0.209047	-0.346545
Jensen's Alpha	n.a	n.a	n.a	n.a	n.a	n.a	n.a	n.a	0.000234	-0.000352
Sortino Ratio	n.a	n.a	n.a	n.a	n.a	n.a	n.a	n.a	0.416200	-0.376585
Omega Ratio	n.a	n.a	n.a	n.a	n.a	n.a	n.a	n.a	1.810446	0.399246
3-Year										
Sharpe Ratio	n.a	n.a	n.a	n.a	n.a	n.a	n.a	n.a		
Treynor Ratio	n.a	n.a	n.a	n.a	n.a	n.a	n.a	n.a		
Information Ratio	n.a	n.a	n.a	n.a	n.a	n.a	n.a	n.a		
Jensen's Alpha	n.a	n.a	n.a	n.a	n.a	n.a	n.a	n.a		
Sortino Ratio	n.a	n.a	n.a	n.a	n.a	n.a	n.a	n.a		
Omega Ratio	n.a	n.a	n.a	n.a	n.a	n.a	n.a	n.a		
5-Year										
Sharpe Ratio	n.a	n.a	n.a	n.a	n.a	n.a				
Treynor Ratio	n.a	n.a	n.a	n.a	n.a	n.a				
Information Ratio	n.a	n.a	n.a	n.a	n.a	n.a				
Jensen's Alpha	n.a	n.a	n.a	n.a	n.a	n.a				
Sortino Ratio	n.a	n.a	n.a	n.a	n.a	n.a				
Omega Ratio	n.a	n.a	n.a	n.a	n.a	n.a				

Short-term Lease Certificates Funds (Equally Weighted)	2010	2011	2012	2013	2014	2015	2016	2017	2018	2019
2.5-Year										
Sharpe Ratio	-0.112118							-0.112118		
Treynor Ratio	-0.000406							-0.000406		
Information Ratio	-0.076812							-0.076812		
Jensen's Alpha	-0.000097							-0.000097		
Sortino Ratio	-0.102030							-0.102030		
Omega Ratio	0.805630							0.805630		

Source: Authors' calculations

Table 3.22: Short-term lease certificate funds' performance (AuM-weighted returns)

Short-term Lease Certificates Funds (AuM-weighted)	2010	2011	2012	2013	2014	2015	2016	2017	2018	2019
1-Year										
Sharpe Ratio	n.a	n.a	n.a	n.a	n.a	n.a	n.a	n.a	0.268029	-0.357262
Treynor Ratio	n.a	n.a	n.a	n.a	n.a	n.a	n.a	n.a	0.000962	-0.004313
Information Ratio	n.a	n.a	n.a	n.a	n.a	n.a	n.a	n.a	0.214592	-0.329965
Jensen's Alpha	n.a	n.a	n.a	n.a	n.a	n.a	n.a	n.a	0.000256	-0.000312
Sortino Ratio	n.a	n.a	n.a	n.a	n.a	n.a	n.a	n.a	0.438833	-0.363027
Omega Ratio	n.a	n.a	n.a	n.a	n.a	n.a	n.a	n.a	1.844061	0.415605
3-Year										
Sharpe Ratio	n.a	n.a	n.a	n.a	n.a	n.a	n.a	n.a		
Treynor Ratio	n.a	n.a	n.a	n.a	n.a	n.a	n.a	n.a		
Information Ratio	n.a	n.a	n.a	n.a	n.a	n.a	n.a	n.a		
Jensen's Alpha	n.a	n.a	n.a	n.a	n.a	n.a	n.a	n.a		
Sortino Ratio	n.a	n.a	n.a	n.a	n.a	n.a	n.a	n.a		
Omega Ratio	n.a	n.a	n.a	n.a	n.a	n.a	n.a	n.a		
5-Year										
Sharpe Ratio	n.a	n.a	n.a	n.a	n.a	n.a				
Treynor Ratio	n.a	n.a	n.a	n.a	n.a	n.a				
Information Ratio	n.a	n.a	n.a	n.a	n.a	n.a				
Jensen's Alpha	n.a	n.a	n.a	n.a	n.a	n.a				
Sortino Ratio	n.a	n.a	n.a	n.a	n.a	n.a				
Omega Ratio	n.a	n.a	n.a	n.a	n.a	n.a				

Short-term Lease Certificates Funds (AuM-weighted)	**2010**	**2011**	**2012**	**2013**	**2014**	**2015**	**2016**	**2017**	**2018**	**2019**
2.5-Year										
Sharpe Ratio	-0.070509							-0.070509		
Treynor Ratio	-0.000263							-0.000263		
Information Ratio	-0.061305							-0.061305		
Jensen's Alpha	0.000000							0.000000		
Sortino Ratio	-0.083154							-0.083154		
Omega Ratio	0.841534							0.841534		

Source: Authors' calculations

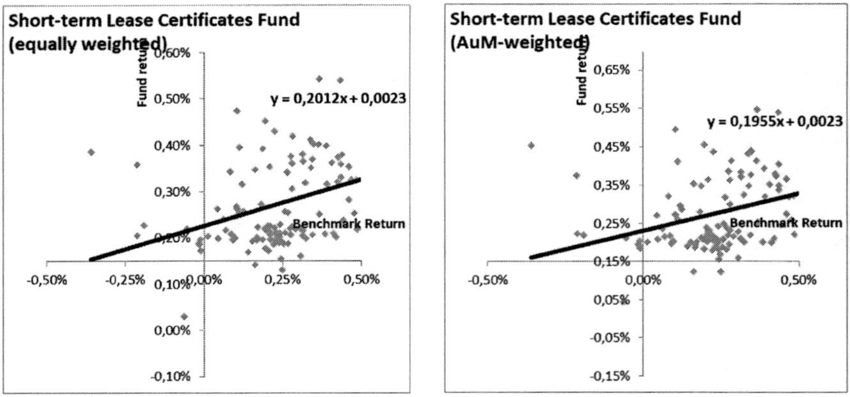

Figure 3.27: Short-term lease certificate funds' Treynor ratio graphics
Source: Author's calculations

In 2018 all the measures yield a positive (and the Omega greater than 1) result and in 2019 it is vice versa (Tables 3.21 and 3.22). The 2.5-year results are all negative as well.

The Treynor scatter diagrams in Figure 3.27 show that there is no significant relationship between the fund category's aggregate returns and those of the defined category benchmark.

There is a positive alpha starting in November 2018. Then we observe a deep dive in Jensen's alpha starting in September 2019 and decreasing below zero just after a year since it turned positive in November 2019 (Figure 3.28).

The Omega ratios show that the possibility of the short-term lease funds yielding a below-benchmark return is about 55 % (Figure 3.29).

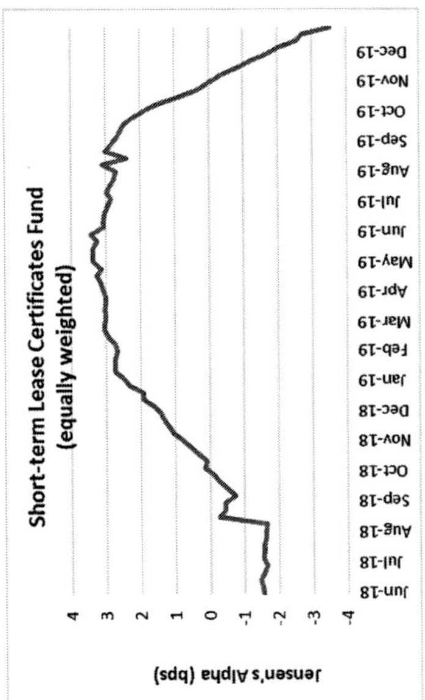

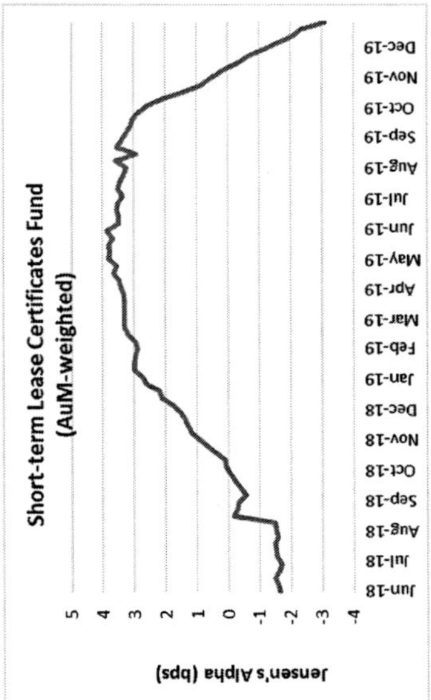

Figure 3.28: Short-term lease certificate funds' Jensen's alpha ratio graphics
Source: Authors' calculations

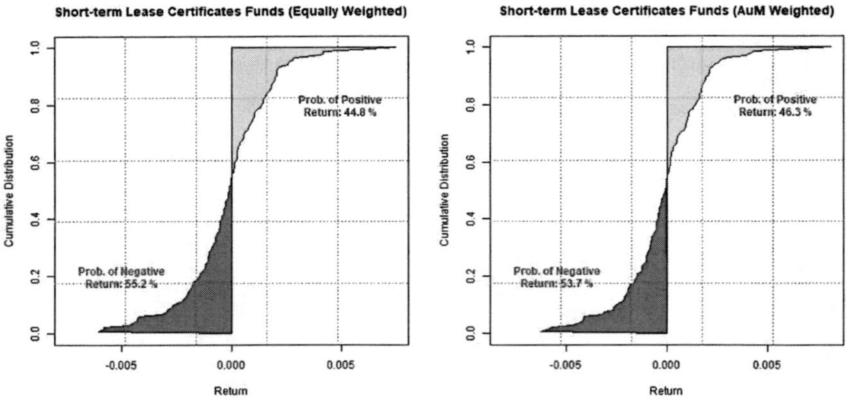

Figure 3.29: Short-term lease certificate funds' Omega ratio graphics
Source: Authors' calculations

3.1.8 Money market funds

Money market funds have always been either the largest or the second largest category in the fund management industry reaching 56 % of the market in 2019.

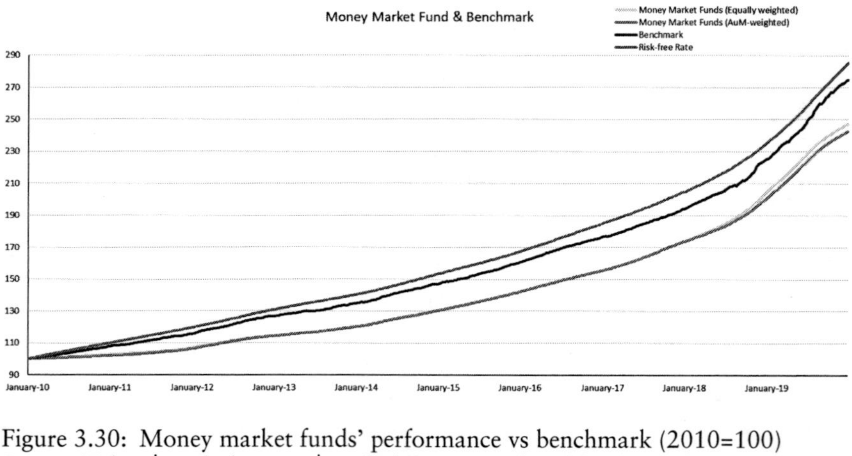

Figure 3.30: Money market funds' performance vs benchmark (2010=100)
Source: Takas İstanbul, Borsa İstanbul, Finnet; indexed by the authors

Table 3.23: Money market funds' performance (equally weighted returns)

Money Market Funds (Equally Weighted)	2010	2011	2012	2013	2014	2015	2016	2017	2018	2019
1-Year										
Sharpe Ratio	-5.640507	-2.786715	-1.258906	-1.144753	-0.183726	-0.009344	-0.833083	**0.557117**	**0.704288**	-0.134264
Treynor Ratio	-0.014589	-0.009545	-0.002091	-0.006965	-0.001657	-0.000011	-0.020907	**0.002255**	**0.002509**	-0.000995
Information Ratio	-2.805840	-0.717200	-0.639302	-0.220160	-0.100801	-0.035131	-0.144348	**0.369519**	**0.177906**	-0.114509
Jensen's Alpha	-0.001256	-0.000836	-0.000444	-0.000376	-0.000134	-0.000002	-0.000207	**0.000164**	**0.000472**	-0.000137
Sortino Ratio	-0.942986	-0.652379	-0.585606	-0.273507	-0.135388	-0.050524	-0.181148	**0.828640**	**0.285435**	-0.154337
Omega Ratio	0.000000	0.181180	0.200398	0.551216	0.736749	0.902819	0.665118	**2.757628**	**1.706351**	0.739061
3-Year										
Sharpe Ratio	-1.884216	-1.430329	-0.609437	-0.350857	-0.248783	-0.067192	**0.275317**	**0.246123**		
Treynor Ratio	-0.003673	-0.003709	-0.002110	-0.001206	-0.001792	-0.000282	**0.000495**	**0.000699**		
Information Ratio	-0.959791	-0.481031	-0.273301	-0.126449	-0.091874	**0.080277**	**0.144627**	**0.077978**		
Jensen's Alpha	-0.000814	-0.000541	-0.000312	-0.000167	-0.000112	-0.000013	**0.000157**	**0.000168**		
Sortino Ratio	-0.735700	-0.502639	-0.326664	-0.165941	-0.122881	**0.128703**	**0.235136**	**0.115995**		
Omega Ratio	0.111429	0.294357	0.470112	0.693466	0.759854	**1.252307**	**1.583081**	**1.253339**		
5-Year										
Sharpe Ratio	-1.051593	-0.711568	-0.529895	-0.261811	**0.116099**	**0.111930**				
Treynor Ratio	-0.003781	-0.002148	-0.001567	-0.000718	**0.000208**	**0.000198**				
Information Ratio	-0.515465	-0.307436	-0.209807	-0.035243	**0.070777**	**0.038974**				

(Continued)

Table 3.23: Continued

Money Market Funds (Equally Weighted)	2010	2011	2012	2013	2014	2015	2016	2017	2018	2019
Jensen's Alpha	-0.000596	-0.000351	-0.000226	-0.000102	**0.000069**	**0.000063**				
Sortino Ratio	-0.530141	-0.359922	-0.258953	-0.049594	**0.109329**	**0.057343**				
Omega Ratio	0.268700	0.434199	0.552709	0.904314	**1.246157**	**1.127135**				
10-Year										
Sharpe Ratio	-0.404127									
Treynor Ratio	-0.000630									
Information Ratio	-0.171059									
Jensen's Alpha	-0.000245									
Sortino Ratio	-0.225073									
Omega Ratio	0.613517									

Source: Authors' calculations

This fund category heavily invests in reverse repo and T-bills. Hence, we use the government 91-days bond index as benchmark. As observed in Figure 3.30, the fund category's returns have always been below the benchmark and the risk-free rate. This is due to the high management fees which has an average of 1.18 % in 2019.

Annually all the measures produced negative (Omega less than 1) results until 2017 both as per equally and AuM-weighted data (Tables 3.23 and 3.24). In 2017 all measures resulted in positive (Omega greater than 1) ratios again as per both data structures. In 2018, though, while equally weighted data yielded positive results in all measures, AuM-weighted data yielded negative Information and Sortino ratios and below 1 Omega ratio. In 2019, all measures yielded negative returns as per both equally and AuM-weighted data.

Table 3.24: Money market funds' performance (AuM-weighted returns)

Money Market Funds (AuM-Weighted)	2010	2011	2012	2013	2014	2015	2016	2017	2018	2019
					1-Year					
Sharpe Ratio	-5.957530	-2.489170	-1.050946	-1.416237	-0.538186	-0.090500	-0.766931	**0.580931**	**0.238849**	-0.128764
Treynor Ratio	-0.025567	-0.010802	-0.001629	-0.005351	-0.001793	-0.000120	-0.148483	**0.002383**	**0.000874**	-0.000978
Information Ratio	-3.139054	-0.658865	-0.533146	-0.243673	-0.124288	-0.042123	-0.119654	**0.377556**	-0.019499	-0.111913
Jensen's Alpha	-0.001406	-0.000805	-0.000361	-0.000390	-0.000130	-0.000008	-0.000191	**0.000171**	**0.000117**	-0.000131
Sortino Ratio	-0.953665	-0.626858	-0.525454	-0.294031	-0.172331	-0.060167	-0.153899	**0.853376**	-0.027452	-0.151127
Omega Ratio	0.000000	0.200305	0.257285	0.525110	0.709940	0.885148	0.718330	**2.817899**	0.942714	0.744246
					3-Year					
Sharpe Ratio	-1.625242	-1.383328	-0.947291	-0.656243	-0.503505	-0.044373	**0.089642**	**0.096410**		
Treynor Ratio	-0.003552	-0.003117	-0.001759	-0.001199	-0.001960	-0.000199	**0.000169**	**0.000262**		
Information Ratio	-0.919135	-0.450624	-0.279131	-0.146482	-0.096571	**0.087721**	**0.053988**	**0.009365**		
Jensen's Alpha	-0.000819	-0.000505	-0.000288	-0.000172	-0.000107	-0.000007	**0.000042**	**0.000052**		
Sortino Ratio	-0.722108	-0.479076	-0.332308	-0.190790	-0.131594	**0.141643**	**0.079432**	**0.013262**		
Omega Ratio	0.119865	0.316834	0.476879	0.667617	0.762103	**1.277953**	**1.189493**	**1.027571**		
					5-Year					
Sharpe Ratio	-1.159074	-0.882690	-0.747455	-0.377097	-0.009464	-0.000980				
Treynor Ratio	-0.003601	-0.001961	-0.001374	-0.000690	-0.000014	-0.000002				
Information Ratio	-0.549782	-0.306845	-0.207296	-0.036221	**0.011445**	-0.009665				

Money Market Funds (AuM-Weighted)	**2010**	**2011**	**2012**	**2013**	**2014**	**2015**	**2016**	**2017**	**2018**	**2019**
Jensen's Alpha	-0.000601	-0.000330	-0.000210	-0.000100	**0.000000**	-0.000005				
Sortino Ratio	-0.549069	-0.359948	-0.256926	-0.051516	**0.016648**	-0.013604				
Omega Ratio	0.257484	0.443969	0.567783	0.905071	**1.035857**	0.970726				
10-Year										
Sharpe Ratio	-0.504436									
Treynor Ratio	-0.000751									
Information Ratio	-0.205935									
Jensen's Alpha	-0.000315									
Sortino Ratio	-0.261823									
Omega Ratio	0.556936									

Source: Authors' calculations

In 3-yearly analysis, we observe that the first 5 periods of the 8 periods produce negative results in terms of all measures both as per equally and AuM-weighted data. In period 2015–2017, both the equally and AuM-weighted returns data yielded positive Information and Sortino ratios, and an Omega ratio greater than 1 while all other measures resulted in negative ratios which means the fund category returned better than the benchmark while returning less than the risk-free rate. The last two periods, namely 2016–2018 and 2017–2019, yielded all positive results in terms of all measures as per both equally and AuM-weighted data.

In 5-yearly analysis, the first four periods resulted in negative ratios in terms of all measures as per both equally and AuM-weighted data. As per equally weighted data, the last two periods yielded all successful results. But it is not the case as per AuM-weighted data: in the period 2014–2018, the absolute return measures were negative while the others were positive, and the Omega was greater than 1. In the last period, namely 2015–2019, all measures turned out to be negative as per AuM-weighted data which means the larger funds must have performed worse than the smaller ones dragging the returns to below-the-benchmark level.

In the decade-long analysis, all measures show unsuccessful results as per both equally and AuM-weighted data.

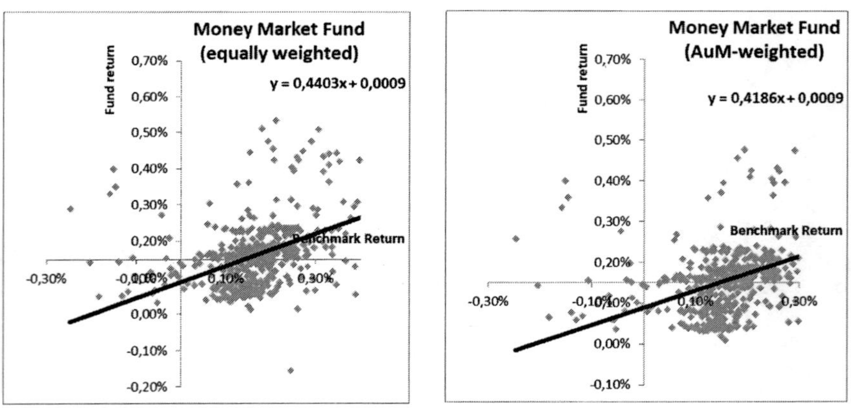

Figure 3.31: Money market funds' Treynor ratio graphics
Source: Author's calculations

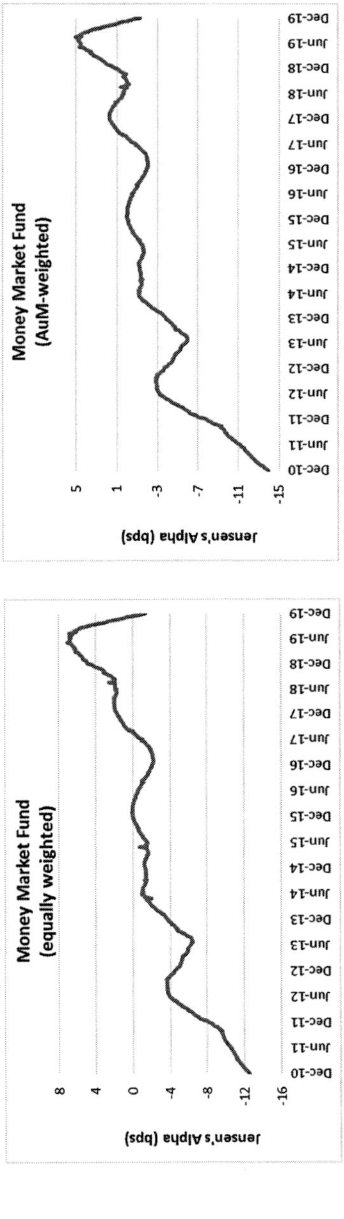

Figure 3.32: Money market Jensen's alpha ratio graphics
Source: Authors' calculations

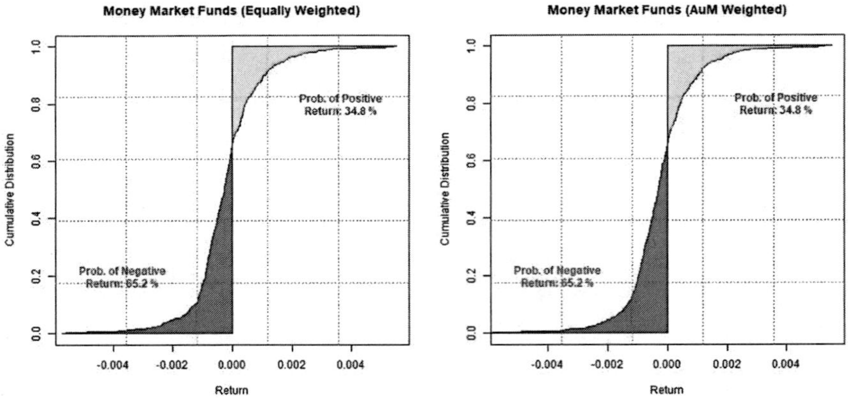

Figure 3.33: Money market funds' Omega ratio graphics
Source: Authors' calculations

The Treynor ratio scatter diagrams demonstrate that there is a somewhat strong relationship between the funds' aggregate returns and the category benchmark (Figure 3.31).

The Jensen's alpha is negative until October 2017. Then the alpha continues to increase until it starts a deep dive in September 2019 decreasing to below zero line by the end of the year (Figure 3.32).

The Omega ratio graphics show that the money market funds category's possibility of yielding a negative risk-adjusted return compared to the category benchmark is 65 % as per both equally and AuM-weighted data (Figure 3.33).

3.2 Pension fund categories vs. defined benchmarks

We calculated the excess return of each fund compared to its own benchmark, i.e., "the fund's return – the category benchmark's return." Then we analyzed whether the excess return is statistically significant for the relevant period. We ran this analysis for four different time periods: (1) Annual analysis for 10 years (Table 3.26), (2) Three-yearly analysis for 8 periods between 2010–2019 (Table 3.28), (3) Five-yearly analysis for 6 periods between 2010–2019 (Table 3.29), and (4) Ten-yearly analysis (Table 3.31).

According to annual analysis, there are statistically significant positive returns over the benchmark only for "initiation," "initiation participation," "government contribution," "government contribution participation," "equity," and "money market" funds and only in 2017, 2018, and 2019 for the first two categories while only in 2017 in respect of the other categories both with equally weighted and AuM-weighted returns analysis (Table 3.26).

However, as observed in Table 3.25, there are many periods with positive access returns in all fund categories other than gold, fixed income, and FC denominated government bonds.

Table 3.25: Annual excess returns

Excess Return (Equally weighted)	2010	2011	2012	2013	2014	2015	2016	2017	2018	2019
Gold Fund	n.a	n.a	n.a	n.a	-0.000468706	-0.000399036	-0.000358507	-0.000323621	-0.00028428	-0.000496388
Initiation Fund	n.a	n.a	n.a	n.a	n.a	n.a	n.a	**0.000181662**	**0.000204162**	**0.000113062**
Initiation Participation Fund	n.a	n.a	n.a	n.a	n.a	n.a	n.a	**0.00017295**	**0.000759282**	**0.000626366**
Fixed Income Fund	n.a	n.a	-0.000067	-0.000473	-0.000044	-0.00053029	-0.000135502	-0.000329099	-0.000285293	-0.000086
Government Contribution Fund	n.a	n.a	n.a	n.a	-0.000470747	**0.000157055**	**0.000022**	**0.000595401**	-0.000194962	**0.000155636**
Equity Fund	**0.002765085**	-0.005183301	**0.005186847**	-0.001049998	**0.00178368**	-0.000971797	-0.000046	**0.006669224**	-0.002979205	**0.000808068**
Government Bonds Fund	-0.000515691	-0.00020638	-0.00066489	-0.000118704	-0.000866343	**0.000293815**	-0.000227977	**0.00021834**	**0.000694425**	-0.000881785
FC Denominated Government Bonds Fund	-0.000246348	-0.000906487	-0.000637182	-0.000817795	-0.00059047	-0.000248509	-0.000358067	-0.001165655	-0.000113891	-0.000166638
Government Contribution Participation Fund	n.a	n.a	n.a	n.a	**0.000269645**	-0.000086	-0.000116	**0.000283**	**0.000149**	-0.000013
Standard Participation Fund	n.a	n.a	n.a	n.a	**0.000177238**	-0.000523972	-0.000948459	-0.000208754	-0.000900141	-0.000058
Private Sector Fixed Income Fund	n.a	n.a	n.a	-0.000778333	**0.000013**	-0.000181908	-0.000191292	-0.00026449	-0.000254524	-0.000472257
Money Market Fund	-0.000463423	-0.000264559	-0.000564568	-0.000229568	-0.000083	-0.000017	-0.000124	**0.000288**	**0.000334**	-0.000079
Standard Fund	-0.000725048	-0.001110945	**0.000001**	-0.000122	-0.000378	-0.000490137	-0.000495433	-0.000063	-0.000488	-0.000644

Excess Return (AuM-weighted)	2010	2011	2012	2013	2014	2015	2016	2017	2018	2019
Gold Fund	n.a	n.a	n.a	n.a	-0.000470143	-0.000368247	-0.000359673	-0.000296324	-0.000254178	-0.000508605
Initiation Fund	n.a	n.a	n.a	n.a	n.a	n.a	n.a	**0.000203755**	**0.00024644**	**0.000135076**
Initiation Participation Fund	n.a	n.a	n.a	n.a	n.a	n.a	n.a	-0.001553205	-0.002071742	-0.002820357
Fixed Income Fund	n.a	n.a	-0.000132	-0.000679	-0.000104	-0.000791084	-0.000226974	-0.000483311	-0.000867749	-0.000327
Government Contribution Fund	n.a	n.a	n.a	n.a	-0.000338573	-0.000003	**0.000032**	**0.000621157**	-0.000462366	**0.000079**
Equity Fund	**0.002689069**	-0.005517598	**0.005440356**	-0.00139371	**0.001758341**	-0.00124936	-0.000081	**0.00692831**	-0.00331629	**0.000866369**
Government Bonds Fund	-0.000584865	-0.00027833	-0.000664623	-0.000140049	-0.000901541	**0.000184889**	-0.000177347	**0.000158111**	**0.000522438**	-0.001075812
FC Denominated Government Bonds Fund	-0.000246581	-0.000760211	-0.000160752	-0.001104816	-0.000160259	-0.000132729	-0.000333395	-0.001349652	-0.000228998	-0.00012052
Government Contribution Participation Fund	n.a	n.a	n.a	n.a	**0.000020**	**0.000023**	-0.000130	**0.000234**	**0.000185**	-0.000060
Standard Participation Fund	n.a	n.a	n.a	n.a	**0.000392139**	-0.000549885	-0.000880051	-0.000329574	-0.000660812	-0.000325
Private Sector Fixed Income Fund	n.a	n.a	n.a	-0.000802786	**0.000002**	-0.000269415	-0.000251033	-0.00027901	-0.00043239	-0.000556403
Money Market Fund	-0.000415031	-0.000185593	-0.000477495	-0.000167109	-0.000040	**0.000009**	-0.000064	**0.000338**	**0.000380**	-0.000058
Standard Fund	-0.000780193	-0.00106632	-0.000155	-0.000067	-0.000280	-0.000631163	-0.000409659	-0.000153	-0.000671	-0.000544

Source: Authors' calculations

Table 3.26: Annual excess returns' t-test analysis

Excess Return Equally Returns	2010		2011		2012		2013		2014		2015		2016		2017		2018		2019	
	P-Value	t-test	P-Value	t-test	P-Value	t-test	P-Value	t-test	P-Value	t-test	P-Value	t-test	P-Value	t-test	P-Value	t-test	P-Value	t-test	P-Value	t-test
Gold Fund	n.a	n.a	n.a	n.a	n.a	n.a	n.a	n.a	0.99281	-2.53431	0.99115	-2.45154	0.99996	-4.30308	0.93873	-1.57030	0.74229	-0.65498	0.81314	-0.89740
Initiation Fund	n.a	n.a	n.a	n.a	n.a	n.a	n.a	n.a	n.a	n.a	n.a	n.a	n.a	n.a	0.0000	4.4832	0.0005	3.5008	0.0122	2.3210
Initiation Participation Fund	n.a	n.a	n.a	n.a	n.a	n.a	n.a	n.a	n.a	n.a	n.a	n.a	n.a	n.a	0.0003	3.6725	0.0000	8.4180	0.0000	9.1151
Fixed Income Fund	n.a	n.a	n.a	n.a	0.69064	-0.50073	0.92082	-1.43162	0.58456	-0.21468	0.96650	-1.87158	0.66725	-0.43486	0.94372	-1.61466	0.70095	-0.53045	0.59390	-0.23882
Government Contribution Fund	n.a	n.a	n.a	n.a	n.a	n.a	n.a	n.a	0.90914	-1.35394	0.28009	0.58642	0.46114	0.09804	0.0083	2.4787	0.65082	-0.38972	0.43207	0.17197
Equity Fund	0.21127	0.80852	0.87136	-1.14567	0.05497	1.62678	0.59179	-0.23337	0.27671	0.59659	0.60225	-0.26053	0.50713	-0.01797	0.0094	2.4250	0.78092	-0.78143	0.40158	0.25056
Government Bonds Fund	0.93178	-1.51307	0.78584	-0.79844	0.99894	-3.23663	0.67882	-0.46717	0.93871	-1.57009	0.28481	0.57231	0.71823	-0.58140	0.21632	0.79095	0.23452	0.72949	0.94392	-1.61647
Foreign Currency Denominated Government Bonds Fund	0.65548	-0.40245	0.94354	-1.61302	0.97311	-1.97430	0.97656	-2.03682	0.96345	-1.82997	0.72649	-0.60626	0.87486	-1.16291	0.99990	-4.00749	0.57331	-0.18576	0.67791	-0.46461
Government Contribution Participation Fund	n.a	n.a	n.a	n.a	n.a	n.a	n.a	n.a	0.06696	1.52304	0.70653	-0.54673	0.81371	-0.89958	0.0138	2.2677	0.26956	0.61831	0.51398	-0.03523
Standard Participation Fund	n.a	n.a	n.a	n.a	n.a	n.a	n.a	n.a	0.41616	0.21280	0.75324	-0.68967	0.90656	-1.33782	0.63984	-0.36001	0.71083	-0.55938	0.53196	-0.08059
Private Sector Fixed Income Fund	n.a	n.a	n.a	n.a	0.21837	0.78388	0.96175	-1.80800	0.48047	0.04922	0.90263	-1.31398	0.97532	-2.01344	0.99861	-3.14244	0.91278	-1.37726	0.99792	-3.00056
Money Market Fund	1.00000	-9.38699	0.99089	-2.43948	1.00000	-5.93754	0.95473	-1.72527	0.76324	-0.72212	0.56812	-0.17247	0.91268	-1.37666	0.0075	2.5160	0.09842	1.30771	0.61443	-0.29244
Standard Fund	0.98114	-2.13342	0.98591	-2.25912	0.49916	0.00212	0.59645	-0.24544	0.83519	-0.98430	0.85900	-1.08732	0.90329	-1.31789	0.58096	-0.20541	0.74224	-0.65483	0.88760	-1.22877

Excess Return Weighted Average	2010		2011		2012		2013		2014		2015		2016		2017		2018		2019	
	P-Value	t-test	P-Value	t-test	P-Value	t-test	P-Value	t-test	P-Value	t-test	P-Value	t-test	P-Value	t-test	P-Value	t-test	P-Value	t-test	P-Value	t-test
Gold Fund	n.a	n.a	n.a	n.a	n.a	n.a	n.a	n.a	0.99863	-3.14911	0.98860	-2.34788	0.99992	-4.08481	0.92253	-1.44370	0.71726	-0.57850	0.81816	-0.91658
Initiation Fund	n.a	n.a	n.a	n.a	n.a	n.a	n.a	n.a	n.a	n.a	n.a	n.a	n.a	n.a	0.0000	5.0530	0.0001	4.2056	0.0035	2.8117
Initiation Participation Fund	n.a	n.a	n.a	n.a	n.a	n.a	n.a	n.a	n.a	n.a	n.a	n.a	n.a	n.a	0.0001	3.9612	0.0000	9.5176	0.0000	9.8818
Fixed Income Fund	n.a	n.a	n.a	n.a	0.84938	-1.04438	0.95667	-1.74693	0.63296	-0.34157	0.96470	-1.84667	0.72505	-0.60191	0.95332	-1.70991	0.94659	-1.64167	0.86939	-1.13610
Government Contribution Fund	n.a	n.a	n.a	n.a	n.a	n.a	n.a	n.a	0.91792	-1.41153	0.50488	-0.01231	0.43516	0.16408	0.0042	2.7425	0.74987	-0.67892	0.46467	0.08911
Equity Fund	0.22084	0.77542	0.87441	-1.16068	0.05203	1.65507	0.61710	-0.29948	0.28501	0.57173	0.62563	-0.32204	0.51237	-0.03116	0.0088	2.4525	0.79380	-0.82644	0.39707	0.26231
Government Bonds Fund	0.99627	-2.78647	0.86358	-1.10851	0.99811	-3.03433	0.73806	-0.64179	0.94639	-1.63974	0.33190	0.43722	0.71383	-0.56828	0.26246	0.64018	0.25642	0.65904	0.91582	-1.39734
Foreign Currency Denominated Government Bonds Fund	0.68819	-0.49374	0.94900	-1.66526	0.63302	-0.34174	0.98990	-2.39769	0.66562	-0.43035	0.58047	-0.20414	0.81212	-0.89356	0.99946	-3.46617	0.61845	-0.30303	0.61588	-0.29625
Government Contribution Participation Fund	n.a	n.a	n.a	n.a	n.a	n.a	n.a	n.a	0.43435	0.16615	0.43125	0.17406	0.88636	-1.22214	0.0355	1.8444	0.18262	0.91356	0.55934	-0.15004
Standard Participation Fund	n.a	n.a	n.a	n.a	n.a	n.a	n.a	n.a	0.33851	0.41894	0.72851	-0.61241	0.87538	-1.16552	0.72540	-0.60297	0.66012	-0.41516	0.67691	-0.46180
Private Sector Fixed Income Fund	n.a	n.a	n.a	n.a	0.21837	0.78388	0.96320	-1.82675	0.49721	0.00704	0.91730	-1.40731	0.95815	-1.76410	0.99913	-3.30683	0.97448	-1.99814	0.99948	-3.47709
Money Market Fund	1.00000	-8.50636	0.95808	-1.76326	1.00000	-5.18981	0.89586	-1.27447	0.63669	-0.35155	0.46417	0.09037	0.75759	-0.70370	0.0026	2.9231	0.06951	1.50297	0.58410	-0.21349
Standard Fund	0.98812	-2.33073	0.98197	-2.15314	0.70050	-0.52916	0.55618	-0.14201	0.74717	-0.67034	0.88873	-1.23488	0.86036	-1.09355	0.70304	-0.53654	0.82682	-0.95048	0.86644	-1.12198

Source: Authors' calculations

According to three-yearly analysis, there are statistically significant positive returns over the benchmarks for "initiation" and "initiation participation" funds for the last period, i.e., 2017–2019 with both equally- and AuM-weighted returns analysis. There is also one for "government contribution" funds in the period 2015–2017 as per equally weighted returns, but this single statistically significant return disappears when the analysis is run with AuM-weighted returns (Table 3.28). However, as observed in Table 3.27, there are many periods with positive access returns in many fund categories which just fail the t-test.

According to five-yearly analysis, there is no statistically significant positive return for any period for any fund category (Table 3.29). However, as observed in Table 3.30, there are five fund categories with positive access returns in more than one period.

Table 3.27: 3-Yearly excess returns

Excess Return (Equally weighted)	2010-2012	2011-2013	2012-2014	2013-2015	2014-2016	2015-2017	2016-2018	2017-2019
Gold Fund	n.a	n.a	n.a	n.a	-0.0004087496	-0.0003603881	-0.000322136	-0.0003680963
Initiation Fund	n.a	n.a	n.a	n.a	n.a	n.a	n.a	0.0001660959
Initiation Participation Fund	n.a	n.a	n.a	n.a	n.a	n.a	n.a	0.0005240335
Fixed Income Fund	n.a	n.a	-0.0001948067	-0.0003493559	-0.0002367513	-0.0003316303	-0.0002499647	-0.0002333101
Government Contribution Fund	n.a	n.a	n.a	n.a	-0.000097	0.0002581517	0.0001408129	0.0001853582
Equity Fund	0.0009228768	-0.0003488173	0.0019735097	-0.000079	0.0002553652	0.0018838797	0.0012147437	0.0014993623
Government Bonds Fund	-0.00046232	-0.0003299913	-0.0005499789	-0.0002304106	-0.0002668348	0.000095	0.000228	0.000010
FC Denominated Government Bonds Fund	-0.0005966725	-0.0007871549	-0.0006818156	-0.000552258	-0.0003990152	-0.0005907436	-0.0005458708	-0.0004820613
Government Contribution Participation Fund	n.a	n.a	n.a	n.a	0.000023	0.000027	0.0001054077	0.0001397271
Standard Participation Fund	n.a	n.a	n.a	n.a	-0.000432	-0.000560	-0.0006857847	-0.0003891215
Private Sector Fixed Income Fund	n.a	n.a	n.a	-0.0003157587	-0.000120	-0.000213	-0.0002367688	-0.0003304235
Money Market Fund	-0.00043085	-0.0003528985	-0.000292276	-0.0001098043	-0.000074	0.000049	0.0001658781	0.0001807166
Standard Fund	-0.0005932032	-0.0004109354	-0.000166722	-0.0003303019	-0.0004546247	-0.0003495887	-0.000348908	-0.0003985037

(Continued)

Table 3.27: Continued

Excess Return (AuM-weighted)	2010-2012	2011-2013	2012-2014	2013-2015	2014-2016	2015-2017	2016-2018	2017-2019
Gold Fund	n.a	n.a	n.a	n.a	-0.0003993545	-0.0003414148	-0.0003033917	-0.0003530356
Initiation Fund	n.a	n.a	n.a	n.a	n.a	n.a	n.a	**0.0001949778**
Initiation Participation Fund	n.a	n.a	n.a	n.a	n.a	n.a	n.a	-0.002156165
Fixed Income Fund	n.a	n.a	-0.0003051261	-0.0005247872	-0.0003740495	-0.0005004563	-0.0005260115	-0.000559206
Government Contribution Fund	n.a	n.a	n.a	n.a	-0.000103	**0.0002167407**	**0.000064**	**0.000079**
Equity Fund	**0.000870609**	-0.0004903173	**0.0019349958**	-0.000295	**0.0001427911**	**0.001866114**	**0.001177**	**0.001493**
Government Bonds Fund	-0.0005092725	-0.0003610006	-0.0005687377	-0.000285567	-0.0002979995	**0.000055**	**0.000168**	-0.000132
FC Denominated Government Bonds Fund	-0.0003891814	-0.0006752599	-0.000475276	-0.0004659348	-0.0002087942	-0.0006052585	-0.0006373485	-0.0005663902
Government Contribution Participation Fund	n.a	n.a	n.a	n.a	-0.000029	**0.000042**	**0.000097**	**0.000120**
Standard Participation Fund	n.a	n.a	n.a	n.a	-0.000346	-0.000587	-0.000623	-0.000439
Private Sector Fixed Income Fund	n.a	n.a	n.a	-0.0003568013	-0.000173	-0.000266	-0.0003208111	-0.000422601
Money Market Fund	-0.0003593732	-0.0002767326	-0.000228267	-0.000066	-0.000032	**0.000095**	**0.0002181449**	**0.0002202647**
Standard Fund	-0.0006486699	-0.0004293784	-0.0001672655	-0.0003259394	-0.0004402677	-0.0003980316	-0.0004113142	-0.0004560776

Source: Authors' calculations

Table 3.28: 3-Yearly excess returns' t-test analysis

Excess Return Equally Returns	2010		2011		2012		2013		2014		2015		2016		2017		2018		2019	
	P-Value	t-test	P-Value	t-test	P-Value	t-test	P-Value	t-test	P-Value	t-test	P-Value	t-test	P-Value	t-test	P-Value	t-test	P-Value	t-test	P-Value	t-test
Gold Fund	n.a	n.a	n.a	n.a	n.a	n.a	n.a	n.a	0.99281	-2.53431	0.99115	-2.45154	0.99996	-4.30308	0.93873	-1.57030	0.74229	-0.65498	0.81314	-0.89740
Initiation Fund	n.a	n.a	n.a	n.a	n.a	n.a	n.a	n.a	n.a	n.a	n.a	n.a	n.a	n.a	0.0000	4.4832	0.0005	3.5008	0.0122	2.3210
Initiation Participation Fund	n.a	n.a	n.a	n.a	n.a	n.a	n.a	n.a	n.a	n.a	n.a	n.a	n.a	n.a	0.0003	3.6725	0.0000	8.4180	0.0000	9.1151
Fixed Income Fund	n.a	n.a	n.a	n.a	0.69064	-0.50073	0.92082	-1.43162	0.58456	-0.21468	0.96650	-1.87158	0.66725	-0.43486	0.94372	-1.61466	0.70095	-0.53045	0.59390	-0.23882
Government Contribution Fund	n.a	n.a	n.a	n.a	n.a	n.a	n.a	n.a	0.90914	-1.35394	0.28009	0.58642	0.46114	0.09804	0.0083	2.4787	0.65082	-0.38972	0.43207	0.17197
Equity Fund	0.21127	0.80852	0.87136	-1.14567	0.05497	1.62678	0.59179	-0.23337	0.27671	0.59659	0.60225	-0.26053	0.50713	-0.01797	0.0094	2.4250	0.78092	-0.78143	0.40158	0.25056
Government Bonds Fund	0.93178	-1.51307	0.78584	-0.79844	0.99894	-3.23663	0.67882	-0.46717	0.93871	-1.57009	0.28481	0.57231	0.71823	-0.58140	0.21632	0.79095	0.23452	0.72949	0.94392	-1.61647
Foreign Currency Denominated Government Bonds Fund	0.65548	-0.40245	0.94354	-1.61302	0.97311	-1.97430	0.97656	-2.03682	0.96345	-1.82997	0.72649	-0.60626	0.87486	-1.16291	0.99990	-4.00749	0.57331	-0.18576	0.67791	-0.46461
Government Contribution Participation Fund	n.a	n.a	n.a	n.a	n.a	n.a	n.a	n.a	0.06696	1.52304	0.70653	-0.54673	0.81371	-0.89958	0.0138	2.2677	0.26956	0.61831	0.51398	-0.03523
Standard Participation Fund	n.a	n.a	n.a	n.a	n.a	n.a	n.a	n.a	0.41616	0.21280	0.75324	-0.68967	0.90656	-1.33782	0.63984	-0.36001	0.71083	-0.55938	0.53196	-0.08059
Private Sector Fixed Income Fund	n.a	n.a	n.a	n.a	0.21837	0.78388	0.96175	-1.80800	0.48047	0.04922	0.90263	-1.31398	0.97532	-2.01344	0.99861	-3.14244	0.91278	-1.37726	0.99792	-3.00056
Money Market Fund	1.00000	-9.38699	0.99089	-2.43948	1.00000	-5.93754	0.95473	-1.72527	0.76324	-0.72212	0.56812	-0.17247	0.91268	-1.37666	0.0075	2.5160	0.09842	1.30771	0.61443	-0.29244
Standard Fund	0.98114	-2.13342	0.98591	-2.25912	0.49916	0.00212	0.59645	-0.24544	0.83519	-0.98430	0.85900	-1.08732	0.90329	-1.31789	0.58096	-0.20541	0.74224	-0.65483	0.88760	-1.22877

Excess Return Weighted Average	2010		2011		2012		2013		2014		2015		2016		2017		2018		2019	
	P-Value	t-test	P-Value	t-test	P-Value	t-test	P-Value	t-test	P-Value	t-test	P-Value	t-test	P-Value	t-test	P-Value	t-test	P-Value	t-test	P-Value	t-test
Gold Fund	n.a	n.a	n.a	n.a	n.a	n.a	n.a	n.a	0.99863	-3.14911	0.98860	-2.34788	0.99992	-4.08481	0.92253	-1.44370	0.71726	-0.57850	0.81816	-0.91658
Initiation Fund	n.a	n.a	n.a	n.a	n.a	n.a	n.a	n.a	n.a	n.a	n.a	n.a	n.a	n.a	0.0000	5.0530	0.0001	4.2056	0.0035	2.8117
Initiation Participation Fund	n.a	n.a	n.a	n.a	n.a	n.a	n.a	n.a	n.a	n.a	n.a	n.a	n.a	n.a	0.0001	3.9612	0.0000	9.5176	0.0000	9.8818
Fixed Income Fund	n.a	n.a	n.a	n.a	0.84938	-1.04438	0.95667	-1.74693	0.63296	-0.34157	0.96470	-1.84667	0.72505	-0.60191	0.95332	-1.70991	0.94659	-1.64167	0.86939	-1.13610
Government Contribution Fund	n.a	n.a	n.a	n.a	n.a	n.a	n.a	n.a	0.91792	-1.41153	0.50488	-0.01231	0.43516	0.16408	0.0042	2.7425	0.74987	-0.67892	0.46467	0.08911
Equity Fund	0.22084	0.77542	0.87441	-1.16068	0.05203	1.65507	0.61710	-0.29948	0.28501	0.57173	0.62563	-0.32204	0.51237	-0.03116	0.0088	2.4525	0.79380	-0.82644	0.39707	0.26231
Government Bonds Fund	0.99627	-2.78647	0.86358	-1.10851	0.99811	-3.03433	0.73806	-0.64179	0.94639	-1.63974	0.33190	0.43722	0.71383	-0.56828	0.26246	0.64018	0.25642	0.65904	0.91582	-1.39734
Foreign Currency Denominated Government Bonds Fund	0.68819	-0.49374	0.94900	-1.66526	0.63302	-0.34174	0.98990	-2.39769	0.66562	-0.43035	0.58047	-0.20414	0.81212	-0.89356	0.99946	-3.46617	0.61845	-0.30303	0.61588	-0.29625
Government Contribution Participation Fund	n.a	n.a	n.a	n.a	n.a	n.a	n.a	n.a	0.43435	0.16615	0.43125	0.17406	0.88636	-1.22214	0.0355	1.8444	0.18262	0.91356	0.55934	-0.15004
Standard Participation Fund	n.a	n.a	n.a	n.a	n.a	n.a	n.a	n.a	0.33851	0.41894	0.72851	-0.61241	0.87538	-1.16552	0.72540	-0.60297	0.66012	-0.41516	0.67691	-0.46180
Private Sector Fixed Income Fund	n.a	n.a	n.a	n.a	0.21837	0.78388	0.96320	-1.82675	0.49721	0.00704	0.91730	-1.40731	0.95815	-1.76410	0.99913	-3.30683	0.97448	-1.99814	0.99948	-3.47709
Money Market Fund	1.00000	-8.50636	0.95808	-1.76326	1.00000	-5.18981	0.89586	-1.27447	0.63669	-0.35155	0.46417	0.09037	0.75759	-0.70370	0.0026	2.9231	0.06951	1.50297	0.58410	-0.21349
Standard Fund	0.98812	-2.33073	0.98197	-2.15314	0.70050	-0.52916	0.55618	-0.14201	0.74717	-0.67034	0.88873	-1.23488	0.86036	-1.09355	0.70304	-0.53654	0.82682	-0.95048	0.86644	-1.12198

Source: Authors' calculations

Table 3.29: 5-Yearly excess returns' t-test analysis

Excess Return	2010-2014		2011-2015		2012-2016		2013-2017		2014-2018		2015-2019	
Weighted Average	P-Value	t-test	P-Value	t-test	P-Value	t-test	P-Value	t-test	P-Value	t-test	P-Value	t-test
Gold Fund	0.00000	0.00000	0.00000	0.00000	0.00000	0.00000	0.00000	0.00000	0.99939	-3.27042	0.99081	-2.37266
Initiation Fund	0.00000	0.00000	0.00000	0.00000	0.00000	0.00000	0.00000	0.00000	0.00000	0.00000	0.00000	0.00000
Initiation Participation Fund	0.00000	0.00000	0.00000	0.00000	0.00000	0.00000	0.00000	0.00000	0.00000	0.00000	0.00000	0.00000
Fixed Income Fund	0.00000	0.00000	0.00000	0.00000	0.99397	-2.52833	0.99758	-2.84221	0.99734	-2.81016	0.99888	-3.08832
Government Contribution Fund	0.00000	0.00000	0.00000	0.00000	0.00000	0.00000	0.00000	0.00000	0.57315	-0.18459	0.41015	0.22738
Equity Fund	0.36714	0.33981	0.54288	-0.10780	0.28715	0.56245	0.22259	0.76463	0.29418	0.54188	0.33851	0.41701
Government Bonds Fund	0.99982	-3.61784	0.98711	-2.24237	0.97992	-2.06236	0.85345	-1.05347	0.57501	-0.18934	0.62164	-0.31012
Foreign Currency Denominated Government Bonds Fund	0.99143	-2.39900	0.98238	-2.11663	0.96187	-1.77986	0.99839	-2.97396	0.96723	-1.84930	0.96342	-1.79905
Government Contribution Participation Fund	0.00000	0.00000	0.00000	0.00000	0.00000	0.00000	0.00000	0.00000	0.14786	1.04777	0.30386	0.51397
Standard Participation Fund	0.00000	0.00000	0.00000	0.00000	0.00000	0.00000	0.00000	0.00000	0.81680	-0.90480	0.89830	-1.27511

Excess Return	2010-2014		2011-2015		2012-2016		2013-2017		2014-2018		2015-2019	
Weighted Average	P-Value	t-test	P-Value	t-test	P-Value	t-test	P-Value	t-test	P-Value	t-test	P-Value	t-test
Private Sector Fixed Income Fund	0.00000	0.00000	0.00000	0.00000	0.98745	-2.25279	0.99734	-2.81124	0.99820	-2.93803	1.00000	-4.85437
Money Market Fund	1.00000	-5.53327	0.99969	-3.46807	0.99871	-3.04332	0.38157	0.30168	0.03102	1.87408	0.07121	1.47127
Standard Fund	0.99172	-2.41183	0.98622	-2.21583	0.95007	-1.65141	0.95028	-1.65346	0.97712	-2.00731	0.98559	-2.19806

Source: Authors' calculations

Table 3.30: 5-Yearly excess returns

Excess Return (Equally weighted)	2010-2014	2011-2015	2012-2016	2013-2017	2014-2018	2015-2019
Gold Fund	n.a	n.a	n.a	n.a	-0.000367	-0.000372
Initiation Fund	n.a	n.a	n.a	n.a	n.a	n.a
Initiation Participation Fund	n.a	n.a	n.a	n.a	n.a	n.a
Fixed Income Fund	n.a	n.a	-0.0002500424	-0.0003025337	-0.0002649292	-0.0002731445
Government Contribution Fund	n.a	n.a	n.a	n.a	**0.000022**	**0.000147**
Equity Fund	**0.0007004626**	-0.000047	**0.0009805889**	**0.0012770643**	**0.000891**	**0.000696**
Government Bonds Fund	-0.0004744015	-0.0003125002	-0.0003168196	-0.0001401737	**0.000022**	**0.000019**
FC Denominated Government Bonds Fund	-0.0006396564	-0.0006400887	-0.0005304046	-0.000636099	-0.000495	-0.000411
Government Contribution Participation Fund	n.a	n.a	n.a	n.a	**0.0001000231**	**0.000043**
Standard Participation Fund	n.a	n.a	n.a	n.a	-0.0004808176	-0.0005279591
Private Sector Fixed Income Fund	n.a	n.a	n.a	-0.0002806116	-0.0001758499	-0.0002728942
Money Market Fund	-0.000320962	-0.000231708	-0.0002034984	-0.000033	**0.000080**	**0.000080**
Standard Fund	-0.0004434	-0.0004202495	-0.0002971471	-0.000309907	-0.0003830331	-0.0004362161

Excess Return (AuM-weighted)	2010-2014	2011-2015	2012-2016	2013-2017	2014-2018	2015-2019
Gold Fund	n.a	n.a	n.a	n.a	-0.000350	-0.000357
Initiation Fund	n.a	n.a	n.a	n.a	n.a	n.a
Initiation Participation Fund	n.a	n.a	n.a	n.a	n.a	n.a
Fixed Income Fund	n.a	n.a	-0.0003866873	-0.0004569294	-0.0004946417	-0.0005391352
Government Contribution Fund	n.a	n.a	n.a	n.a	-0.000030	**0.000053**
Equity Fund	**0.0005952917**	-0.000192	**0.0008950039**	**0.0011925948**	**0.000808**	**0.000630**
Government Bonds Fund	-0.0005138815	-0.0003599307	-0.0003397342	-0.0001751874	-0.000043	-0.000078
FC Denominated Government Bonds Fund	-0.000486524	-0.0004637535	-0.0003783903	-0.0006161703	-0.000441	-0.000433
Government Contribution Participation Fund	n.a	n.a	n.a	n.a	**6.65886736231165E-005**	**0.000051**
Standard Participation Fund	n.a	n.a	n.a	n.a	-0.0004056364	-0.0005491092
Private Sector Fixed Income Fund	n.a	n.a	n.a	-0.0003200895	-0.0002460103	-0.0003576503
Money Market Fund	-0.0002570851	-0.0001722691	-0.0001479465	**0.000015**	**0.000125**	**0.000121**
Standard Fund	-0.0004409572	-0.0004398558	-0.0003085237	-0.0003081499	-0.0004290173	-0.000481811

Source: Authors' calculations

In a decade-long analysis only the "initiation" and "initiation participation" funds show statistically significant positive returns over the benchmarks (Table 3.32). However, as observed in Table 3.31, in addition to the stated fund categories, the "equity" and "government contribution participation" fund categories also yield positive access returns as per AuM-weighted data, the "government contribution" fund category joins them as per equally weighted data – these fund categories just fail the t test.

Table 3.31: 10-Yearly excess returns' t-test analysis

Excess Return Equally Returns	P-Value	t-test
Gold Fund	0.00091	-3.34576
Initiation Fund	0.0000	5.7634
Initiation Participation Fund	0.0000	11.4775
Fixed Income Fund	0.01275	-2.50032
Government Contribution Fund	0.87510	0.15731
Equity Fund	0.53170	0.62584
Government Bonds Fund	0.13407	-1.50060
Foreign Currency Denominated Government Bonds Fund	0.00016	-3.80876
Government Contribution Participation Fund	0.73268	0.34184
Standard Participation Fund	0.19825	-1.28910
Private Sector Fixed Income Fund	0.00070	-3.41558
Money Market Fund	0.01305	-2.49092
Standard Fund	0.00313	-2.96938

Excess Return Weighted Average	P-Value	t-test
Gold Fund	0.00069	-3.42476
Initiation Fund	0.0000	6.7709
Initiation Participation Fund	0.0000	12.5085
Fixed Income Fund	0.00005	-4.07208
Government Contribution Fund	0.90558	-0.11870
Equity Fund	0.59623	0.53016
Government Bonds Fund	0.04047	-2.05403
Foreign Currency Denominated Government Bonds Fund	0.00360	-2.92429
Government Contribution Participation Fund	0.82953	0.21547
Standard Participation Fund	0.23508	-1.18950
Private Sector Fixed Income Fund	0.00010	-3.93623
Money Market Fund	0.15709	-1.41697
Standard Fund	0.00167	-3.16045

Source: Authors' calculations

Table 3.32: 10-Yearly excess returns

Excess Return (Equally weighted)	2010-2019
Gold Fund	-0.0004227477
Initiation Fund	**0.0001660959**
Initiation Participation Fund	**0.0005240335**
Fixed Income Fund	-0.0002425
Government Contribution Fund	**0.000028**
Equity Fund	**0.0006982815**
Government Bonds Fund	-0.0002275188
FC Denominated Government Bonds Fund	-0.0005251042
Government Contribution Participation Fund	**0.000030**
Standard Participation Fund	-0.0004722036
Private Sector Fixed Income Fund	-0.0002683586
Money Market Fund	-0.0001203324
Standard Fund	-0.0004396494

Excess Return (AuM-weighted)	2010-2019
Gold Fund	-0.0004219987
Initiation Fund	**0.0001949778**
Initiation Participation Fund	**0.0005789262**
Fixed Income Fund	-0.0004501681
Government Contribution Fund	-0.000021
Equity Fund	**0.000612488**
Government Bonds Fund	-0.0002957128
FC Denominated Government Bonds Fund	-0.0004597914
Government Contribution Participation Fund	**0.000017**
Standard Participation Fund	-0.000456466
Private Sector Fixed Income Fund	-0.0003283808
Money Market Fund	-0.000068
Standard Fund	-0.0004622865

Source: Authors' calculations

3.2.1 Gold funds

It is clearly observed in Figure 3.34 that the gold pension funds performed below the defined category benchmark between 2010–2019. This is mainly due to high management fees which averaged 1 % in 2019. We shall evaluate via six different single-index performance measures whether this conclusion holds from a risk-adjusted point of view as well in the following tables (Tables 3.33 and 3.34).

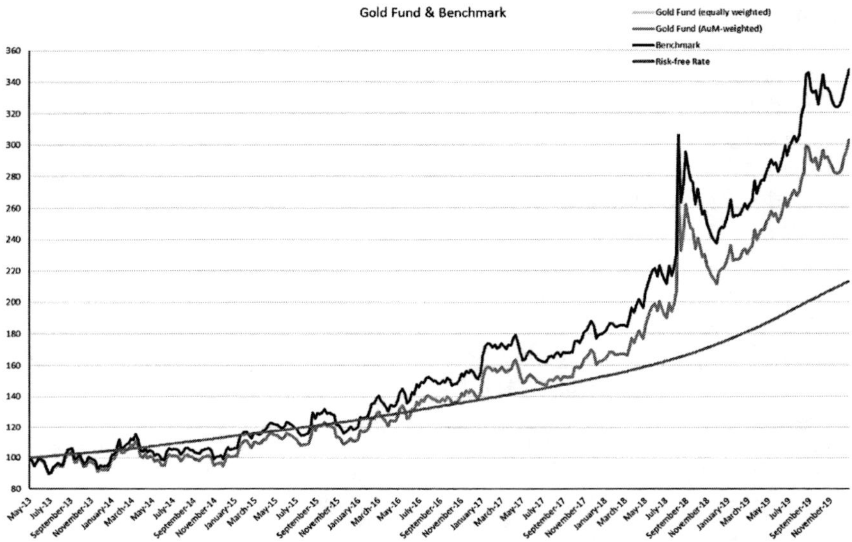

Figure 3.34: Gold funds' performance vs benchmark (May 2013=100)
Source: Takas İstanbul, Borsa İstanbul, Finnet; indexed by the authors

In annual analysis, gold pension funds yielded the same results both as per equally and AuM-weighted data (other than positive negligible Jensen's alphas with AuM-weighted data). In 2014, all measures yielded negative (and in case of Omega less than 1) ratios. In the following years, however, just the absolute measures (Sharpe and Treynor) became positive which means gold pension funds achieved an aggregate return above the risk-free rate of return.

In 3-, 5-yearly, and the decade-long analysis, again, only the absolute performance measures are positive while all others are negative (and Omega ratios less than 1) as per both equally and AuM-weighted data which is line with the trend exhibited in Figure 3.34.

Table 3.33: Gold funds' performance (equally weighted returns)

Gold Funds (Equally Weighted)	2010	2011	2012	2013	2014	2015	2016	2017	2018	2019
1-Year										
Sharpe Ratio	n.a	n.a	n.a	n.a	-0.011269	0.021393	0.135621	0.062851	0.089063	0.119225
Treynor Ratio	n.a	n.a	n.a	n.a	-0.000281	0.000457	0.002656	0.001207	0.004955	0.002436
Information Ratio	n.a	n.a	n.a	n.a	-0.351446	-0.339967	-0.659684	-0.217761	-0.090829	-0.124447
Jensen's Alpha	n.a	n.a	n.a	n.a	-0.000458	-0.000367	-0.000274	-0.000279	-0.000195	-0.000251
Sortino Ratio	n.a	n.a	n.a	n.a	-0.387653	-0.387139	-0.597289	-0.277252	-0.127871	-0.156407
Omega Ratio	n.a	n.a	n.a	n.a	0.384329	0.372533	0.194603	0.360173	0.723278	0.703873
3-Year										
Sharpe Ratio	n.a	n.a	n.a	n.a	0.043051	0.071267	0.081922	0.078993		
Treynor Ratio	n.a	n.a	n.a	n.a	0.000957	0.001444	0.002931	0.002826		
Information Ratio	n.a	n.a	n.a	n.a	-0.379617	-0.316116	-0.159162	-0.121401		
Jensen's Alpha	n.a	n.a	n.a	n.a	-0.000355	-0.000304	-0.000255	-0.000287		
Sortino Ratio	n.a	n.a	n.a	n.a	-0.410230	-0.367886	-0.214952	-0.157543		
Omega Ratio	n.a	n.a	n.a	n.a	0.329686	0.313052	0.522560	0.655918		
5-Year										
Sharpe Ratio	n.a	n.a	n.a	n.a	0.057629	0.075670				
Treynor Ratio	n.a	n.a	n.a	n.a	0.001804	0.002319				
Information Ratio	n.a	n.a	n.a	n.a	-0.209687	-0.154029				
Jensen's Alpha	n.a	n.a	n.a	n.a	-0.000313	-0.000301				
Sortino Ratio	n.a	n.a	n.a	n.a	-0.269213	-0.196836				
Omega Ratio	n.a	n.a	n.a	n.a	0.454523	0.564733				
6.5 - Year										
Sharpe Ratio	0.049268									
Treynor Ratio	0.001458									
Information Ratio	-0.179869									
Jensen's Alpha	-0.000357									
Sortino Ratio	-0.224714									
Omega Ratio	0.531890									

Source: Authors' calculations

Table 3.34: Gold funds' performance (AuM-weighted returns)

Gold Funds (AuM-Weighted) Gold Funds (AuM-Weighted)	2010	2011	2012	2013	2014	2015	2016	2017	2018	2019
1-Year										
Sharpe Ratio	n.a	n.a	n.a	n.a	-0.011214	0.022791	0.135845	0.064267	0.089534	0.117363
Treynor Ratio	n.a	n.a	n.a	n.a	-0.000280	0.000486	0.002659	0.001234	0.004981	0.002400
Information Ratio	n.a	n.a	n.a	n.a	-0.436703	-0.325592	-0.614026	-0.200205	-0.080224	-0.127106
Jensen's Alpha	n.a	n.a	n.a	n.a	0.000171	0.000825	0.002845	0.001469	0.005091	0.002434
Sortino Ratio	n.a	n.a	n.a	n.a	-0.443878	-0.382510	-0.570442	-0.257862	-0.112896	-0.157055
Omega Ratio	n.a	n.a	n.a	n.a	0.302450	0.388597	0.219824	0.386825	0.748935	0.692021
3-Year										
Sharpe Ratio	n.a	n.a	n.a	n.a	0.043274	0.072147	0.082407	0.079286		
Treynor Ratio	n.a	n.a	n.a	n.a	0.000962	0.001462	0.002949	0.002836		
Information Ratio	n.a	n.a	n.a	n.a	-0.412467	-0.302316	-0.148270	-0.115737		
Jensen's Alpha	n.a	n.a	n.a	n.a	0.001270	0.001711	0.003138	0.003047		
Sortino Ratio	n.a	n.a	n.a	n.a	-0.434479	-0.357686	-0.200637	-0.148846		
Omega Ratio	n.a	n.a	n.a	n.a	0.304414	0.331280	0.546161	0.663465		
5-Year										
Sharpe Ratio	n.a	n.a	n.a	n.a	0.058068	0.076043				
Treynor Ratio	n.a	n.a	n.a	n.a	0.001818	0.002330				

Gold Funds (AuM-Weighted) Gold Funds (AuM-Weighted)	2010	2011	2012	2013	2014	2015	2016	2017	2018	2019
Information Ratio	n.a	n.a	n.a	n.a	-0.202823	-0.147146				
Jensen's Alpha	n.a	n.a	n.a	n.a	0.002082	0.002563				
Sortino Ratio	n.a	n.a	n.a	n.a	-0.261768	-0.186873				
Omega Ratio	n.a	n.a	n.a	n.a	0.456637	0.574059				
6.5 - Year										
Sharpe Ratio	0.049091									
Treynor Ratio	0.001453									
Information Ratio	-0.184116									
Jensen's Alpha	0.001752									
Sortino Ratio	-0.227867									
Omega Ratio	0.514948									

Source: Authors' calculations

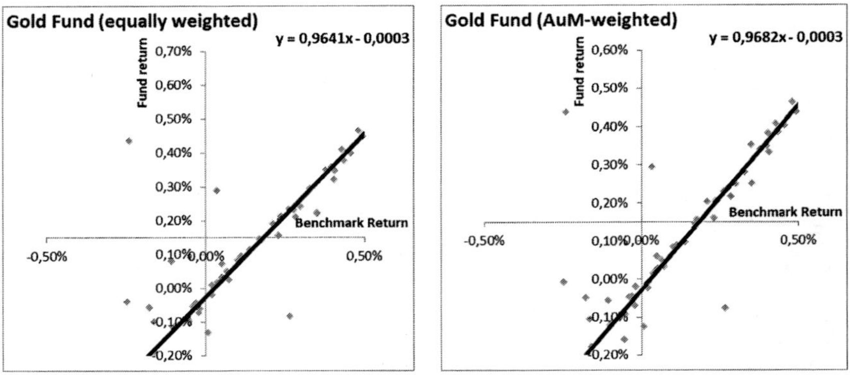

Figure 3.35: Gold funds' Treynor ratio graphics
Source: Authors' calculations

The Treynor ratio scatter diagrams demonstrate that there is a strong positive relationship between the funds' aggregate returns and the category benchmark as would be expected (Figure 3.35).

The Jensen's alpha is negative for the whole period as per both equally and AuM-weighted data (Figure 3.36).

The Omega ratio graphics exhibit that the gold funds category's possibility of yielding a positive return compared to the category benchmark is 33 % as per both equally and AuM-weighted data (Figure 3.37). This is due to high management fees as explained earlier.

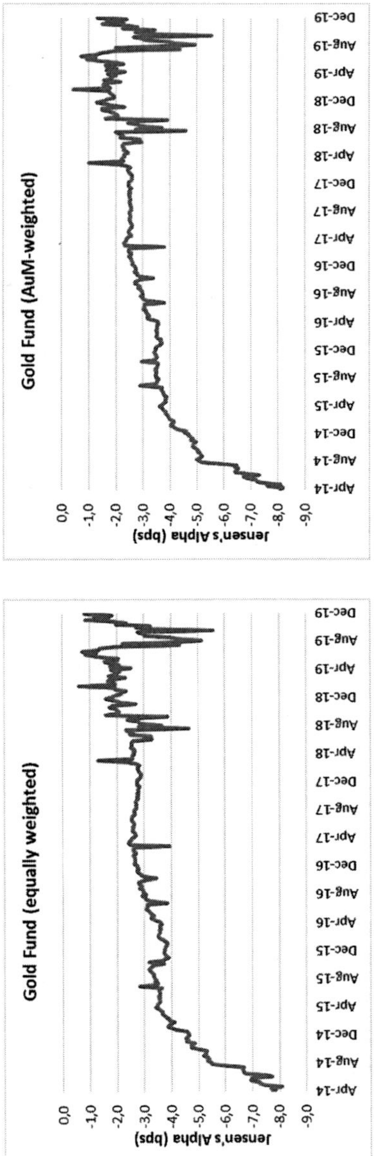

Figure 3.36: Gold funds' Jensen's alpha ratio graphics
Source: Authors' calculations

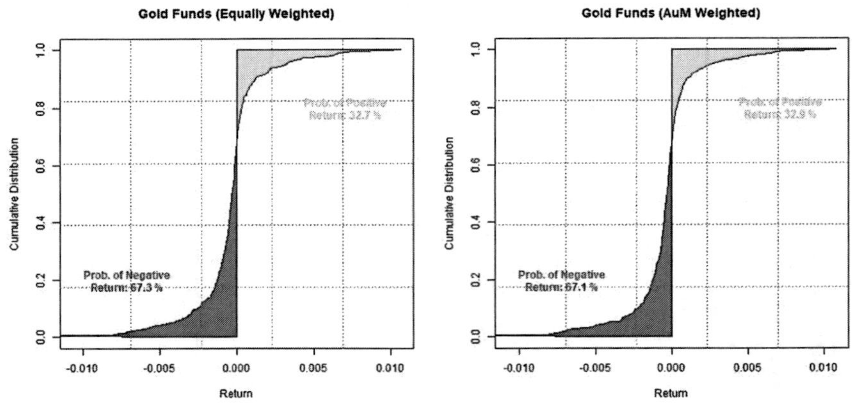

Figure 3.37: Gold funds' Omega ratio graphics
Source: Authors' calculations

3.2.2 Fixed income funds

It is clearly observed in Figure 3.38 that the fixed income pension funds performed below the defined category benchmark and the risk-free rate of return between 2010–2019. This result can be attributed to high management fees which is 1.58 % on average in 2019. The risk-adjusted performance ratios listed in Tables 3.35 and 3.36 also exhibit these unsuccessful results.

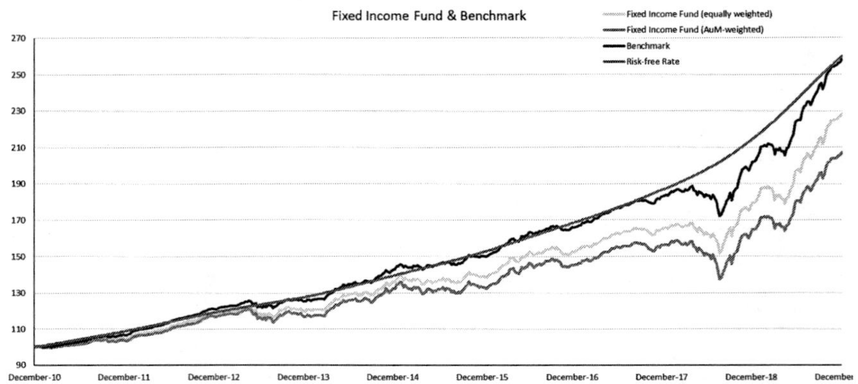

Figure 3.38: Fixed income funds' performance vs benchmark (2010=100)
Source: Authors' calculations

As per equally weighted data, there are only three annual periods (namely 2012, 2014, and 2019) and one 3-yearly period (2012–2014) when absolute performance measures are positive. All other performance measures for all other periods are negative (and less than 1 in case of Omega ratios).

As per AuM-weighted data, the annual periods with the positive absolute performance measures remain the same but the only 3-year period with positive ratios also become negative. Unlike the equally weighted data, there are some positive Jensen's alphas, but they are negligible.

Table 3.35: Fixed income funds' performance (equally weighted returns)

Fixed Income Funds (Equally Weighted)	2010	2011	2012	2013	2014	2015	2016	2017	2018	2019
1-Year										
Sharpe Ratio	n.a	n.a	**0.233354**	-0.161269	**0.135921**	-0.184303	-0.015426	-0.119973	-0.084702	**0.087995**
Treynor Ratio	n.a	n.a	**0.000482**	-0.000775	**0.000602**	-0.000896	-0.000063	-0.000354	-0.000921	**0.000776**
Information Ratio	n.a	n.a	-0.069439	-0.198531	-0.029770	-0.259541	-0.060123	-0.223913	-0.073561	-0.033119
Jensen's Alpha	n.a	n.a	-0.000212	-0.000156	-0.000240	-0.000246	-0.000157	-0.000286	-0.000227	-0.000350
Sortino Ratio	n.a	n.a	-0.097782	-0.233970	-0.038273	-0.299471	-0.083438	-0.291778	-0.102155	-0.044831
Omega Ratio	n.a	n.a	0.818451	0.585023	0.922874	0.535984	0.923979	0.578775	0.801972	0.916463
3-Year										
Sharpe Ratio	n.a	n.a	**0.012051**	-0.083984	-0.032106	-0.105610	-0.065135	-0.017154		
Treynor Ratio	n.a	n.a	**0.000048**	-0.000398	-0.000144	-0.000425	-0.000452	-0.000142		
Information Ratio	n.a	n.a	-0.113492	-0.174134	-0.121236	-0.170759	-0.092053	-0.083187		
Jensen's Alpha	n.a	n.a	-0.000287	-0.000275	-0.000251	-0.000217	-0.000207	-0.000244		
Sortino Ratio	n.a	n.a	-0.138835	-0.206608	-0.152820	-0.215222	-0.126260	-0.113340		
Omega Ratio	n.a	n.a	0.719587	0.633529	0.731449	0.650864	0.779199	0.784366		
5-Year										
Sharpe Ratio	n.a	n.a	-0.039244	-0.073625	-0.056423	-0.043514				
Treynor Ratio	n.a	n.a	-0.000165	-0.000316	-0.000345	-0.000305				
Information Ratio	n.a	n.a	-0.131790	-0.154479	-0.111252	-0.106794				

Fixed Income Funds (Equally Weighted)	2010	2011	2012	2013	2014	2015	2016	2017	2018	2019
Jensen's Alpha	n.a	n.a	-0.000258	-0.000248	-0.000237	-0.000254				
Sortino Ratio	n.a	n.a	-0.163060	-0.190845	-0.146857	-0.141760				
Omega Ratio	n.a	n.a	0.698920	0.668757	0.727816	0.743005				
10-Year										
Sharpe Ratio	-0.027377									
Treynor Ratio	-0.000166									
Information Ratio	-0.106623									
Jensen's Alpha	-0.000251									
Sortino Ratio	-0.138825									
Omega Ratio	0.737149									

Source: Authors' calculations

Table 3.36: Fixed income funds' performance (AuM-weighted returns)

Fixed Income Funds (AuM-Weighted)	2010	2011	2012	2013	2014	2015	2016	2017	2018	2019
1-Year										
Sharpe Ratio	n.a	n.a	**0.204217**	-0.179122	**0.107709**	-0.191537	-0.028088	-0.134038	-0.116529	**0.069296**
Treynor Ratio	n.a	n.a	**0.000338**	-0.000860	**0.000473**	-0.000929	-0.000114	-0.000389	-0.001220	**0.000610**
Information Ratio	n.a	n.a	-0.144830	-0.242256	-0.047367	-0.256086	-0.083764	-0.237122	-0.227658	-0.157548
Jensen's Alpha	n.a	n.a	**0.000853**	-0.001105	**0.001040**	-0.001111	**0.000071**	-0.000164	-0.001286	**0.001148**
Sortino Ratio	n.a	n.a	-0.207390	-0.270645	-0.062150	-0.296807	-0.113575	-0.291835	-0.273928	-0.196346
Omega Ratio	n.a	n.a	0.668880	0.497063	0.882502	0.540762	0.884765	0.563853	0.549589	0.653791
3-Year										
Sharpe Ratio	n.a	n.a	-0.007583	-0.098722	-0.047834	-0.118843	-0.087332	-0.047828		
Treynor Ratio	n.a	n.a	-0.000030	-0.000466	-0.000213	-0.000476	-0.000587	-0.000388		
Information Ratio	n.a	n.a	-0.143528	-0.192835	-0.138901	-0.189246	-0.178645	-0.202673		
Jensen's Alpha	n.a	n.a	**0.000382**	-0.000297	**0.000060**	-0.000420	-0.000518	-0.000181		
Sortino Ratio	n.a	n.a	-0.171390	-0.225787	-0.172429	-0.231210	-0.222058	-0.245671		
Omega Ratio	n.a	n.a	0.652645	0.602327	0.704584	0.626598	0.641907	0.578270		
5-Year										
Sharpe Ratio	n.a	n.a	-0.056356	-0.088716	-0.076591	-0.069163				
Treynor Ratio	n.a	n.a	-0.000236	-0.000379	-0.000457	-0.000479				
Information Ratio	n.a	n.a	-0.156800	-0.176266	-0.174279	-0.191529				

Fixed Income Funds (AuM-Weighted)	2010	2011	2012	2013	2014	2015	2016	2017	2018	2019
Jensen's Alpha	n.a	n.a	**0.000034**	-0.000206	-0.000309	-0.000298				
Sortino Ratio	n.a	n.a	-0.189494	-0.212317	-0.213274	-0.232626				
Omega Ratio	n.a	n.a	0.651503	0.634873	0.638063	0.608789				
10-Year										
Sharpe Ratio	-0.050867									
Treynor Ratio	-0.000305									
Information Ratio	-0.174823									
Jensen's Alpha	-0.000073									
Sortino Ratio	-0.211398									
Omega Ratio	0.621032									

Source: Authors' calculations

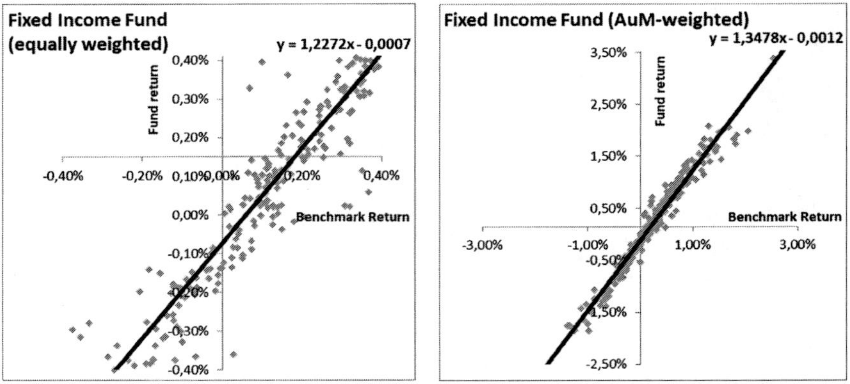

Figure 3.39: Fixed income funds' Treynor ratio graphics
Source: Authors' calculations

The Treynor ratio scatter diagrams demonstrate that there is a very strong positive relationship between the funds' aggregate return and the category benchmark as would be expected (Figure 3.39), because both the fund category and the benchmark returns are basically government bonds' returns.

The Jensen's alpha is negative for the whole period as per AuM-weighted data and only positive for about a year between July 2013–May 2014 (Figure 3.40).

The Omega ratio graphics exhibit that the fixed income pension funds category's possibility of yielding a positive return compared to the category benchmark is 44 % as per equally and 40 % as per AuM-weighted data (Figure 3.41).

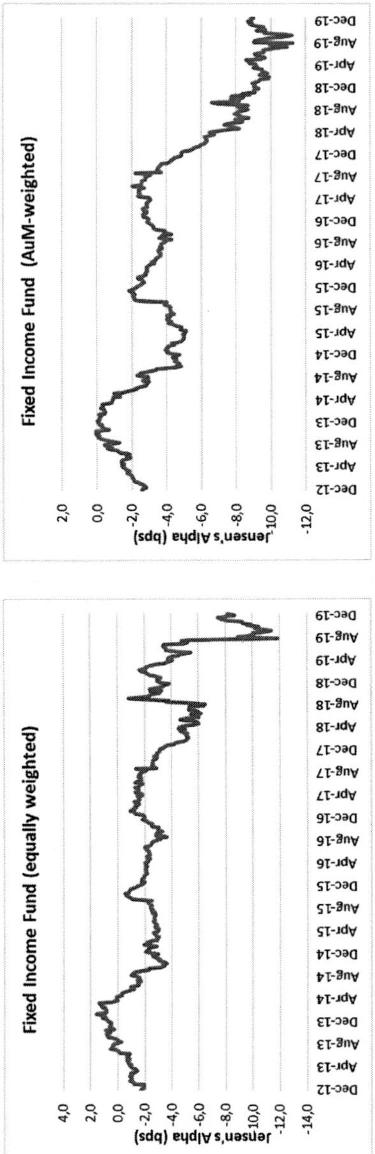

Figure 3.40: Fixed income funds' Jensen's alpha ratio graphics
Source: Authors' calculations

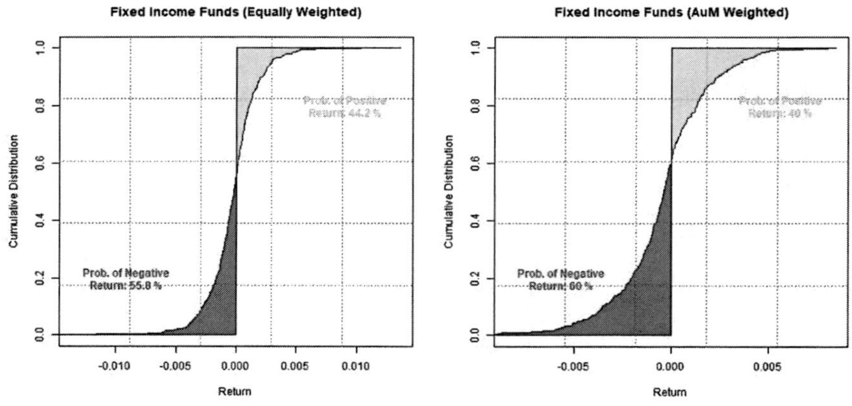

Figure 3.41: Fixed income funds' Omega ratio graphics
Source: Authors' calculations

3.2.3 Government bonds funds

It is clearly observed in Figure 3.42 that the government bonds pension funds performed below the defined category benchmark and the risk-free rate of return between 2010–2019. This result can be attributed to high management fees which is on average 1.6 % in 2019. The risk-adjusted performance ratios listed in Tables 3.37 and 3.38 also exhibit these unsuccessful results.

Government bonds pension fund graph is like that of fixed income pension funds (Figures 3.38 and 3.42). The distinguishing factor between the two is expected to be more asset allocation to private sector bonds in the fixed income pension funds compared to government bonds pension funds. Therefore, we defined the benchmark for government bonds fund category as 100 % "BIST-KYD Government All" while that of fixed income funds as 50 % the same benchmark and 50 % private sector bonds. However, in reality, the fixed income pension fund category's allocation to private sector bonds has been only 6 % for the analyzed 10 years.

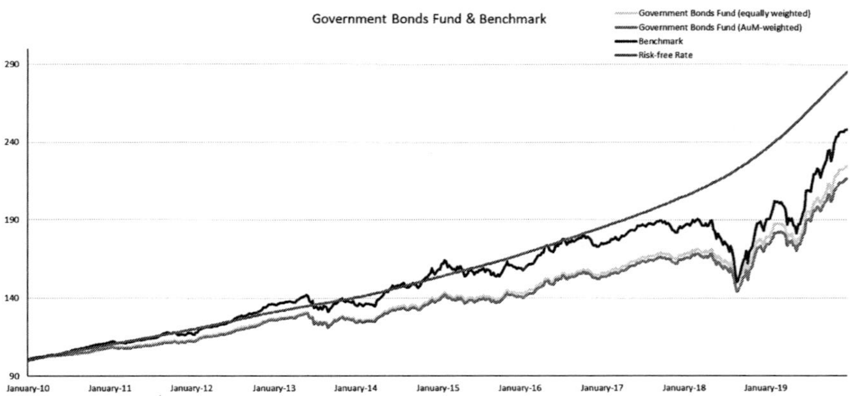

Figure 3.42: Government bonds funds' performance vs benchmark (2010=100)
Source: Authors' calculations

In annual analysis, the results as per both equally and AuM-weighted data are the same (other than negligible positive Jensen's alpha ratios): The absolute return measures are positive in years 2012, 2014 and 2019, though the Treynor ratios are negligible, while all other measures are negative (and less than 1 in Omega ratios). In 2015, 2017 and 2018, Information and Sortino ratios are positive and Omega ratios are greater than 1 indicating that the fund category performed above its category benchmark. In 2016, though, all measures are negative (and Omega less than 1).

In 3-yearly analysis, the first five periods of the 8 periods have resulted in negative (and less than 1 Omega) ratios as per both equally and AuM-weighted data. In the following two periods (2015–2017 and 2016–2018), Information and Sortino ratios are positive, and the Omega ratios are above 1 as per both equally and AuM-weighted data indicating that the fund category performed above its category benchmark. In the last 3-year period (2017–2019), the same risk-adjusted performance of the previous period continued as per equally weighted data, but it did not as per AuM-weighted data which means the larger funds performed worse than the smaller ones and dragged down the aggregate return.

Table 3.37: Government bonds funds' performance (equally weighted returns)

Government Bonds Funds (Equally Weighted)	2010	2011	2012	2013	2014	2015	2016	2017	2018	2019
					1-Year					
Sharpe Ratio	-0.139002	-0.327652	**0.183329**	-0.186974	**0.103931**	-0.207777	-0.047180	-0.141845	-0.101465	**0.059185**
Treynor Ratio	-0.011629	-0.001323	**0.000674**	-0.001778	**0.000916**	-0.002034	-0.000379	-0.000812	-0.002058	**0.001038**
Information Ratio	-0.209825	-0.110724	-0.448840	-0.064785	-0.217732	**0.079365**	-0.080166	**0.109686**	**0.101161**	-0.224164
Jensen's Alpha	-0.000279	-0.000441	-0.000256	-0.000319	-0.000254	-0.000293	-0.000236	-0.000034	**0.000009**	-0.000526
Sortino Ratio	-0.260240	-0.149475	-0.450099	-0.089133	-0.262032	**0.119674**	-0.104377	**0.172732**	**0.174864**	-0.271125
Omega Ratio	0.592422	0.729247	0.290550	0.841589	0.569108	**1.214221**	0.817635	**1.301400**	**1.303437**	0.537552
					3-Year					
Sharpe Ratio	-0.080518	-0.124201	-0.034911	-0.116492	-0.061916	-0.134048	-0.083221	-0.032205		
Treynor Ratio	-0.000383	-0.000790	-0.000278	-0.001114	-0.000553	-0.001070	-0.001084	-0.000510		
Information Ratio	-0.234426	-0.189652	-0.205877	-0.069297	-0.075244	**0.032496**	**0.051317**	**0.002185**		
Jensen's Alpha	-0.000358	-0.000390	-0.000449	-0.000398	-0.000294	-0.000185	-0.000086	-0.000096		
Sortino Ratio	-0.282844	-0.236068	-0.246889	-0.092207	-0.099568	**0.046949**	**0.083834**	**0.003383**		
Omega Ratio	0.532174	0.595727	0.553723	0.832691	0.827189	**1.084929**	**1.160633**	**1.006297**		
					5-Year					
Sharpe Ratio	-0.062912	-0.100806	-0.074475	-0.105685	-0.077616	-0.055101				
Treynor Ratio	-0.000479	-0.000787	-0.000625	-0.000908	-0.000905	-0.000743				

Government Bonds Funds (Equally Weighted)	2010	2011	2012	2013	2014	2015	2016	2017	2018	2019
Information Ratio	-0.191103	-0.112155	-0.107703	-0.046717	**0.005332**	**0.004607**				
Jensen's Alpha	-0.000432	-0.000384	-0.000351	-0.000293	-0.000192	-0.000141				
Sortino Ratio	-0.233043	-0.146274	-0.140285	-0.062791	**0.008048**	**0.006973**				
Omega Ratio	0.585648	0.732031	0.749303	0.885217	**1.014684**	**1.012838**				
10-Year										
Sharpe Ratio	-0.045467									
Treynor Ratio	-0.000610									
Information Ratio	-0.065806									
Jensen's Alpha	-0.000287									
Sortino Ratio	-0.093446									
Omega Ratio	0.828495									

Source: Authors' calculations

Table 3.38: Government bonds funds' performance (AuM-weighted returns)

Government Bonds Funds (AuM-Weighted)	2010	2011	2012	2013	2014	2015	2016	2017	2018	2019
1-Year										
Sharpe Ratio	-0.139095	-0.449873	**0.188970**	-0.184681	**0.096210**	-0.203437	-0.033693	-0.149040	-0.104452	**0.050881**
Treynor Ratio	-0.000853	-0.001679	**0.000536**	-0.001751	**0.000849**	-0.001991	-0.000270	-0.000850	-0.002122	**0.000896**
Information Ratio	-0.386414	-0.153722	-0.420786	-0.089001	-0.227391	**0.060632**	-0.077891	**0.088777**	**0.091393**	-0.193776
Jensen's Alpha	-0.000230	-0.000646	**0.000622**	-0.001263	**0.000614**	-0.001178	-0.000026	-0.000579	-0.001556	**0.000994**
Sortino Ratio	-0.402554	-0.197039	-0.433797	-0.126070	-0.271525	**0.089961**	-0.104556	**0.139901**	**0.154729**	-0.234785
Omega Ratio	0.358479	0.662808	0.301702	0.784624	0.558698	**1.164886**	0.822860	**1.236689**	**1.268309**	0.596405
3-Year										
Sharpe Ratio	-0.080621	-0.129359	-0.037540	-0.119324	-0.062394	-0.128549	-0.082486	-0.044871		
Treynor Ratio	-0.000474	-0.000820	-0.000299	-0.001139	-0.000559	-0.001025	-0.001076	-0.000710		
Information Ratio	-0.311018	-0.217146	-0.216365	-0.093868	-0.093753	**0.022934**	**0.045311**	-0.027833		
Jensen's Alpha	-0.000065	-0.000350	**0.000109**	-0.000532	-0.000175	-0.000596	-0.000724	-0.000440		
Sortino Ratio	-0.347225	-0.264776	-0.257757	-0.121832	-0.121608	**0.033262**	**0.073451**	-0.039326		
Omega Ratio	0.431804	0.553854	0.531896	0.775408	0.785375	**1.059363**	**1.139147**	0.925150		
5-Year										
Sharpe Ratio	-0.063022	-0.106070	-0.074297	-0.105433	-0.079236	-0.064438				
Treynor Ratio	-0.000527	-0.000824	-0.000622	-0.000904	-0.000926	-0.000868				

Government Bonds Funds (AuM-Weighted)	2010	2011	2012	2013	2014	2015	2016	2017	2018	2019
Information Ratio	-0.224369	-0.139066	-0.127902	-0.065333	-0.011743	-0.019233				
Jensen's Alpha	-0.000067	-0.000311	-0.000194	-0.000440	-0.000517	-0.000520				
Sortino Ratio	-0.265637	-0.176365	-0.163470	-0.086464	-0.017230	-0.027191				
Omega Ratio	0.522598	0.678156	0.705471	0.840264	0.968520	0.947628				
10-Year										
Sharpe Ratio	-0.045729									
Treynor Ratio	-0.000696									
Information Ratio	-0.090075									
Jensen's Alpha	-0.000292									
Sortino Ratio	-0.121357									
Omega Ratio	0.768708									

Source: Authors' calculations

In 5-yearly analysis, the first four periods out of six periods have yielded negative results as per both equally and AuM-weighted data. The negative results prevail for the last two periods as well as per the AuM-weighted data. However, we notice positive Information and Sortino ratios, and above 1 Omega ratios as per equally weighted data although Information and Sortino ratios are negligible. The smaller funds must have performed better than the larger ones in the last two 5-yearly periods to push up the aggregate fund category return.

In a decade-long analysis, all ratios are negative as per both equally and AuM-weighted data. High management fees (averaging 1.60 % in 2019) are to be blamed for these unsuccessful risk-adjusted performances.

The Treynor ratio scatter diagrams demonstrate that there is a strong positive relationship between the funds' aggregate return and the category benchmark as would be expected (Figure 3.43), because both the fund category and the benchmark returns are basically government bonds' returns.

The Jensen's alpha is negative until mid-October 2018 as per both equally and AuM-weighted data. It stays above the zero line until mid-August 2019 as per equally and until November 2019 as per AuM-weighted data (Figure 3.44).

The Omega ratio graphics exhibit that the funds category's possibility of yielding a positive return compared to the category benchmark is 44 % as per both equally AuM-weighted data (Figure 3.45).

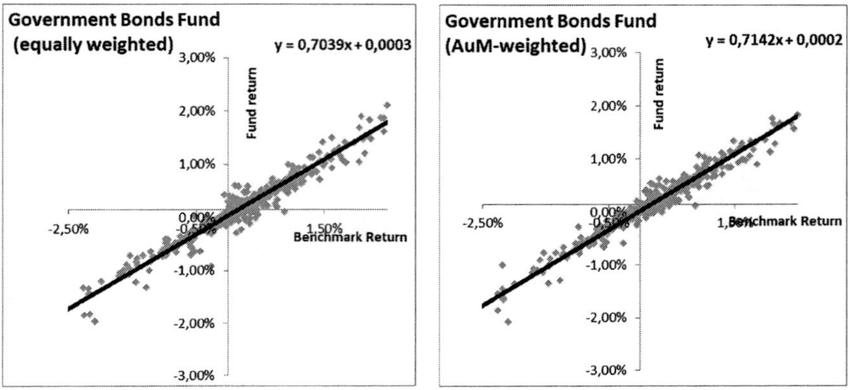

Figure 3.43: Government bonds funds' Treynor ratio graphics
Source: Authors' calculations

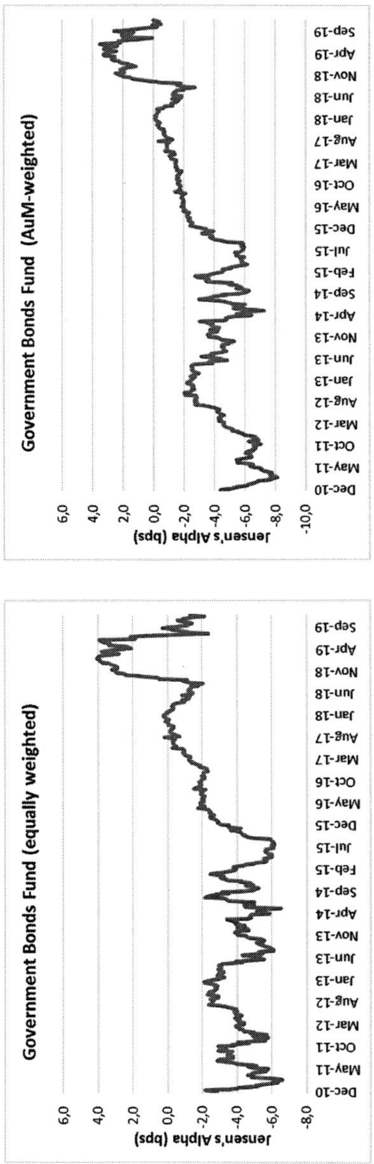

Figure 3.44: Government bonds funds' Jensen's alpha ratio graphics
Source: Author's calculations

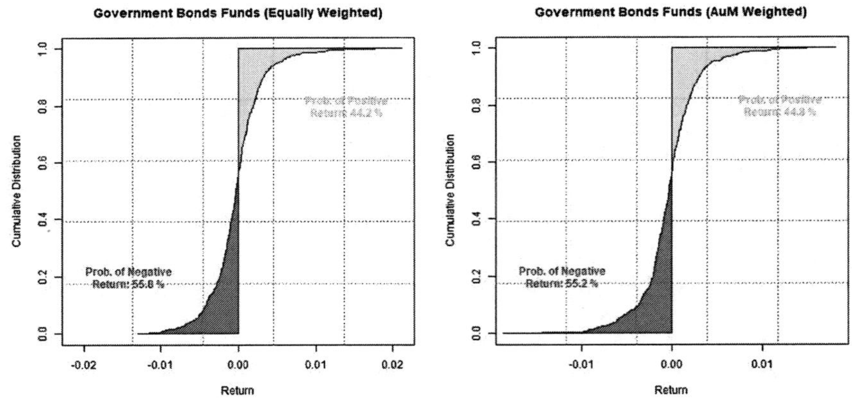

Figure 3.45: Government bonds funds' Omega ratio graphics
Source: Authors' calculations

3.2.4 Foreign currency denominated government bonds funds

It is clearly observed in Figure 3.46 that the foreign currency denominated government bonds pension funds performed below the defined category benchmark and except the first two years, above the risk-free rate of return between 2010–2019.

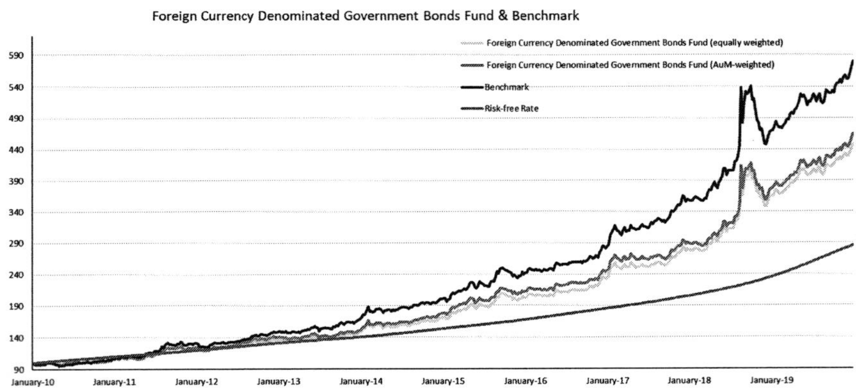

Figure 3.46: FC denominated government bonds funds' performance vs benchmark (2010=100)
Source: Authors' calculations

Table 3.39: FC denominated government bonds funds' performance (equally weighted)

Foreign Currency Denominated Government Bonds Funds (Equally Weighted)	2010	2011	2012	2013	2014	2015	2016	2017	2018	2019
1-Year										
Sharpe Ratio	-0.139385	0.125914	0.019463	0.054826	0.078440	0.120383	0.093973	0.102989	0.092348	0.038031
Treynor Ratio	-0.000928	0.001804	0.000179	0.000664	0.001027	0.001928	0.000964	0.001468	0.003522	0.000453
Information Ratio	-0.055810	-0.223686	-0.273786	-0.282456	-0.253771	-0.084074	-0.158898	-0.555739	-0.025760	-0.064430
Jensen's Alpha	-0.000335	-0.000541	-0.000519	-0.000590	-0.000394	-0.000007	-0.000225	-0.000985	0.000216	-0.000100
Sortino Ratio	-0.080392	-0.267874	-0.309937	-0.334538	-0.316604	-0.108032	-0.207553	-0.505459	-0.034078	-0.091266
Omega Ratio	0.873789	0.572913	0.502393	0.471747	0.503700	0.809948	0.676748	0.190248	0.917414	0.840368
3-Year										
Sharpe Ratio	-0.079451	0.073590	0.054252	0.087956	0.098617	0.106350	0.082146	0.074822		
Treynor Ratio	0.000360	0.000884	0.000625	0.001210	0.001308	0.001454	0.001991	0.001823		
Information Ratio	-0.161378	-0.249462	-0.270968	-0.202068	-0.158988	-0.238935	-0.174219	-0.150089		
Jensen's Alpha	-0.000457	-0.000549	-0.000502	-0.000334	-0.000208	-0.000396	-0.000314	-0.000273		
Sortino Ratio	-0.206412	-0.292991	-0.319282	-0.249099	-0.202026	-0.278041	-0.213557	-0.187541		
Omega Ratio	0.665721	0.523042	0.490973	0.590459	0.660654	0.530819	0.580091	0.625581		

(Continued)

Table 3.39: Continued

Foreign Currency Denominated Government Bonds Funds (Equally Weighted)	2010	2011	2012	2013	2014	2015	2016	2017	2018	2019
5-Year										
Sharpe Ratio	-0.060869	**0.085907**	**0.077921**	**0.092014**	**0.085488**	**0.080623**				
Treynor Ratio	**0.000556**	**0.001122**	**0.000958**	**0.001216**	**0.001777**	**0.001666**				
Information Ratio	-0.193694	-0.215904	-0.207787	-0.251770	-0.168805	-0.137821				
Jensen's Alpha	-0.000472	-0.000414	-0.000348	-0.000434	-0.000280	-0.000217				
Sortino Ratio	-0.243435	-0.259490	-0.253408	-0.296604	-0.208602	-0.173348				
Omega Ratio	0.604795	0.570319	0.582761	0.511830	0.609746	0.668923				
10-Year										
Sharpe Ratio	-0.040566									
Treynor Ratio	**0.001109**									
Information Ratio	-0.167025									
Jensen's Alpha	-0.000355									
Sortino Ratio	-0.209927									
Omega Ratio	0.632613									

Source: Authors' calculations

Table 3.40: FC denominated government bonds funds' performance (AuM-weighted)

Foreign Currency Denominated Government Bonds Funds (AuM-Weighted)	2010	2011	2012	2013	2014	2015	2016	2017	2018	2019
1-Year										
Sharpe Ratio	-0.139393	0.140856	0.078580	0.023500	0.119221	0.138113	0.094823	0.089743	0.090982	0.041574
Treynor Ratio	-0.000934	0.001979	0.001102	0.000290	0.001566	0.002264	0.000990	0.001291	0.003475	0.000500
Information Ratio	-0.068469	-0.230930	-0.047390	-0.332500	-0.059678	-0.028309	-0.122526	-0.480671	-0.042022	-0.041083
Jensen's Alpha	-0.000496	0.002139	0.000925	0.000811	0.001654	0.001810	0.001085	0.002079	0.002864	0.000535
Sortino Ratio	-0.095682	-0.270702	-0.063719	-0.381268	-0.082221	-0.037885	-0.152106	-0.459866	-0.054840	-0.056955
Omega Ratio	0.843834	0.565242	0.890868	0.415063	0.849949	0.930882	0.774656	0.256470	0.877390	0.903000
3-Year										
Sharpe Ratio	-0.079084	0.081578	0.072398	0.095739	0.119362	0.108277	0.079376	0.072207		
Treynor Ratio	0.000610	0.000987	0.000850	0.001341	0.001608	0.001507	0.001930	0.001765		
Information Ratio	-0.113829	-0.202338	-0.150364	-0.127076	-0.060285	-0.171232	-0.163650	-0.143828		
Jensen's Alpha	0.000896	0.001336	0.001176	0.001412	0.001510	0.001628	0.001978	0.001801		
Sortino Ratio	-0.147474	-0.245762	-0.191077	-0.163142	-0.079201	-0.206938	-0.198051	-0.177552		

(Continued)

Table 3.40: Continued

Foreign Currency Denominated Government Bonds Funds (AuM-Weighted)	2010	2011	2012	2013	2014	2015	2016	2017	2018	2019
Omega Ratio	0.756790	0.603594	0.678129	0.713396	0.852972	0.637385	0.621681	0.655016		
5-Year										
Sharpe Ratio	-0.060518	0.102304	0.092177	0.094039	0.090574	0.081115				
Treynor Ratio	0.000728	0.001353	0.001156	0.001262	0.001894	0.001686				
Information Ratio	-0.148779	-0.131268	-0.110382	-0.184437	-0.114689	-0.111573				
Jensen's Alpha	0.001029	0.001489	0.001277	0.001466	0.001893	0.001663				
Sortino Ratio	-0.189125	-0.166646	-0.141785	-0.223921	-0.143993	-0.140386				
Omega Ratio	0.686411	0.713687	0.751780	0.613165	0.722399	0.733260				
10-Year										
Sharpe Ratio	-0.040357									
Treynor Ratio	0.001205									
Information Ratio	-0.128239									
Jensen's Alpha	0.001358									
Sortino Ratio	-0.161887									
Omega Ratio	0.710367									

Source: Authors' calculations

As per both equally and AuM-weighted data, other than the absolute risk-adjusted performance measures (i.e., Sharpe and Treynor), all measures are negative (and less than 1 in case of Omega ratios) in the analysis of all periods. Jensen' alphas become positive as per AuM-weighted data, but they are negligibly small. The Treynor ratios are also negligibly small. So basically, the only measure yielding positive results is the Sharpe ratio which is positive all periods other than the first period in annual, 3-yearly, and 5-yearly analysis. In a decade-long analysis, even the Sharpe ratios turns into negative.

The reason why the relative risk-adjusted performance measures yield negative ratios is the high management fee of 1.52 % on average in 2019 to the already small excess returns.

The Treynor ratio scatter diagrams demonstrate that there is a strong positive relationship between the funds' aggregate return and the category benchmark as would be expected (Figure 3.47), because both the fund category and the benchmark returns are basically foreign currency–denominated government bonds' returns.

The Jensen's alpha is negative for most of the 10-year period as per equally weighted data: we notice a positive Jensen's alpha during the second half of 2015 and after October 2018 to December 2019. As per AuM-weighted data, the positive periods are longer: there is a 7 months period between June 2012–January 2013 and two 13 months period between January 2015–February 2016 and November 2018–December 2019 (Figure 3.48).

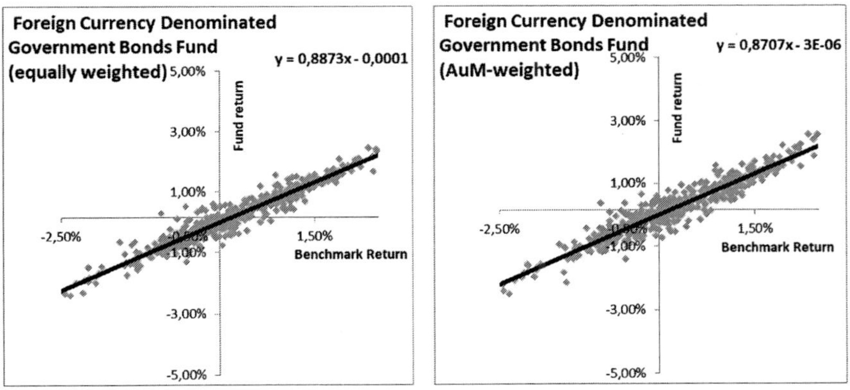

Figure 3.47: FC denominated government bonds funds' Treynor ratio graphics
Source: Authors' calculations

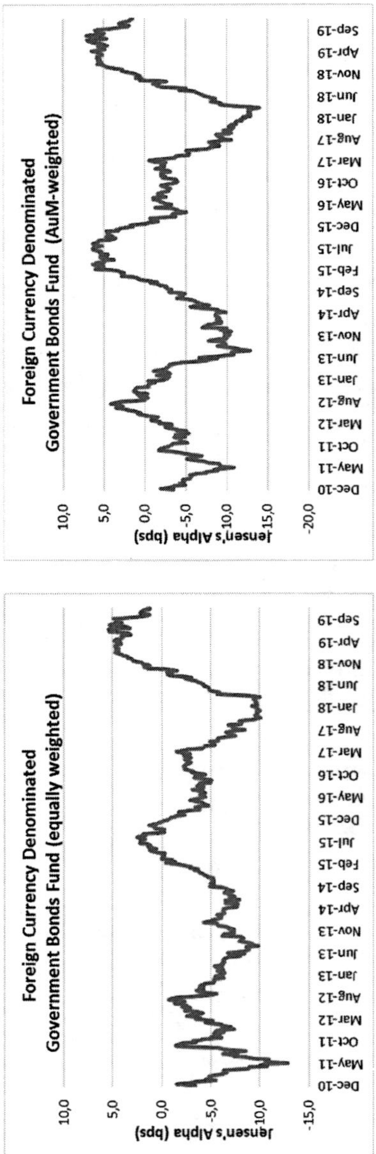

Figure 3.48: FC denominated government bonds funds' Jensen's alpha ratio graphics
Source: Authors' calculations

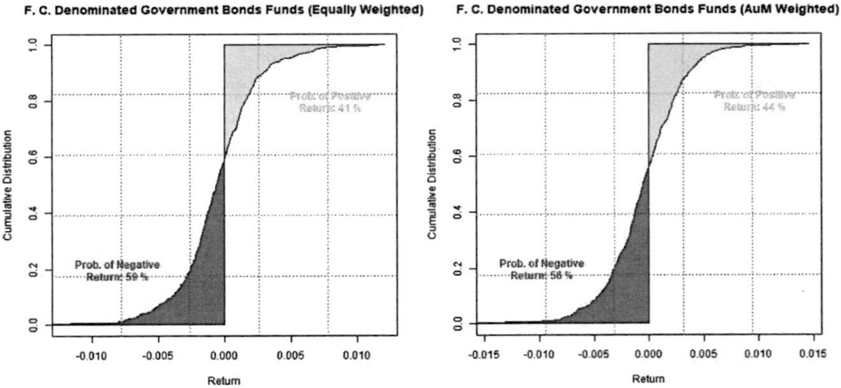

Figure 3.49: FC denominated government bonds funds' Omega ratio graphics
Source: Author's calculations

The Omega ratio graphics exhibit that the funds category's possibility of yielding a positive return compared to the category benchmark is 41 % and 44 % as per equally and AuM-weighted data, respectively (Figure 3.49).

3.2.5 Private sector fixed income funds

It is observed in Figure 3.50 that the private sector fixed income pension funds performed below the defined category benchmark and the risk-free rate of return between 2010–2019.

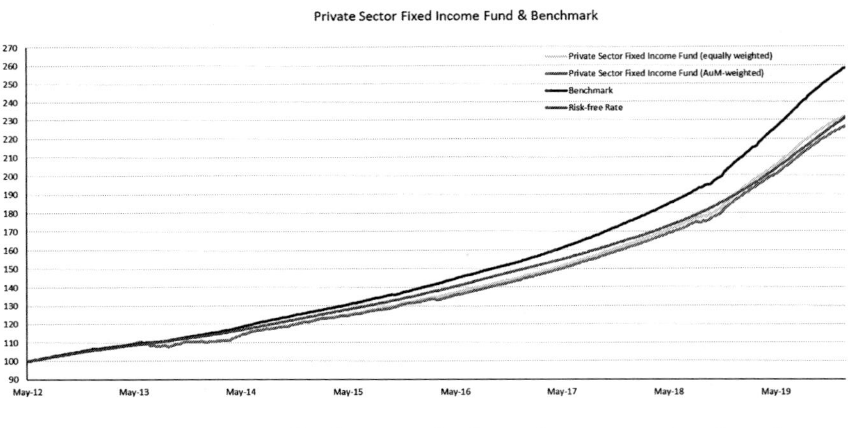

Figure 3.50: Private sector fixed income funds' performance vs benchmark (May 2012=100)
Source: Authors' calculations

Table 3.41: Private sector fixed income funds' performance (equally weighted returns)

Private Sector Fixed Income Funds (Equally Weighted)	2010	2011	2012	2013	2014	2015	2016	2017	2018	2019
1-Year										
Sharpe Ratio	n.a	n.a	n.a	-0.218854	**0.116820**	-0.077334	-0.154595	**0.744588**	**0.273643**	-0.077147
Treynor Ratio	n.a	n.a	n.a	-0.000180	**0.000198**	**0.000491**	-0.001729	-0.002727	**0.000534**	-0.000189
Information Ratio	n.a	n.a	n.a	-0.250724	**0.006826**	-0.182216	-0.276717	-0.435778	-0.190991	-0.416103
Jensen's Alpha	n.a	n.a	n.a	-0.000972	-0.000019	-0.000041	-0.000098	**0.000265**	-0.000084	-0.000197
Sortino Ratio	n.a	n.a	n.a	-0.267797	**0.010190**	-0.264756	-0.315269	-0.520336	-0.233333	-0.456894
Omega Ratio	n.a	n.a	n.a	0.482455	**1.018334**	0.583966	0.408735	0.275478	0.557718	0.295443
3-Year										
Sharpe Ratio	n.a	n.a	n.a	-0.080086	**0.022032**	**0.046128**	**0.189119**	**0.189041**		
Treynor Ratio	n.a	n.a	n.a	-0.000135	**0.000105**	**0.000181**	**0.000248**	**0.000299**		
Information Ratio	n.a	n.a	n.a	-0.144128	-0.092693	-0.273296	-0.253948	-0.309535		
Jensen's Alpha	n.a	n.a	n.a	-0.000362	-0.000011	-0.000009	-0.000111	-0.000134		
Sortino Ratio	n.a	n.a	n.a	-0.168475	-0.132587	-0.350976	-0.303511	-0.360762		
Omega Ratio	n.a	n.a	n.a	0.642307	0.752321	0.426714	0.438864	0.384618		
5-Year										
Sharpe Ratio	n.a	n.a	n.a	-0.045835	**0.119531**	**0.094321**				
Treynor Ratio	n.a	n.a	n.a	-0.000084	**0.000208**	**0.000125**				

Private Sector Fixed Income Funds (Equally Weighted)	2010	2011	2012	2013	2014	2015	2016	2017	2018	2019
Information Ratio	n.a	n.a	n.a	-0.160948	-0.146989	-0.276283				
Jensen's Alpha	n.a	n.a	n.a	-0.000274	-0.000073	-0.000151				
Sortino Ratio	n.a	n.a	n.a	-0.187774	-0.198883	-0.332964				
Omega Ratio	n.a	n.a	n.a	0.577823	0.632878	0.421371				
7.5 - Year										
Sharpe Ratio	**0.007655**									
Treynor Ratio	**0.000015**									
Information Ratio	-0.171207									
Jensen's Alpha	-0.000213									
Sortino Ratio	-0.201791									
Omega Ratio	0.565641									

Source: Authors' calculations

In annual analysis, the fund category yielded all negative (and below 1 Omega) ratios as per both equally and AuM-weighted data (ignoring the negligible Jensen's alpha) in 2013. It was vice versa the next year in 2014. Then for the next two years (in 2015 and 2016), the category could not generate positive risk-adjusted performance (other than negligible Treynor ratios) based on any measure as per both equally and AuM-weighted data. Then while the negative results continue to hold in terms of other measures, the category achieved positive and high Sharpe ratios (and negligible positive Treynor ratios) in 2017 and 2018 as per both data structures. In 2019, all measures resulted in negative (and below 1 Omegas) again.

In 3-yearly analysis, the first period (2013–2015) resulted in all negative (and below 1 Omega) ratios as per both equally and AuM-weighted data. In the following two periods, while all negative ratios continued as per AuM-weighted data, the absolute risk-adjusted return measures turned to be positive (though negligible in Treynor ratios) as per equally weighted data. The smaller funds must have performed better and dragged the category return above the risk-free rate of return. In last two periods, the Sharpe ratios turned into positive also as per AuM-weighted data while all other ratios were still negative (and Omegas below 1) – ignoring the negligible Jensen's alpha ratios.

In 5-yearly analysis, the first period (2013–2017) yielded all negative (and below 1 Omega) ratios as per both equally and AuM-weighted data. In the next period the Sharpe ratios turned into positive while all others remained negative as per both data structures. In the last period, the absolute measures (Sharpe and Treynor) remained positive as per equally weighted data while they also turned into negative like the other measures as per AuM-weighted data. We observe the better performance effect of smaller funds in the longer terms as well.

In the decade-long analysis, the equally weighted data yield positive Sharpe and Treynor ratios although both are negligible while it is all negative as per AuM-weighted data (albeit a negligible positive Jensen's alpha).

The Treynor ratio scatter diagrams demonstrate that there is a strong positive relationship between the funds' aggregate return and the category benchmark (Figure 3.51).

The Jensen's alpha is positive for most of the 10-year period as per both equally and AuM-weighted data (Figure 3.52).

Table 3.42: Private sector fixed income funds' performance (AuM-weighted returns)

Private Sector Fixed Income Funds (AuM-Weighted)	2010	2011	2012	2013	2014	2015	2016	2017	2018	2019
1-Year										
Sharpe Ratio	n.a	n.a	n.a	-0.221827	**0.114710**	-0.124051	-0.153579	**0.583914**	**0.130624**	-0.171939
Treynor Ratio	n.a	n.a	n.a	-0.000180	**0.000133**	-0.000407	**0.001268**	**0.000565**	**0.000247**	-0.000648
Information Ratio	n.a	n.a	n.a	-0.253324	**0.000976**	-0.195159	-0.242799	-0.458575	-0.277092	-0.482185
Jensen's Alpha	n.a	n.a	n.a	**0.003261**	**0.000441**	-0.000115	-0.000163	**0.000194**	**0.000317**	-0.000105
Sortino Ratio	n.a	n.a	n.a	-0.269965	**0.001430**	-0.253857	-0.258690	-0.523611	-0.304723	-0.488196
Omega Ratio	n.a	n.a	n.a	0.473757	**1.002554**	0.598294	0.395561	0.278353	0.434928	0.269405
3-Year										
Sharpe Ratio	n.a	n.a	n.a	-0.095231	-0.018210	-0.030476	**0.081294**	**0.084753**		
Treynor Ratio	n.a	n.a	n.a	-0.000133	-0.000043	-0.000065	**0.000118**	**0.000143**		
Information Ratio	n.a	n.a	n.a	-0.157065	-0.119141	-0.254611	-0.282984	-0.360517		
Jensen's Alpha	n.a	n.a	n.a	**0.000438**	**0.000005**	-0.000003	**0.000185**	**0.000190**		
Sortino Ratio	n.a	n.a	n.a	-0.181851	-0.156699	-0.300729	-0.308489	-0.385977		
Omega Ratio	n.a	n.a	n.a	0.630907	0.706461	0.448499	0.385493	0.337408		
5-Year										
Sharpe Ratio	n.a	n.a	n.a	-0.064802	**0.053018**	-0.002445				
Treynor Ratio	n.a	n.a	n.a	-0.000105	**0.000090**	-0.000004				

(*Continued*)

Table 3.42: Continued

Private Sector Fixed Income Funds (AuM-Weighted)	2010	2011	2012	2013	2014	2015	2016	2017	2018	2019
Information Ratio	n.a	n.a	n.a	-0.174346	-0.182209	-0.301055				
Jensen's Alpha	n.a	n.a	n.a	0.000229	0.000147	0.000110				
Sortino Ratio	n.a	n.a	n.a	-0.200225	-0.225534	-0.335911				
Omega Ratio	n.a	n.a	n.a	0.564980	0.578564	0.399185				
10-Year										
Sharpe Ratio	-0.028649									
Treynor Ratio	-0.000058									
Information Ratio	-0.197305									
Jensen's Alpha	0.000137									
Sortino Ratio	-0.225696									
Omega Ratio	0.531557									

Source: Authors' calculations

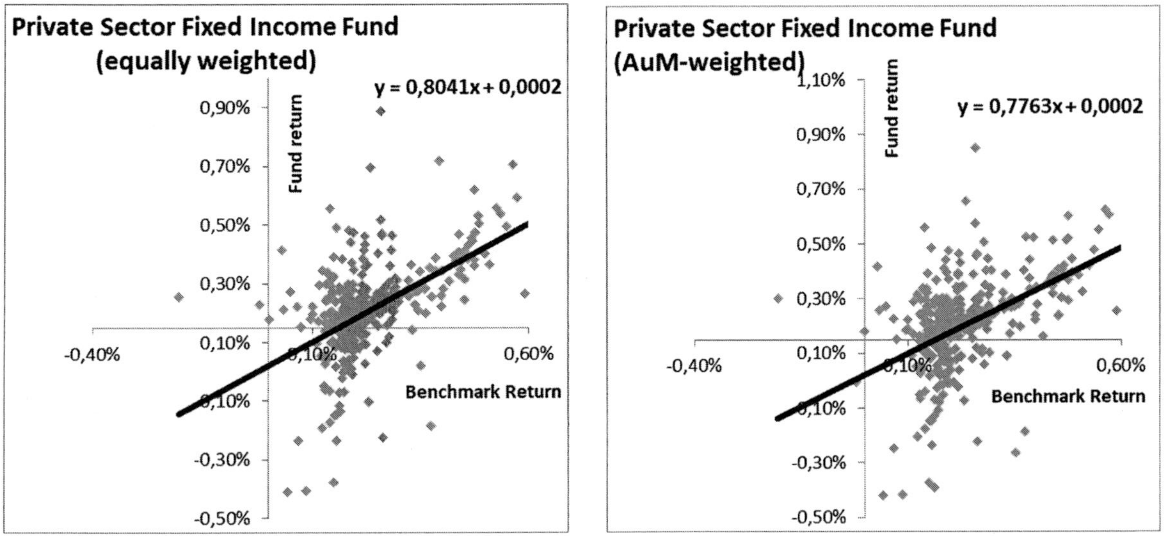

Figure 3.51: Private sector fixed income funds' Treynor ratio graphics
Source: Authors' calculations

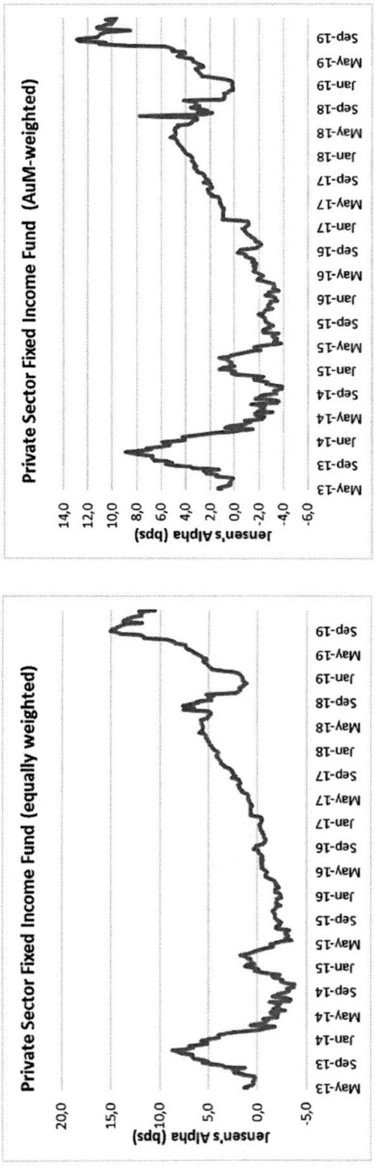

Figure 3.52: Private sector fixed income funds' Jensen's alpha ratio graphics
Source: Authors' calculations

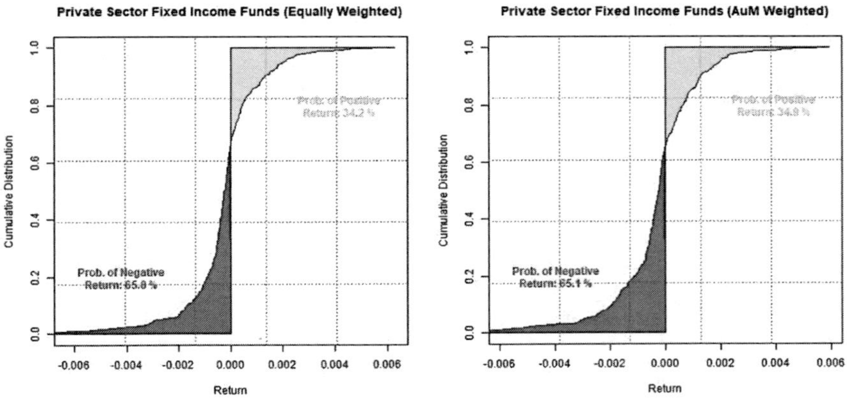

Figure 3.53: Private sector fixed income funds' Omega ratio graphics
Source: Authors' calculations

The Omega ratio graphics exhibit that the funds category's possibility of yielding a positive return compared to the category benchmark is 34 % as per both equally and AuM-weighted data, respectively (Figure 3.53).

3.2.6 Equity funds

Equity pension fund category has its ups and downs around both the category benchmark and the risk-free rate of return (Figure 3.54).

In annual analysis, equity pension fund category has consecutive "success" and "failure" years as per both equally and AuM-weighted returns: 2010 has been a success year where all measures have been positive (and Omega above 1) other than the Sharpe ratio followed by a failure year in 2011 where all measures have been negative (and Omega below 1), and the cycle continued until 2016, which has been another fail year after the failure year of 2015. The Omega ratio in 2016 has been above 1, though, indicating that the positive returns have been more than the negative ones – in a sense making 2016 a success year as it should have been. Then the success and fail years continue to follow one another (Table 3.43). In some of the "failure" years there are some positive Jensen's alphas, but they are negligible.

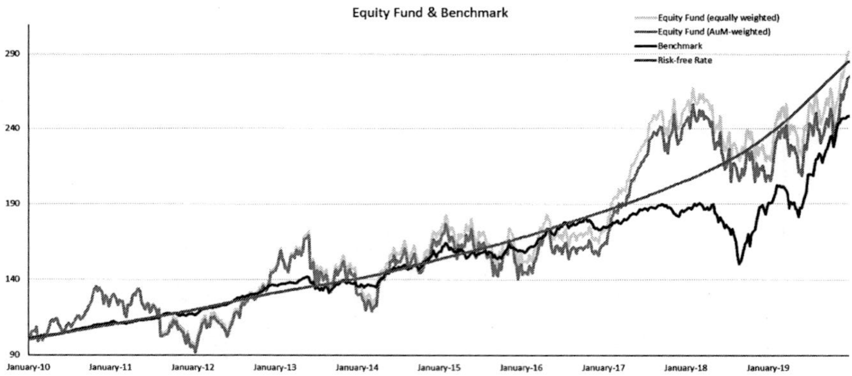

Figure 3.54: Equity funds' performance vs benchmark (2010=100)
Source: Takas İstanbul, Borsa İstanbul, Finnet; indexed by the authors

In 3-yearly analysis, other than the negligible Jensen's alphas, the measures yield the same results as per both equally and AuM-weighted data. The first 3-year period is all positive other than the Sharpe ratio. Then there are consecutive "failure" and "success" periods and the last four periods are all "success" periods with all measures positive (and Omega ratios above 1).

In 5-yearly analysis, again other than the negligible Jensen's alpha ratios, the measures yield the same results as per both equally and AuM-weighted data. The first 5-year period is all positive other than the Sharpe ratio. The following period is a "failure" period. Then the remaining four periods are all "success" periods with all positive (and above 1 Omega) ratios.

The decade-long analysis reveals that the equity pension fund category could not generate a positive Sharpe ratio. The Treynor and Jensen's alpha ratios are negligible. However, the fund category achieved positive Information and Sortino ratios, and an Omega above 1 indicating that the equity pensions funds achieved superior risk-adjusted performance compared to its benchmark which is BIST-100 Total Return Index.

Table 3.43: Equity funds' performance (equally weighted returns)

Equity Funds (Equally Weighted)	2010	2011	2012	2013	2014	2015	2016	2017	2018	2019
1-Year										
Sharpe Ratio	-0.134964	-0.172906	0.257132	-0.063976	0.120731	-0.079217	-0.003026	0.296548	-0.173430	0.085141
Treynor Ratio	0.000531	-0.002096	0.001991	-0.000854	0.001604	-0.001213	-0.000038	0.010866	-0.008258	0.002422
Information Ratio	0.112122	-0.158876	0.225594	-0.032362	0.082732	-0.036130	-0.002604	0.336289	-0.108365	0.034746
Jensen's Alpha	0.001633	-0.004132	0.002853	0.001581	0.000453	0.000737	-0.000028	0.006322	-0.003784	0.000746
Sortino Ratio	0.151680	-0.185278	0.410243	-0.042403	0.122510	-0.052793	-0.003973	0.645372	-0.133091	0.051218
Omega Ratio	1.323484	0.630768	1.784269	0.917278	1.238194	0.913246	1.116410	2.387359	0.756313	1.084824
3-Year										
Sharpe Ratio	-0.077391	-0.019975	0.076719	-0.018835	0.006833	0.043411	0.010886	0.041924		
Treynor Ratio	0.000340	-0.000225	0.000928	-0.000264	0.000094	0.000638	0.000351	0.001430		
Information Ratio	0.033834	-0.011700	0.075692	-0.002919	0.011382	0.085090	0.054421	0.062696		
Jensen's Alpha	0.000332	0.000237	0.001445	0.000620	0.000323	0.002451	0.000966	0.001418		
Sortino Ratio	0.044769	-0.015318	0.108913	-0.004029	0.016551	0.132226	0.077076	0.088722		
Omega Ratio	1.094818	0.968617	1.220956	0.992413	1.029205	1.239983	1.188304	1.169362		
5-Year										
Sharpe Ratio	-0.059363	-0.008572	0.029937	0.028105	0.010708	0.005652				
Treynor Ratio	0.000325	-0.000113	0.000389	0.000389	0.000262	0.000154				

(*Continued*)

Table 3.43: Continued

Equity Funds (Equally Weighted)	2010	2011	2012	2013	2014	2015	2016	2017	2018	2019
Information Ratio	0.025664	-0.001694	0.039467	0.052419	0.038442	0.029622				
Jensen's Alpha	0.000479	0.000261	0.001113	0.001780	0.000939	0.000691				
Sortino Ratio	0.034179	-0.002286	0.056858	0.075406	0.054809	0.042223				
Omega Ratio	1.070924	0.995492	1.107667	1.146012	1.102998	1.076829				
10-Year										
Sharpe Ratio	-0.041473									
Treynor Ratio	0.000391									
Information Ratio	0.027445									
Jensen's Alpha	0.000753									
Sortino Ratio	0.037546									
Omega Ratio	1.073749									

Source: Authors' calculations

Table 3.44: Equity funds' performance (AuM-weighted returns)

Equity Funds (AuM-Weighted)	2010	2011	2012	2013	2014	2015	2016	2017	2018	2019
1-Year										
Sharpe Ratio	-0.135089	-0.174480	**0.260022**	-0.070868	**0.116542**	-0.085071	-0.004581	**0.300764**	-0.174327	**0.084373**
Treynor Ratio	**0.000514**	-0.002223	**0.001549**	-0.000949	**0.001533**	-0.001314	-0.000058	**0.010757**	-0.008383	**0.002362**
Information Ratio	**0.107531**	-0.160958	**0.229516**	-0.041530	**0.079285**	-0.044659	-0.004521	**0.340100**	-0.114606	**0.036376**
Jensen's Alpha	-0.006385	**0.005253**	-0.005489	-0.007464	**0.002206**	-0.004395	-0.000054	**0.002543**	-0.002956	**0.001758**
Sortino Ratio	**0.144858**	-0.186994	**0.417177**	-0.054247	**0.116914**	-0.065169	-0.006821	**0.654222**	-0.139989	**0.053797**
Omega Ratio	**1.311485**	0.624357	**1.793558**	0.895375	**1.226579**	0.893735	**1.111190**	**2.440184**	0.742924	**1.089415**
3-Year										
Sharpe Ratio	-0.077518	-0.023443	**0.073303**	-0.024726	**0.002600**	**0.041577**	**0.008968**	**0.039928**		
Treynor Ratio	**0.000320**	-0.000266	**0.000885**	-0.000347	**0.000036**	**0.000616**	**0.000290**	**0.001354**		
Information Ratio	**0.030798**	-0.015803	**0.071858**	-0.010479	**0.006171**	**0.081703**	**0.050776**	**0.060122**		
Jensen's Alpha	-0.000039	-0.001504	-0.001444	-0.002303	-0.000575	-0.003227	-0.000517	-0.000053		
Sortino Ratio	**0.040514**	-0.020593	**0.103120**	-0.014426	**0.008943**	**0.126701**	**0.071282**	**0.084662**		
Omega Ratio	**1.086550**	0.957810	**1.207788**	0.973058	**1.015748**	**1.230838**	**1.178095**	**1.163445**		
5-Year										
Sharpe Ratio	-0.059692	-0.012773	**0.026267**	**0.024455**	**0.007292**	**0.003082**				
Treynor Ratio	**0.000277**	-0.000169	**0.000342**	**0.000340**	**0.000179**	**0.000084**				

(Continued)

Table 3.44: Continued

Equity Funds (AuM-Weighted)	2010	2011	2012	2013	2014	2015	2016	2017	2018	2019
Information Ratio	0.021074	-0.006686	0.034882	0.047420	0.033606	0.025862				
Jensen's Alpha	-0.000537	-0.001056	-0.001779	-0.003042	-0.000848	-0.000624				
Sortino Ratio	0.027929	-0.008981	0.050111	0.068020	0.047647	0.036707				
Omega Ratio	1.058068	0.982311	1.094452	1.131535	1.089961	1.067214				
10-Year										
Sharpe Ratio	-0.041844									
Treynor Ratio	0.000312									
Information Ratio	0.023249									
Jensen's Alpha	-0.000579									
Sortino Ratio	0.031659									
Omega Ratio	1.062435									

Source: Authors' calculations

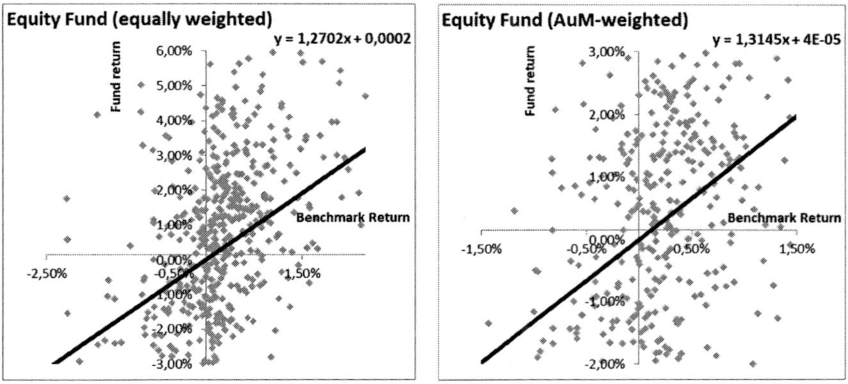

Figure 3.55: Equity funds' Treynor ratio graphics
Source: Authors' calculations

The Treynor ratio scatter diagrams demonstrate that there is a strong positive relationship between the funds' aggregate return and the category benchmark (Figure 3.55).

The Jensen's alpha reflects the up and down nature of the equity fund category. It also demonstrates that there is no size effect in the returns performance as there is no difference between the equally and AuM-weighted graphs (Figure 3.56).

The Omega ratio graphics exhibit that the funds category's possibility of yielding a positive return compared to the category benchmark is 53 % as per both equally and AuM-weighted data, respectively (Figure 3.57).

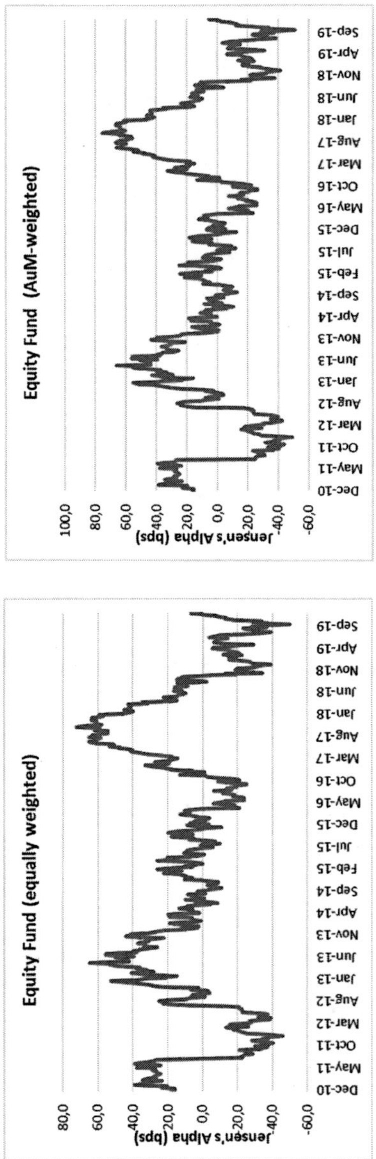

Figure 3.56: Equity funds' Jensen's alpha ratio graphics
Source: Authors' calculations

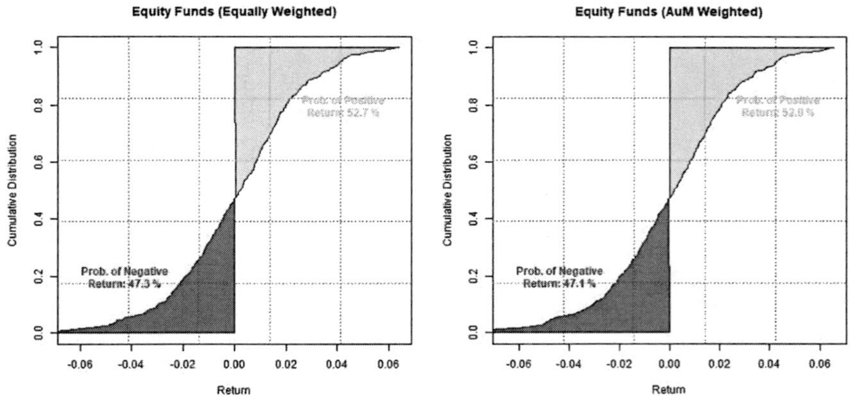

Figure 3.57: Equity funds' Omega ratio graphics
Source: Authors' calculations

3.2.7 Government contribution funds

As mentioned in Section 1.2: An overview of asset management industry in Turkey, by the inauguration of state support[21] for private pensions on January 1, 2013, the government contribution funds were also created, because the government regulated both (i) the asset allocation (minimum 70 % must be invested in government debentures) and the management fee (maximum 36.5 bps per annum).

The Figure 3.58 illustrates that the fund category closely traced its benchmark but underperformed the risk-free rate of return.

These funds are in existence since May 2013, so the end-to-end period is 6.5 years instead of 10 years. Besides, we performed our annual, 3-yearly and 5-yearly analysis starting from January 1, 2014 to have a complete year (i.e., 52 data point) analysis.

21 The state support is implemented as 25 % of monthly contributions of pensioners up to an annual limit of 25 % of the gross annual minimum wage. The maximum annual state support was 8,829.-TL in 2020.

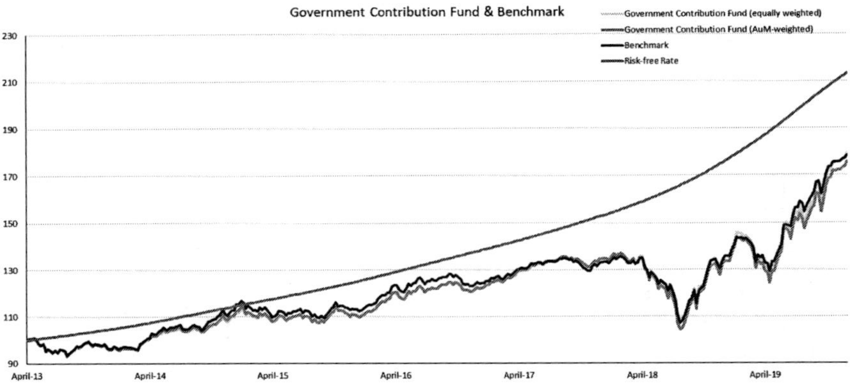

Figure 3.58: Government contribution funds' performance vs benchmark (April 2013=100)
Source: Takas İstanbul, Borsa İstanbul, Finnet; indexed by the authors

In annual analysis, the Sharpe and Treynor ratios are positive in 2014 (although the Treynor ratios are negligible) as per both equally and AuM-weighted data. In 2015, the equally weighted data produce positive Information and Sortino ratios and an Omega above 1. However, all measures are negative (and the Omega is below 1) the same year as per AuM-weighted data, indicating that the larger funds must have performed worse than the smaller ones. In 2016 all performance measures are positive (and Omegas above 1) as per both equally and AuM-weighted data (the Treynor and Jensen's alpha ratios are negligible). In 2017, the Sharpe ratios are negative while Information and Sortino are positive, and Omega is above 1 (and Treynor and Jensen's alpha are negligible) as per both equally and AuM-weighted data. All performance measures are negative (Omega ratio below 1) I 2018 and it is vice versa in 2019 as per both equally and AuM-weighted data (Tables 3.45 and 3.46).

In 3-yearly analysis, the first period yields all negative (and below 1 Omega) ratios while in the following periods the relative performance measures and measures based on downside risk and higher moments become positive (and above 1 in case of Omega) as per both equally and AuM-weighted data (the Jensen's alphas also turn into negative as per AuM-weighted data, but they are negligibly small).

Table 3.45: Government contribution funds' performance (equally weighted returns)

Government Contribution Funds (Equally Weighted)	2010	2011	2012	2013	2014	2015	2016	2017	2018	2019
1-Year										
Sharpe Ratio	n.a	n.a	n.a	n.a	0.137208	-0.164806	0.000287	-0.035835	-0.103923	0.081787
Treynor Ratio	n.a	n.a	n.a	n.a	0.001207	-0.001629	0.000002	-0.000209	-0.002131	0.001454
Information Ratio	n.a	n.a	n.a	n.a	-0.187757	0.081322	0.013909	0.343730	-0.054044	0.023848
Jensen's Alpha	n.a	n.a	n.a	n.a	-0.000125	-0.000055	-0.000005	0.000437	-0.000063	-0.000317
Sortino Ratio	n.a	n.a	n.a	n.a	-0.223388	0.128207	0.020576	0.755331	-0.085505	0.032353
Omega Ratio	n.a	n.a	n.a	n.a	0.608594	1.239141	1.122085	2.453113	0.855507	1.066516
3-Year										
Sharpe Ratio	n.a	n.a	n.a	n.a	-0.022613	-0.076174	-0.059971	-0.010444		
Treynor Ratio	n.a	n.a	n.a	n.a	-0.000203	-0.000615	-0.000793	-0.000168		
Information Ratio	n.a	n.a	n.a	n.a	-0.047273	0.145769	0.056318	0.042096		
Jensen's Alpha	n.a	n.a	n.a	n.a	-0.000110	0.000143	0.000167	0.000237		
Sortino Ratio	n.a	n.a	n.a	n.a	-0.062891	0.244252	0.092122	0.059657		
Omega Ratio	n.a	n.a	n.a	n.a	0.883284	1.453904	1.201144	1.135666		
5-Year										
Sharpe Ratio	n.a	n.a	n.a	n.a	-0.051195	-0.026397				
Treynor Ratio	n.a	n.a	n.a	n.a	-0.000606	-0.000364				
Information Ratio	n.a	n.a	n.a	n.a	0.009055	0.041004				

(Continued)

Table 3.45: Continued

Government Contribution Funds (Equally Weighted)	2010	2011	2012	2013	2014	2015	2016	2017	2018	2019
Jensen's Alpha	n.a	n.a	n.a	n.a	0.000003	0.000196				
Sortino Ratio	n.a	n.a	n.a	n.a	0.013493	0.058400				
Omega Ratio	n.a	n.a	n.a	n.a	1.025538	1.136253				
6.5-Year										
Sharpe Ratio	-0.029735									
Treynor Ratio	-0.000386									
Information Ratio	0.008445									
Jensen's Alpha	0.000052									
Sortino Ratio	0.014445									
Omega Ratio	1.026365									

Source: Authors' calculations

Table 3.46: Government contribution funds' performance (AuM-weighted returns)

Government Contribution Funds (AuM-Weighted)	2010	2011	2012	2013	2014	2015	2016	2017	2018	2019
1-Year										
Sharpe Ratio	n.a	n.a	n.a	n.a	**0.135238**	-0.162365	**0.001548**	-0.027791	-0.106735	**0.079133**
Treynor Ratio	n.a	n.a	n.a	n.a	**0.001187**	-0.001606	**0.000013**	-0.000163	-0.002191	**0.001408**
Information Ratio	n.a	n.a	n.a	n.a	-0.195744	-0.001706	**0.023990**	**0.380323**	-0.094150	**0.012357**
Jensen's Alpha	n.a	n.a	n.a	n.a	**0.001145**	-0.001516	**0.000013**	-0.000517	-0.002461	**0.002182**
Sortino Ratio	n.a	n.a	n.a	n.a	-0.222158	-0.002542	**0.039705**	**0.933667**	-0.135335	**0.016448**
Omega Ratio	n.a	n.a	n.a	n.a	0.577767	0.995338	**1.209427**	**2.787823**	0.770722	**1.033959**
3-Year										
Sharpe Ratio	n.a	n.a	n.a	n.a	-0.020707	-0.073729	-0.060267	-0.015614		
Treynor Ratio	n.a	n.a	n.a	n.a	-0.000186	-0.000596	-0.000797	-0.000251		
Information Ratio	n.a	n.a	n.a	n.a	-0.064453	**0.136809**	**0.020415**	**0.016752**		
Jensen's Alpha	n.a	n.a	n.a	n.a	-0.000071	-0.000702	-0.001079	-0.000579		
Sortino Ratio	n.a	n.a	n.a	n.a	-0.085255	**0.236803**	**0.030651**	**0.023188**		
Omega Ratio	n.a	n.a	n.a	n.a	0.839681	**1.440487**	**1.090264**	**1.050745**		
5-Year										
Sharpe Ratio	n.a	n.a	n.a	n.a	-0.050677	-0.031127				
Treynor Ratio	n.a	n.a	n.a	n.a	-0.000599	-0.000427				
Information Ratio	n.a	n.a	n.a	n.a	-0.011448	**0.014101**				

(Continued)

Table 3.46: Continued

Government Contribution Funds (AuM-Weighted)	2010	2011	2012	2013	2014	2015	2016	2017	2018	2019
Jensen's Alpha	n.a	n.a	n.a	n.a	-0.000642	-0.000715				
Sortino Ratio	n.a	n.a	n.a	n.a	-0.016589	0.019589				
Omega Ratio	n.a	n.a	n.a	n.a	0.964906	1.045886				
6.5-Year										
Sharpe Ratio	-0.031730									
Treynor Ratio	-0.000410									
Information Ratio	-0.006372									
Jensen's Alpha	-0.000514									
Sortino Ratio	-0.010715									
Omega Ratio	0.979571									

Source: Authors' calculations

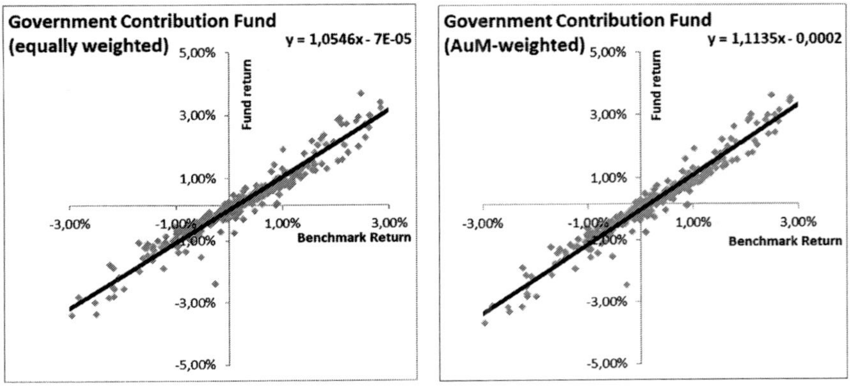

Figure 3.59: Government contribution funds' Treynor ratio graphics
Source: Authors' calculations

There are only two 5-yearly analyses. In the first period (2014–2018), while all performance measures are negative (and Omega below 1) as per AuM-weighted data, as per equally weighted data the Information, Jensen's alpha (though negligible), and Sortino turn into positive, and the Omega becomes greater than 1. In the second period (2015–2019), the absolute performance measures are negative while the others are positive and Omega above 1 as per both equally and AuM-weighted data.

The 6.5 years long analysis yields different results as per equally and AuM-weighted data: while all measures are negative and Omega is below 1 as per AuM-weighted data, as per equally weighted data, the Information, Jensen's alpha (though negligible), and Sortino turn into positive, and the Omega becomes greater than 1. Thus, the smaller funds must have performed better than the larger ones pushing up the risk-adjusted returns above that of the benchmark.

The Treynor ratio scatter diagrams demonstrate that there is a very strong positive relationship between the funds' aggregate return and the category benchmark as expected (Figure 3.59).

The Jensen's alpha illustrates that there has been about two years period between December 2016 and December 2018 when there was a positive Jensen's alpha as per both equally and AuM-weighted data (Figure 3.60).

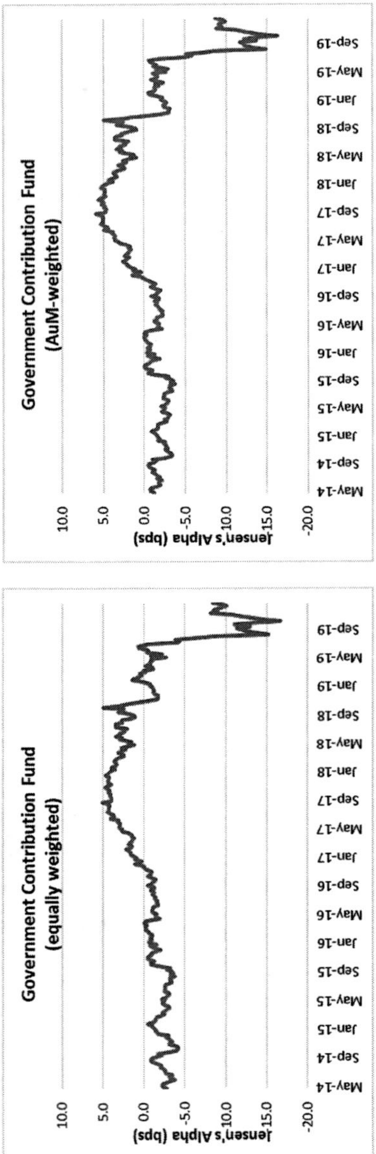

Figure 3.60: Government contribution funds' Jensen's alpha graphics
Source: Authors' calculations

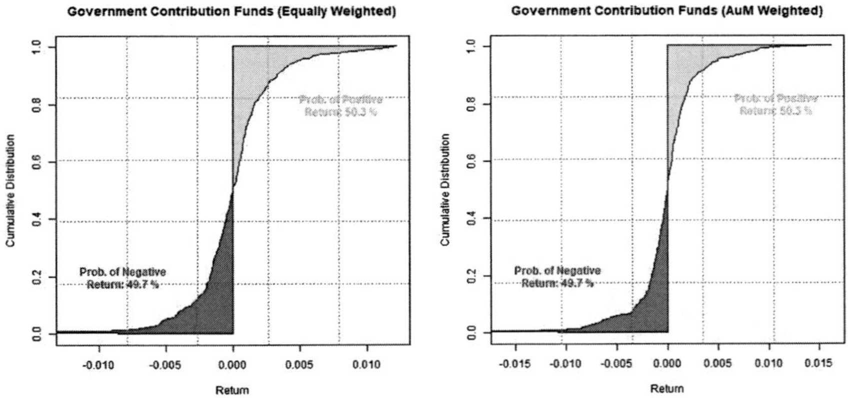

Figure 3.61: Government contribution funds' Omega ratio graphics
Source: Authors' calculations

The Omega ratio graphics exhibit that the funds category's possibility of yielding a positive return compared to the category benchmark is 50 % as per both equally and AuM-weighted data (Figure 3.61).

3.2.8 Government contribution participation funds

As mentioned in Section 1.2: An overview of asset management industry in Turkey, by the inauguration of state support for private pensions on January 1, 2013, the government contribution participation funds were also created, because the government regulated both (i) the asset allocation (minimum 70 % must be invested in government lease certificates) and the management fee (maximum 36.5 bps per annum).

These funds are in existence since May 2013, so the end-to-end period is 6.5 years instead of 10 years. Besides, we performed our annual, 3-yearly and 5-yearly analysis starting from January 1, 2014 to have a complete year (i.e., 52 data point) analysis.

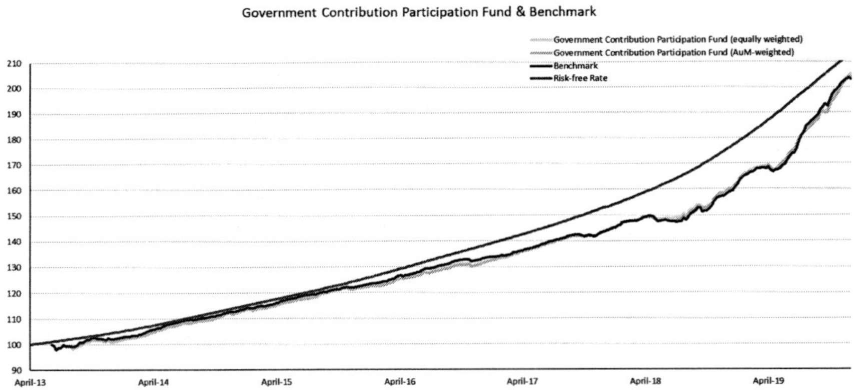

Figure 3.62: Government contribution participation funds' performance vs benchmark (April 2010=100)
Source: Takas İstanbul, Borsa İstanbul, Finnet; indexed by the authors

In annual analysis, all performance measures are positive in 2014 (although Treynor and Jensen's alpha ratios are negligible) as per both equally and AuM-weighted data. In 2015, the equally weighted data produce all negative (and below 1 Omega) ratios while the AuM-weighted data produce positive Information and Sortino ratios and an Omega ratio above 1. In the following years (namely 2016, 2017, 2018 and 2019), both data structures produce the same results. In 2016, all measures are negative (and Omega is below 1). In 2017 and 2018, the Information and Sortino ratios are positive, and the Omega ratios are above 1 while the Sharpe and Treynor are negative. In 2019, the Sharpe and (though negligible) Treynor and Jensen's alpha are positive while the others are negative (and Omega less than 1).

In 3-yearly analysis, the first period (2014–2016) yields all negative results as per AuM-weighted data while only absolute return measures stay negative as per equally weighted data. In the following two periods (other than negligible negative or positive Jensen's alpha) both equally and AuM-weighted data yield positive Information and Sortino and an above 1 Omega ratios. In the last period (2017–2019), all measures yield successful results as per both equally and AuM-weighted data.

Table 3.47: Government contribution participation funds' performance (equally weighted returns)

Government Contribution Participation Fund (Equally Weighted)	2010	2011	2012	2013	2014	2015	2016	2017	2018	2019
					1-Year					
Sharpe Ratio	n.a	n.a	n.a	n.a	**0.262524**	-0.106695	-0.233813	-0.153850	-0.194609	**0.240871**
Treynor Ratio	n.a	n.a	n.a	n.a	**0.000522**	-0.000176	-0.000442	-0.000301	-0.000835	**0.001350**
Information Ratio	n.a	n.a	n.a	n.a	**0.211208**	-0.075818	-0.128284	**0.314478**	**0.085744**	-0.004885
Jensen's Alpha	n.a	n.a	n.a	n.a	0.000000	-0.000063	-0.000090	**0.000152**	-0.000057	**0.000222**
Sortino Ratio	n.a	n.a	n.a	n.a	**0.461312**	-0.098581	-0.172485	**0.628745**	**0.142098**	-0.006847
Omega Ratio	n.a	n.a	n.a	n.a	**1.869260**	0.819305	0.808895	**2.272529**	**1.272961**	0.986127
					3-Year					
Sharpe Ratio	n.a	n.a	n.a	n.a	-0.031262	-0.166255	-0.188990	**0.022583**		
Treynor Ratio	n.a	n.a	n.a	n.a	-0.000058	-0.000308	-0.000560	**0.000095**		
Information Ratio	n.a	n.a	n.a	n.a	**0.020077**	**0.026945**	**0.084228**	**0.073558**		
Jensen's Alpha	n.a	n.a	n.a	n.a	**0.000029**	**0.000020**	-0.000013	**0.000125**		
Sortino Ratio	n.a	n.a	n.a	n.a	**0.030839**	**0.038463**	**0.137393**	**0.109222**		
Omega Ratio	n.a	n.a	n.a	n.a	**1.055669**	**1.071531**	**1.306139**	**1.245658**		
					5-Year					
Sharpe Ratio	n.a	n.a	n.a	n.a	-0.093516	-0.032539				
Treynor Ratio	n.a	n.a	n.a	n.a	-0.000247	-0.000112				
Information Ratio	n.a	n.a	n.a	n.a	**0.080871**	**0.026998**				

(Continued)

Table 3.47: Continued

Government Contribution Participation Fund (Equally Weighted)	2010	2011	2012	2013	2014	2015	2016	2017	2018	2019
Jensen's Alpha	n.a	n.a	n.a	n.a	0.000046	0.000019				
Sortino Ratio	n.a	n.a	n.a	n.a	0.130742	0.039104				
Omega Ratio	n.a	n.a	n.a	n.a	1.251293	1.083115				
6.5 - Year										
Sharpe Ratio	-0.024444									
Treynor Ratio	-0.000181									
Information Ratio	0.018594									
Jensen's Alpha	-0.000040									
Sortino Ratio	0.026695									
Omega Ratio	1.056649									

Source: Authors' calculations

Table 3.48: Government contribution participation funds' performance (AuM-weighted returns)

Government Contribution Participation Fund (AuM-Weighted)	2010	2011	2012	2013	2014	2015	2016	2017	2018	2019
1-Year										
Sharpe Ratio	n.a	n.a	n.a	n.a	**0.165469**	-0.056446	-0.260600	-0.172648	-0.156881	**0.242414**
Treynor Ratio	n.a	n.a	n.a	n.a	**0.000292**	-0.000091	-0.000486	-0.000337	-0.000659	**0.001418**
Information Ratio	n.a	n.a	n.a	n.a	**0.023040**	**0.024138**	-0.168636	**0.255768**	**0.126688**	-0.020806
Jensen's Alpha	n.a	n.a	n.a	n.a	0.000000	-0.000030	-0.000398	-0.000394	-0.000522	**0.000847**
Sortino Ratio	n.a	n.a	n.a	n.a	**0.032784**	**0.034286**	-0.212215	**0.481861**	**0.225096**	-0.028220
Omega Ratio	n.a	n.a	n.a	n.a	**1.060627**	**1.076396**	0.688693	**1.945599**	**1.427702**	0.945392
3-Year										
Sharpe Ratio	n.a	n.a	n.a	n.a	-0.065938	-0.165679	-0.175418	**0.016047**		
Treynor Ratio	n.a	n.a	n.a	n.a	-0.000116	-0.000299	-0.000504	**0.000068**		
Information Ratio	n.a	n.a	n.a	n.a	-0.033222	**0.047850**	**0.087908**	**0.062329**		
Jensen's Alpha	n.a	n.a	n.a	n.a	-0.000142	-0.000305	-0.000436	-0.000046		
Sortino Ratio	n.a	n.a	n.a	n.a	-0.045358	**0.071447**	**0.147275**	**0.089518**		
Omega Ratio	n.a	n.a	n.a	n.a	0.914621	**1.137923**	**1.296731**	**1.202870**		
5-Year										
Sharpe Ratio	n.a	n.a	n.a	n.a	-0.106878	-0.029828				
Treynor Ratio	n.a	n.a	n.a	n.a	-0.000265	-0.000102				
Information Ratio	n.a	n.a	n.a	n.a	**0.064980**	**0.031875**				

(Continued)

Table 3.48: Continued

Government Contribution Participation Fund (AuM-Weighted)	2010	2011	2012	2013	2014	2015	2016	2017	2018	2019
Jensen's Alpha	n.a	n.a	n.a	n.a	-0.000278	-0.000101				
Sortino Ratio	n.a	n.a	n.a	n.a	**0.102163**	**0.045392**				
Omega Ratio	n.a	n.a	n.a	n.a	**1.196628**	**1.103258**				
6.5 - Year										
Sharpe Ratio	-0.029439									
Treynor Ratio	-0.000195									
Information Ratio	**0.011720**									
Jensen's Alpha	-0.000137									
Sortino Ratio	**0.016512**									
Omega Ratio	**1.036909**									

Source: Authors' calculations

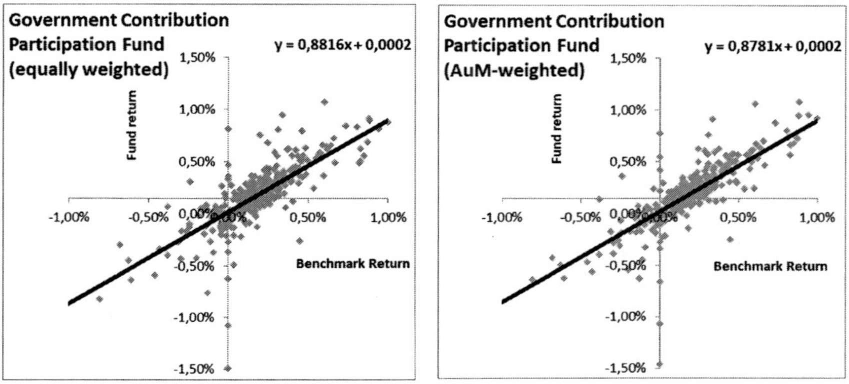

Figure 3.63: Government contribution participation funds' Treynor ratio graphics
Source: Authors' calculations

The two 5-yearly analyses yield the same results as per both equally and AuM-weighted data (other than negative and positive but negligible Jensen's alphas): Information and Sortino are positive, and Omega is above 1 while Sharpe and Treynor are negative indicating that the fund category outperformed its benchmark but not the risk-free rate of return.

The end-to-end (6.5-year) period also reveals the same result as the 5-yearly analyses as per both equally and AuM-weighted data (Jensen's alphas are negative but negligibly small anyway).

The Treynor ratio scatter diagrams demonstrate that there is a strong positive relationship between the funds' aggregate return and the category benchmark as expected (Figure 3.63).

The Jensen's alpha graphs illustrate that the AuM-weighted data smoothens the alpha line compared to the equally weighted one, but the periods of positive alphas does not change (Figure 3.64).

The Omega ratio graphics exhibit that the funds category's possibility of yielding a positive return compared to the category benchmark is 53 and 51 % as per equally and AuM-weighted data, respectively (Figure 3.65).

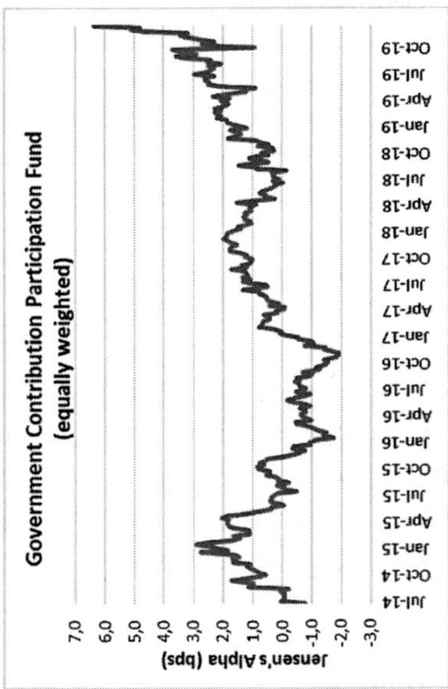

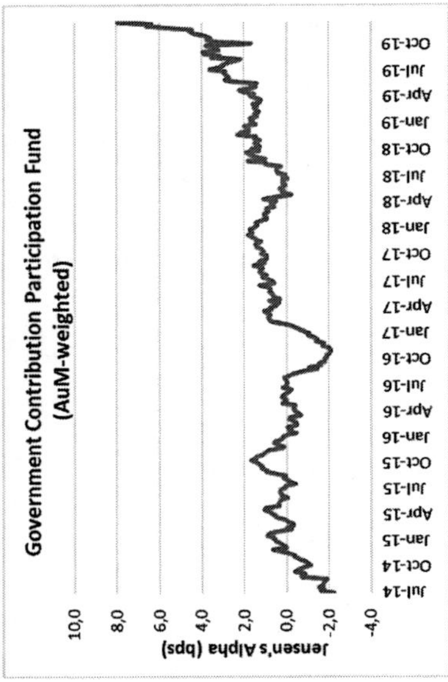

Figure 3.64: Government contribution participation funds' Jensen's alpha ratio graphics
Source: Authors' calculations

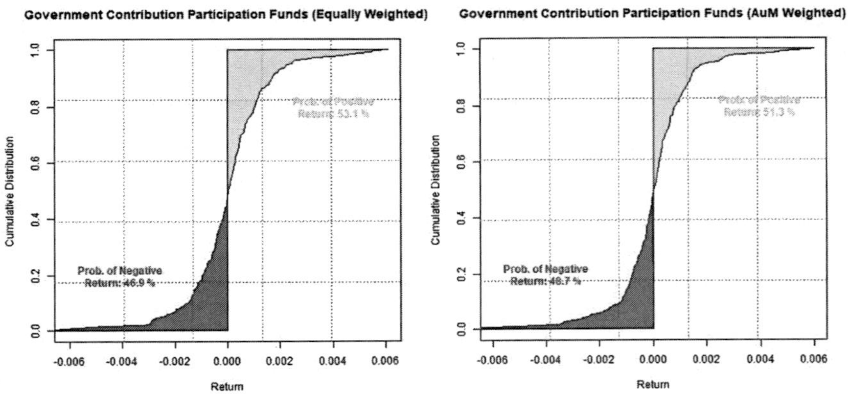

Figure 3.65: Government contribution participation funds' Omega ratio graphics
Source: Authors' calculations

3.2.9 Standard participation funds

Standard pension fund and its participation version, i.e., standard participation pension fund are established as per the private pension regulations. The government required the pension companies to establish the standard funds and defined the asset allocation of these funds to be at least 60 % invested in government debentures (in the form of bonds and/or lease certificates). This fund category is designed to invest the contributions of the pensioners who do not specify a pension plan selection of his own.

As observed in Figure 3.66, standard participation funds performed lower than both the category benchmark and the risk-free rate of return for analyzed 10-year period.

According to the risk-adjusted performance measures listed in Tables 3.49 and 3.50, the fund category returns are not subject to a size effect in any period, i.e., all ratios bear the same sign (negative or positive) as per both equally and AuM-weighted data.

In annual analysis, the first year (2014) is the best year ever for this fund category: four of the calculated six ratios are positive, namely Sharpe, Information, Sortino ratios and Omega ratio above 1. Then for the following four years, other than positive Treynor ratios, all measures yielded negative results (and Omega below 1). In 2019, the Sharpe ratio turned out to be a high positive figure, Jensen's alpha ratio was also positive but negligibly small.

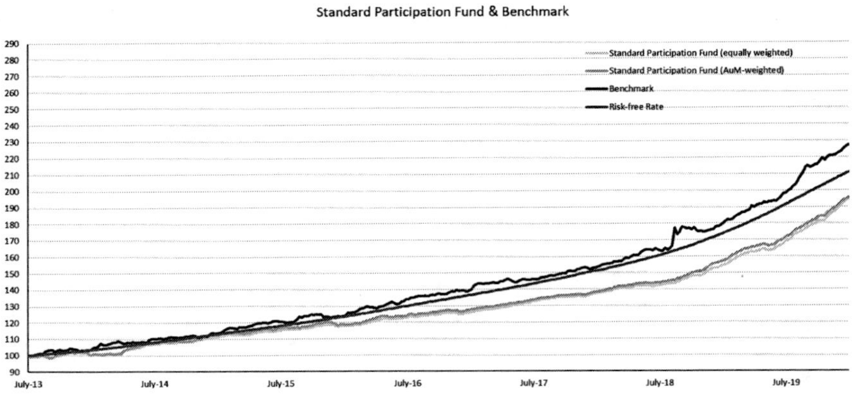

Figure 3.66: Standard participation funds' performance vs benchmark (July 2013=100)
Source: Takas İstanbul, Borsa İstanbul, Finnet; indexed by the authors

In 3-yearly analysis, we can say that all measures yielded in negative (and Omega below 1) results, other than the positive Treynor ratios for the first three periods as per both equally and AuM-weighted data.

There are only two 5-year periods and in both only Treynor ratios are positive as per both equally and AuM-weighted data.

Again, only the Treynor ratio is positive in the decade-long analysis.

Table 3.49: Standard participation funds' performance (equally weighted returns)

Standard Participation Funds (Equally Weighted)	2010	2011	2012	2013	2014	2015	2016	2017	2018	2019
1-Year										
Sharpe Ratio	n.a	n.a	n.a	n.a	**0.096752**	-0.206235	-0.292940	-0.188152	-0.179100	**0.163169**
Treynor Ratio	n.a	n.a	n.a	n.a	-0.002154	**0.004058**	**0.004719**	**0.006166**	**0.009032**	**0.002801**
Information Ratio	n.a	n.a	n.a	n.a	**0.029510**	-0.095641	-0.192072	-0.049925	-0.077573	-0.060811
Jensen's Alpha	n.a	n.a	n.a	n.a	0.000000	-0.000535	-0.000649	-0.000297	-0.000411	**0.000369**
Sortino Ratio	n.a	n.a	n.a	n.a	**0.043574**	-0.118054	-0.240376	-0.067868	-0.089465	-0.084563
Omega Ratio	n.a	n.a	n.a	n.a	**1.081228**	0.770723	0.719258	0.872378	0.753262	0.858943
3-Year										
Sharpe Ratio	n.a	n.a	n.a	n.a	-0.132048	-0.228829	-0.221074	-0.027746		
Treynor Ratio	n.a	n.a	n.a	n.a	**0.002579**	**0.004516**	**0.008630**	-0.013546		
Information Ratio	n.a	n.a	n.a	n.a	-0.078096	-0.113634	-0.089583	-0.061391		
Jensen's Alpha	n.a	n.a	n.a	n.a	-0.000314	-0.000497	-0.000463	-0.000071		
Sortino Ratio	n.a	n.a	n.a	n.a	-0.101417	-0.141159	-0.105280	-0.072934		
Omega Ratio	n.a	n.a	n.a	n.a	0.815337	0.740059	0.769155	0.809321		
5-Year										
Sharpe Ratio	n.a	n.a	n.a	n.a	-0.148259	-0.114496				
Treynor Ratio	n.a	n.a	n.a	n.a	**0.005029**	**0.016185**				
Information Ratio	n.a	n.a	n.a	n.a	-0.069186	-0.085054				

(*Continued*)

Table 3.49: Continued

Standard Participation Funds (Equally Weighted)	2010	2011	2012	2013	2014	2015	2016	2017	2018	2019
Jensen's Alpha	n.a	n.a	n.a	n.a	-0.000332	-0.000283				
Sortino Ratio	n.a	n.a	n.a	n.a	-0.083685	-0.101412				
Omega Ratio	n.a	n.a	n.a	n.a	0.804509	0.763995				
9 - Year										
Sharpe Ratio	-0.097115									
Treynor Ratio	**0.019826**									
Information Ratio	-0.076010									
Jensen's Alpha	-0.000264									
Sortino Ratio	-0.093698									
Omega Ratio	0.794230									

Source: Authors' calculations

Table 3.50: Standard participation funds' performance (AuM-weighted returns)

Standard Participation Funds (AuM-Weighted)	2010	2011	2012	2013	2014	2015	2016	2017	2018	2019
1-Year										
Sharpe Ratio	n.a	n.a	n.a	n.a	**0.128116**	-0.148011	-0.232387	-0.351074	-0.086603	**0.113391**
Treynor Ratio	n.a	n.a	n.a	n.a	-0.002693	**0.002377**	**0.003268**	**0.029655**	**0.004948**	**0.003144**
Information Ratio	n.a	n.a	n.a	n.a	**0.058236**	-0.085628	-0.168848	-0.083846	-0.057510	-0.094064
Jensen's Alpha	n.a	n.a	n.a	n.a	0.000000	-0.000689	-0.000746	-0.000419	-0.000209	**0.000302**
Sortino Ratio	n.a	n.a	n.a	n.a	**0.088176**	-0.107454	-0.215751	-0.110213	-0.066831	-0.130163
Omega Ratio	n.a	n.a	n.a	n.a	**1.169873**	0.799427	0.770409	0.794086	0.812394	0.785119
3-Year										
Sharpe Ratio	n.a	n.a	n.a	n.a	-0.071803	-0.192299	-0.194612	-0.038918		
Treynor Ratio	n.a	n.a	n.a	n.a	**0.001245**	**0.003406**	**0.008607**	-0.019412		
Information Ratio	n.a	n.a	n.a	n.a	-0.056011	-0.110235	-0.082142	-0.064537		
Jensen's Alpha	n.a	n.a	n.a	n.a	-0.000305	-0.000610	-0.000436	-0.000088		
Sortino Ratio	n.a	n.a	n.a	n.a	-0.074250	-0.137419	-0.097102	-0.076934		
Omega Ratio	n.a	n.a	n.a	n.a	0.864676	0.747976	0.795441	0.800264		

(Continued)

Table 3.50: Continued

Standard Participation Funds (AuM-Weighted)	2010	2011	2012	2013	2014	2015	2016	2017	2018	2019
5-Year										
Sharpe Ratio	n.a	n.a	n.a	n.a	-0.093761	-0.105969				
Treynor Ratio	n.a	n.a	n.a	n.a	**0.003293**	**0.010392**				
Information Ratio	n.a	n.a	n.a	n.a	-0.056368	-0.083630				
Jensen's Alpha	n.a	n.a	n.a	n.a	-0.000295	-0.000296				
Sortino Ratio	n.a	n.a	n.a	n.a	-0.069294	-0.100564				
Omega Ratio	n.a	n.a	n.a	n.a	0.841528	0.772159				
10-Year										
Sharpe Ratio	-0.072719									
Treynor Ratio	**0.006062**									
Information Ratio	-0.068012									
Jensen's Alpha	-0.000248									
Sortino Ratio	-0.085044									
Omega Ratio	0.816412									

Source: Authors' calculations

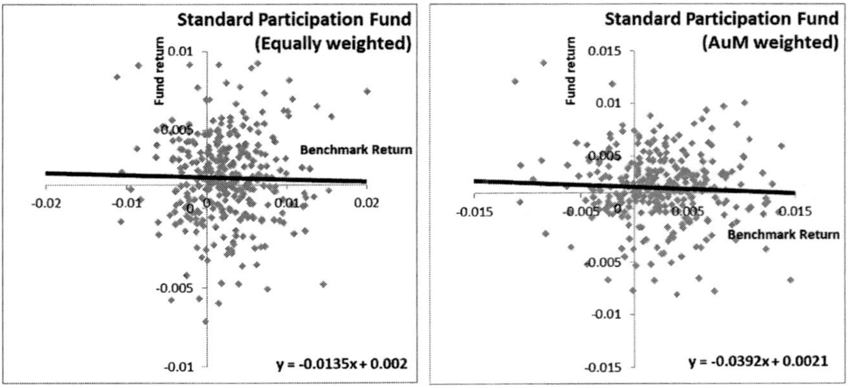

Figure 3.67: Standard participation funds' Treynor ratio graphics
Source: Authors' calculations

The Treynor ratio scatter diagrams demonstrate that there is a weak and negative relationship between the funds' aggregate return and the category benchmark (Figure 3.67).

The Jensen's alpha graphs illustrate that except for the first quarter in 2015, the fund category started to generate positive alphas only after January 2019 (Figure 3.68).

The Omega ratio graphics exhibit that the funds category's possibility of yielding a positive return compared to the category benchmark is 49 % as per both equally and AuM-weighted data (Figure 3.69).

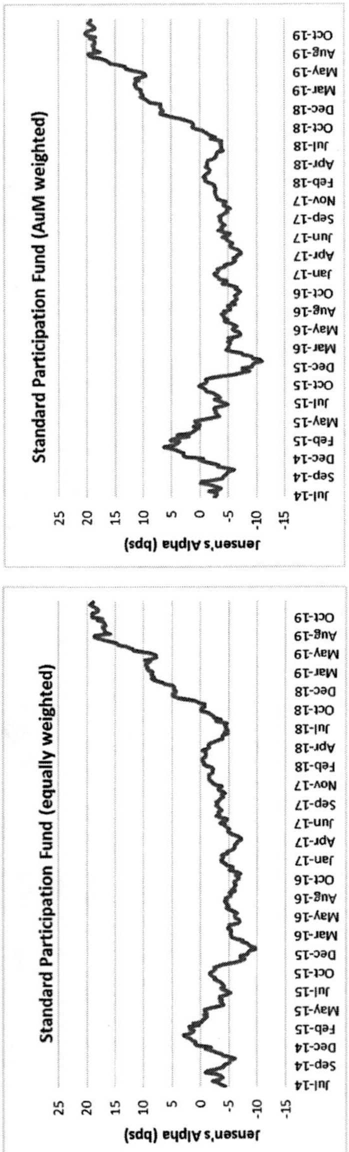

Figure 3.68: Standard participation funds' Jensen's alpha ratio graphics
Source: Authors' calculations

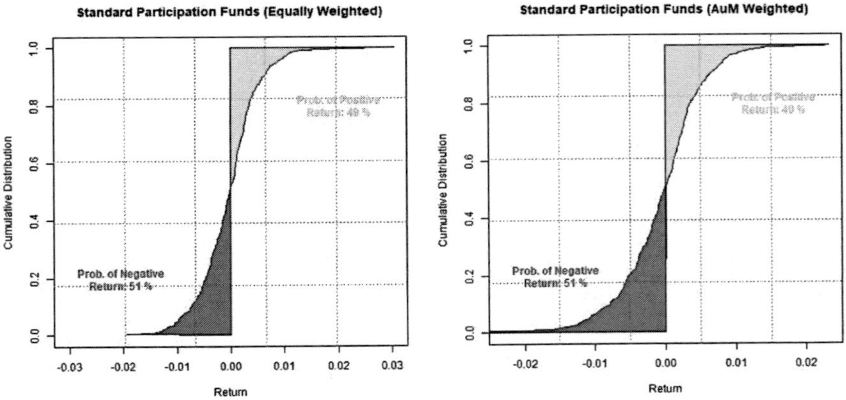

Figure 3.69: Standard participation funds' Omega ratio graphics
Source: Authors' calculations

3.2.10 Standard funds

Standard pension funds are established as per the private pension regulations – as explained in the previous section. It is clearly observed in Figure 3.70 that the fund category performed below the defined category benchmark.

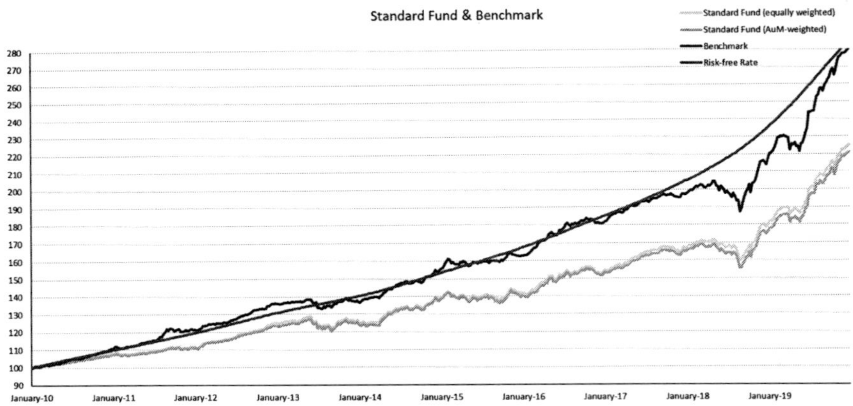

Figure 3.70: Standard funds' performance vs benchmark (2010=100)
Source: Takas İstanbul, Borsa İstanbul, Finnet; indexed by the authors

In the annual analysis, standard funds yielded all negative (and less than 1 Omega) ratios for the first two years as per both equally and AuM-weighted returns. In 2012, while it continued to be all negative as per AuM-weighted data, as per equally weighted data, all ratios were positive (and Omega above 1), though Treynor, Information, Jensen's alpha and Sortino ratios were negligible. In 2013, all measures yielded unsuccessful results as per both equally and AuM-weighted data. In 2014, only absolute risk-adjusted performance measures were positive (though Treynor ratios were negligible) as per both data structures. Then the following four years resulted in all negative ratios as per both data structures again (neglecting the negligible Jensen's alpha in 2016 as per AuM-weighted data). In 2019, only Sharpe and Treynor ratios were positive – though Treynor ratios were negligible.

All the periods in 3-yearly and in 5-yearly analysis, and the decade-long analysis reveal negative (and below 1 in case of Omega) ratios.

The Treynor ratio scatter diagrams demonstrate that there is a strong positive relationship between the funds' aggregate return and the category benchmark (Figure 3.71).

The Jensen's alpha graphs illustrate that the fund category could not generate positive alpha almost ever during the analyzed 10 years (Figure 3.72).

Table 3.51: Standard funds' performance (equally weighted returns)

Standard Funds (Equally Weighted)	2010	2011	2012	2013	2014	2015	2016	2017	2018	2019
1-Year										
Sharpe Ratio	-0.182687	-0.429958	**0.153119**	-0.192409	**0.084996**	-0.193474	-0.043666	-0.108159	-0.137226	**0.074486**
Treynor Ratio	-0.002185	-0.003097	**0.000609**	-0.001242	**0.000425**	-0.001146	-0.000219	-0.000435	-0.001676	**0.000793**
Information Ratio	-0.389507	-0.313284	**0.000295**	-0.034037	-0.136498	-0.150785	-0.189421	-0.028485	-0.090809	-0.170399
Jensen's Alpha	-0.000357	-0.001011	**0.000139**	-0.000021	-0.000427	-0.000350	-0.000529	-0.000099	-0.000697	-0.000289
Sortino Ratio	-0.548409	-0.340230	**0.000409**	-0.048519	-0.176343	-0.187416	-0.232479	-0.040287	-0.117896	-0.216863
Omega Ratio	0.367876	0.422630	**1.000749**	0.909038	0.697882	0.670492	0.729411	0.922816	0.745068	0.634666
3-Year										
Sharpe Ratio	-0.086654	-0.141058	-0.031391	-0.115150	-0.063028	-0.118735	-0.096219	-0.047218		
Treynor Ratio	-0.000776	-0.000834	-0.000165	-0.000676	-0.000336	-0.000595	-0.000786	-0.000454		
Information Ratio	-0.217614	-0.129788	-0.058255	-0.102982	-0.156628	-0.127182	-0.094986	-0.099973		
Jensen's Alpha	-0.000393	-0.000464	-0.000167	-0.000289	-0.000464	-0.000318	-0.000409	-0.000374		
Sortino Ratio	-0.269093	-0.162429	-0.079657	-0.135553	-0.192624	-0.158634	-0.122647	-0.129461		
Omega Ratio	0.549197	0.697509	0.853045	0.757486	0.666382	0.713039	0.777665	0.734139		
5-Year										
Sharpe Ratio	-0.065272	-0.106845	-0.072823	-0.098587	-0.086578	-0.077420				
Treynor Ratio	-0.000447	-0.000608	-0.000389	-0.000528	-0.000631	-0.000652				

(*Continued*)

Table 3.51: Continued

Standard Funds (Equally Weighted)	2010	2011	2012	2013	2014	2015	2016	2017	2018	2019
Information Ratio	-0.150805	-0.135678	-0.102192	-0.105725	-0.111858	-0.120805				
Jensen's Alpha	-0.000412	-0.000431	-0.000289	-0.000288	-0.000407	-0.000452				
Sortino Ratio	-0.196141	-0.169755	-0.132227	-0.137115	-0.142134	-0.153206				
Omega Ratio	0.661168	0.691681	0.761882	0.752202	0.719246	0.702555				
10-Year										
Sharpe Ratio	-0.045614									
Treynor Ratio	-0.000552									
Information Ratio	-0.133061									
Jensen's Alpha	-0.000431									
Sortino Ratio	-0.171022									
Omega Ratio	0.683948									

Source: Authors' calculations

Table 3.52: Standard funds' performance (AuM-weighted returns)

Standard Funds (AuM-Weighted)	2010	2011	2012	2013	2014	2015	2016	2017	2018	2019
1-Year										
Sharpe Ratio	-0.182710	-0.428771	**0.106100**	-0.188338	**0.097099**	-0.197206	-0.028242	-0.143263	-0.147042	**0.079423**
Treynor Ratio	-0.003399	-0.003106	**0.000579**	-0.001200	**0.000486**	-0.001170	-0.000141	-0.000569	-0.001779	**0.000849**
Information Ratio	-0.425531	-0.298587	-0.073381	-0.019693	-0.092959	-0.171247	-0.158960	-0.074404	-0.131808	-0.155591
Jensen's Alpha	-0.000422	-0.000621	**0.000182**	-0.001267	**0.001030**	-0.001035	**0.000453**	-0.000394	-0.000796	**0.000883**
Sortino Ratio	-0.583085	-0.327322	-0.094127	-0.028619	-0.123179	-0.209666	-0.199504	-0.100427	-0.161983	-0.203071
Omega Ratio	0.336179	0.434126	0.823672	0.947867	0.783236	0.637101	0.797030	0.808934	0.627813	0.677238
3-Year										
Sharpe Ratio	-0.086707	-0.150566	-0.031469	-0.109954	-0.057191	-0.122517	-0.101507	-0.051575		
Treynor Ratio	-0.001111	-0.000889	-0.000166	-0.000644	-0.000305	-0.000613	-0.000814	-0.000492		
Information Ratio	-0.236785	-0.138264	-0.058288	-0.097045	-0.140091	-0.138114	-0.117599	-0.121918		
Jensen's Alpha	-0.000248	-0.000314	**0.000001**	-0.000408	**0.000189**	-0.000339	-0.000325	-0.000090		
Sortino Ratio	-0.288944	-0.171719	-0.079408	-0.127335	-0.173589	-0.169923	-0.145880	-0.152979		
Omega Ratio	0.514400	0.681403	0.854569	0.773117	0.693706	0.687636	0.717130	0.681093		
5-Year										
Sharpe Ratio	-0.065268	-0.107431	-0.072736	-0.095614	-0.088666	-0.078680				
Treynor Ratio	-0.000475	-0.000615	-0.000389	-0.000511	-0.000641	-0.000657				

(Continued)

Table 3.52: Continued

Standard Funds (AuM-Weighted)	2010	2011	2012	2013	2014	2015	2016	2017	2018	2019
Information Ratio	-0.149576	-0.137420	-0.102416	-0.102543	-0.124488	-0.136318				
Jensen's Alpha	-0.000050	-0.000173	-0.000110	-0.000250	-0.000210	-0.000173				
Sortino Ratio	-0.194446	-0.171252	-0.131693	-0.132472	-0.154033	-0.168676				
Omega Ratio	0.664347	0.689104	0.761610	0.759006	0.689895	0.670487				
10-Year										
Sharpe Ratio	-0.045655									
Treynor Ratio	-0.000560									
Information Ratio	-0.141623									
Jensen's Alpha	-0.000107									
Sortino Ratio	-0.179254									
Omega Ratio	0.667716									

Source: Authors' calculations

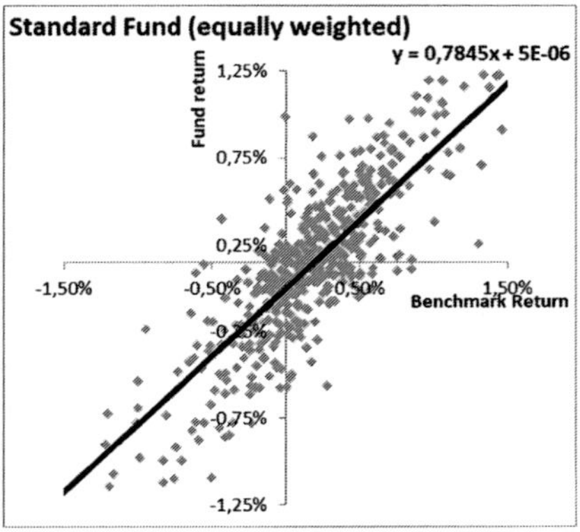

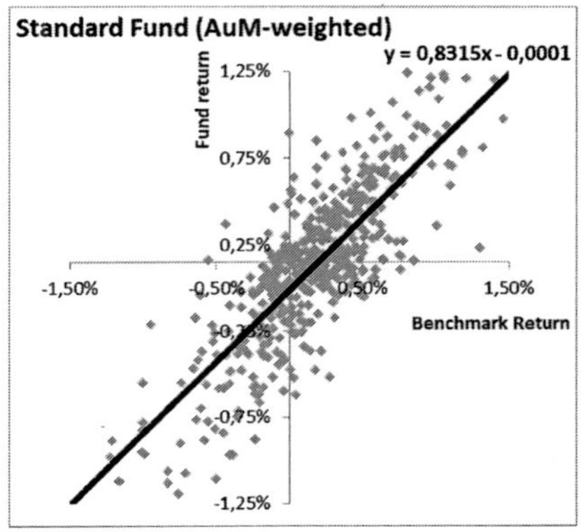

Figure 3.71: Standard funds' Treynor ratio graphics
Source: Authors' calculations

The Omega ratio graphics exhibit that the funds category's possibility of yielding a positive return compared to the category benchmark is 47 % as per both equally and AuM-weighted data (Figure 3.73).

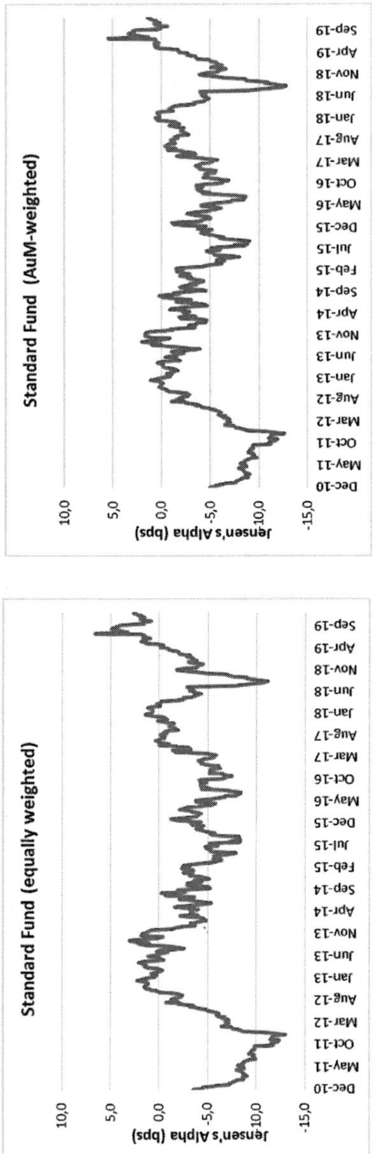

Figure 3.72: Standard funds' Jensen's alpha ratio graphics
Source: Authors' calculations

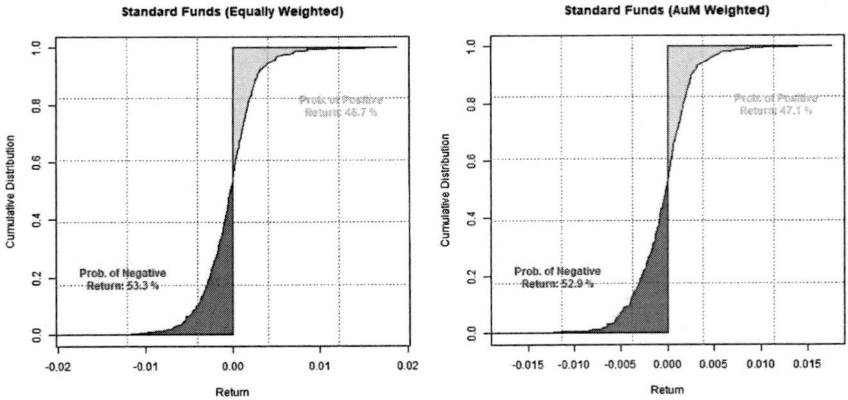

Figure 3.73: Standard funds' Omega ratio graphics
Source: Authors' calculations

3.2.11 Money market funds

It is clearly observed in Figure 3.74 that the fund category performed below the defined category benchmark and the risk-free rate for the whole analyzed period. We attribute it to the high management fee of almost 1 % which is eliminating the excess return which is already a narrow margin in money market funds.

In annual analysis, it is observed that the fund category generated negative (and below 1 for Omega) risk-adjusted return measures every year for the first five years as per both equally and AuM-weighted data. In 2015, while the AuM-weighted data yielded all positive (and above 1 Omega) ratios (albeit Treynor and Jensen's alpha being negligible), as per equally weighted data, it was just the Sharpe ratio (and negligible Treynor and Jensen's alpha) that was positive. The larger funds must have performed better to drag especially the relative risk-adjusted measures above the defined category benchmark. In 2016, all measures yielded negative results followed by positive results for the next two years as per both equally and AuM-weighted data. In 2019, there was only the Sharpe ratio positive (other than negligible Treynor and Jensen's alpha ratios).

In 3-yearly analysis, for the first five periods out of 8, all risk-adjusted performance measures resulted in negative (and below 1 in case of Omega)

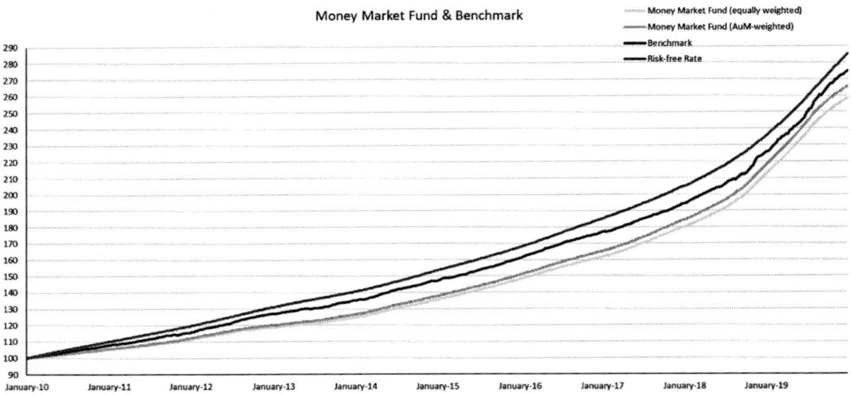

Figure 3.74: Money market funds' performance vs benchmark (2010=100)
Source: Takas İstanbul, Borsa İstanbul, Finnet; indexed by the authors

ratios as per both equally and AuM-weighted data. In 2015–2017 period, as per AuM-weighted data all measures yielded positive results while as per equally weighted data the Sharpe, Treynor and Jensen's alpha ratios turned into negative figures (though the latter two ratios being negligible). The last two 3-year periods resulted in positive ratios (and above 1 Omega ratio).

In 5-yearly analysis, the first three periods yielded in negative (and below 1 Omega) ratios as per both equally and AuM-weighted data. In 2013–2017 period, all measures continued to be negative (and Omega below 1) as per equally weighted data, as per AuM-weighted data, Information and Sortino ratios turned into positive and Omega increased above 1. The larger funds must have performed better than the smaller ones in this period dragging the fund category's aggregate return above the benchmark return. The last two 5-year periods yielded all positive (and above 1 Omega) ratios as per both equally and AuM-weighted data.

However, in a decade-long analysis, as per both equally and AuM-weighted data, all measures are negative (and Omega less than 1).

The Treynor ratio scatter diagrams demonstrate that there is a strong positive relationship between the funds' aggregate return and the category benchmark (Figure 3.75).

Table 3.53: Money market funds' performance (equally weighted returns)

Money Market Funds (Equally Weighted)	2010	2011	2012	2013	2014	2015	2016	2017	2018	2019
1-Year										
Sharpe Ratio	-0.139227	-1.760590	-1.527074	-1.253233	-0.411752	**0.085323**	-0.889280	**0.464065**	**0.685759**	**0.041599**
Treynor Ratio	-0.008849	-0.003993	-0.002152	-0.002542	-0.000931	**0.000081**	-0.003670	**0.001386**	**0.002545**	**0.000195**
Information Ratio	-1.301741	-0.338295	-0.823389	-0.239251	-0.100140	-0.023917	-0.187264	**0.348900**	**0.181346**	-0.040554
Jensen's Alpha	-0.000804	-0.000499	-0.000547	-0.000355	-0.000105	**0.000006**	-0.000225	**0.000143**	**0.000481**	**0.000016**
Sortino Ratio	-0.802764	-0.407114	-0.668821	-0.292949	-0.141868	-0.034740	-0.226640	**0.765224**	**0.294003**	-0.058877
Omega Ratio	0.031137	0.391590	0.130752	0.534351	0.755517	0.932920	0.586363	**2.610963**	**1.727078**	0.897869
3-Year										
Sharpe Ratio	-0.080789	-1.478469	-0.964154	-0.554729	-0.457055	-0.114405	**0.240737**	**0.304861**		
Treynor Ratio	-0.003233	-0.002590	-0.001698	-0.000776	-0.001066	-0.000311	**0.000435**	**0.000736**		
Information Ratio	-0.670222	-0.427447	-0.343755	-0.130823	-0.101955	**0.065379**	**0.133834**	**0.111657**		
Jensen's Alpha	-0.000598	-0.000460	-0.000332	-0.000149	-0.000106	-0.000023	**0.000144**	**0.000214**		
Sortino Ratio	-0.615899	-0.462193	-0.392162	-0.173787	-0.138300	**0.103555**	**0.218040**	**0.174201**		
Omega Ratio	0.172844	0.328807	0.407840	0.696938	0.748787	**1.201419**	**1.537671**	**1.384295**		
5-Year										
Sharpe Ratio	-0.062720	-0.872533	-0.754941	-0.378504	**0.134960**	**0.149887**				
Treynor Ratio	-0.002485	-0.001545	-0.001261	-0.000554	**0.000198**	**0.000239**				

(Continued)

Table 3.53: Continued

Money Market Funds (Equally Weighted)	2010	2011	2012	2013	2014	2015	2016	2017	2018	2019
Information Ratio	-0.420276	-0.283922	-0.256518	-0.040594	**0.074025**	**0.060394**				
Jensen's Alpha	-0.000449	-0.000295	-0.000240	-0.000098	**0.000069**	**0.000088**				
Sortino Ratio	-0.461166	-0.339248	-0.307061	-0.058012	**0.117355**	**0.092617**				
Omega Ratio	0.329620	0.466425	0.499169	0.894051	**1.260607**	**1.204668**				
10-Year										
Sharpe Ratio	-0.044252									
Treynor Ratio	-0.000413									
Information Ratio	-0.109234									
Jensen's Alpha	-0.000159									
Sortino Ratio	-0.153067									
Omega Ratio	0.723725									

Source: Authors' calculations

Table 3.54: Money market funds' performance (AuM-weighted returns)

Money Market Funds (AuM-Weighted)	2010	2011	2012	2013	2014	2015	2016	2017	2018	2019
1-Year										
Sharpe Ratio	-0.139195	-1.259419	-1.323419	-0.971221	-0.249717	0.301294	-0.652483	0.634953	0.731177	0.063096
Treynor Ratio	-0.006116	-0.002425	-0.001345	-0.001901	-0.000554	0.000337	-0.003524	0.002105	0.002629	0.000294
Information Ratio	-1.179620	-0.244519	-0.719697	-0.176738	-0.048751	0.012532	-0.095719	0.405358	0.208425	-0.029606
Jensen's Alpha	-0.000687	-0.000362	-0.000270	-0.000255	-0.000053	0.000034	-0.000162	0.000167	0.000461	0.000058
Sortino Ratio	-0.777096	-0.313766	-0.624631	-0.226297	-0.072274	0.018688	-0.124006	0.942532	0.342635	-0.043505
Omega Ratio	0.041684	0.498331	0.163872	0.629633	0.872188	1.037248	0.765443	3.078934	1.870858	0.924331
3-Year										
Sharpe Ratio	-0.080707	-1.174421	-0.796825	-0.399027	-0.282057	0.053925	0.328163	0.351836		
Treynor Ratio	-0.002427	-0.001899	-0.001298	-0.000551	-0.000664	0.000157	0.000590	0.000858		
Information Ratio	-0.574741	-0.343538	-0.273488	-0.079276	-0.043248	0.124833	0.176739	0.136384		
Jensen's Alpha	-0.000428	-0.000309	-0.000207	-0.000084	-0.000056	0.000017	0.000141	0.000202		
Sortino Ratio	-0.563660	-0.394053	-0.329589	-0.109684	-0.061406	0.207965	0.295443	0.216236		
Omega Ratio	0.215408	0.403692	0.487722	0.803437	0.884413	1.422362	1.761343	1.485670		
5-Year										
Sharpe Ratio	-0.062626	-0.705677	-0.601978	-0.218297	0.227733	0.212987				
Treynor Ratio	-0.001947	-0.001164	-0.000949	-0.000321	0.000334	0.000343				

(Continued)

Table 3.54: Continued

Money Market Funds (AuM-Weighted)	2010	2011	2012	2013	2014	2015	2016	2017	2018	2019
Information Ratio	-0.343159	-0.215080	-0.188739	0.018709	0.116226	0.091244				
Jensen's Alpha	-0.000320	-0.000187	-0.000145	-0.000047	0.000086	0.000100				
Sortino Ratio	-0.399158	-0.270808	-0.238150	0.028077	0.189722	0.142734				
Omega Ratio	0.399281	0.558205	0.599121	1.053047	1.438287	1.324149				
10-Year										
Sharpe Ratio	-0.044143									
Treynor Ratio	-0.000300									
Information Ratio	-0.062138									
Jensen's Alpha	-0.000066									
Sortino Ratio	-0.090188									
Omega Ratio	0.830486									

Source: Authors' calculations

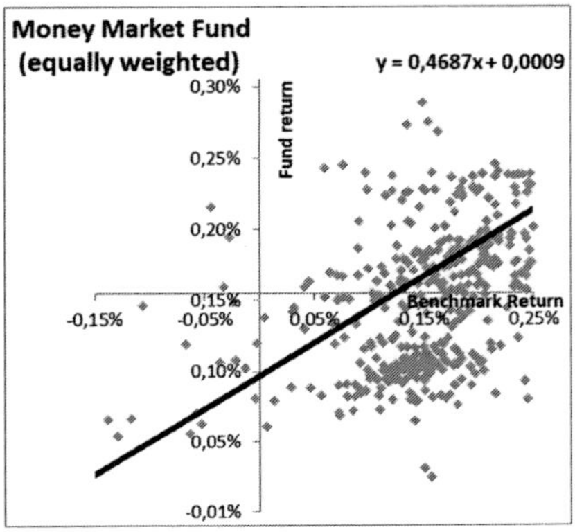

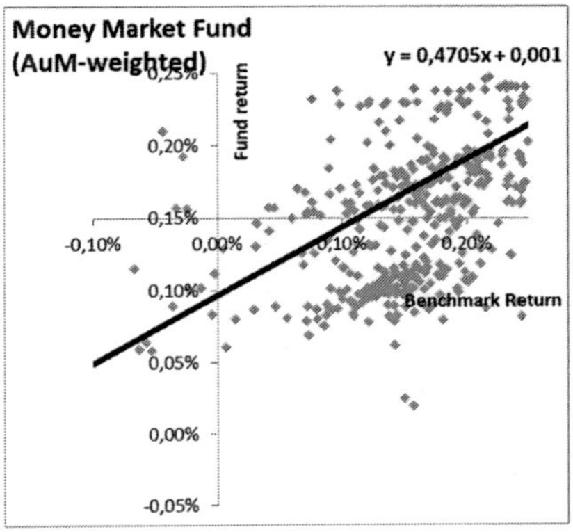

Figure 3.75: Money market funds' Treynor ratio graphics
Source: Authors' calculations

The Jensen's alpha graphs illustrate that the fund category could not generate positive alpha before August 2017 as per both equally and AuM-weighted data. The upward trend is turned downward since September 2019, but still in the positive area of the graph (Figure 3.76).

The Omega ratio graphics exhibit that the funds category's possibility of yielding a positive return compared to the category benchmark is 37 and 40 % as per equally and AuM-weighted data, respectively (Figure 3.77).

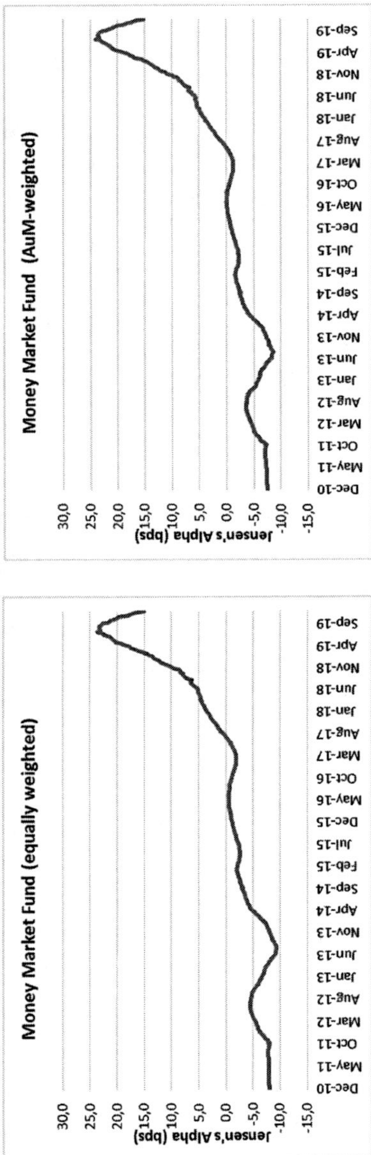

Figure 3.76: Money market funds' Jensen's alpha ratio graphics
Source: Author's calculations

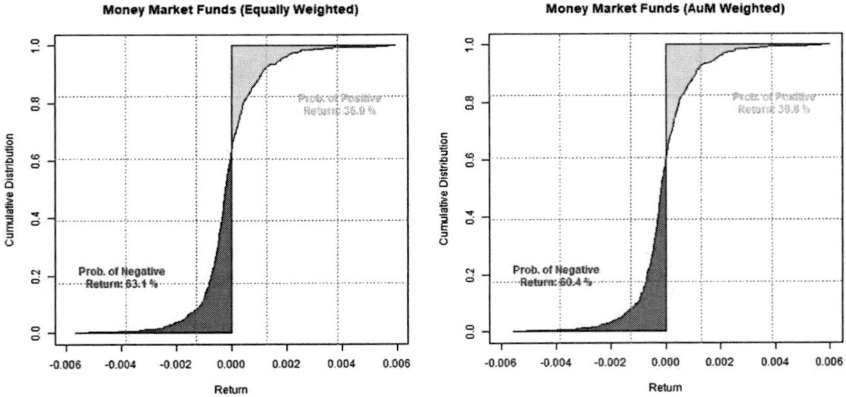

Figure 3.77: Money market funds' Omega ratio graphics
Source: Authors' calculations

3.2.12 Initiation funds

The so-called *initiation* funds are introduced by the regulator with inauguration of auto-enrolment system in January 2017. The regulation requires the employers to enroll all of their employees who are younger than 45 years to the auto-enrolment pension system and avail them with a conventional (i.e., interest bearing) or a participation pension fund through a pension company. The employees then have two months to terminate their enrolment and get their money back without any deduction or continue contributing to the system – any termination after two months will be subject to the system's early termination provisions. The pension companies have to establish an initiation fund (or the participation version) and channel the pensioners' contributions into these funds for those two-months period when the pensioners can terminate their pension contract. If the pensioner does not terminate his contract after two months and does not instruct the pension company to change his fund allocation, the pension company has to keep the contributions within the initial fund for another 10 months. If after one year, the pensioner still does not instruct the pension company to change his fund allocation, the pension company has to transfer that pensioner's funds to a standard fund (or the participation version of it). The pensioners can at any time instruct the pension company and change their fund allocations (the pensioners have a right to alter their fund allocations six times in a calendar year).

As summarized above, initiation funds are mandatory at entrance into the auto-enrolment pension system and the pensioners can withdraw their contributions within two months without any deduction. It means the initiation funds should not lose value in those two months otherwise the pension company would have to compensate for the loss. In order to prevent any such problematic situations, the asset allocation within the initiation funds are regulated: a minimum of 60 % of conventional initiation funds must be invested in bank accounts and a further minimum of 20 % in government debentures and similarly a minimum of 60 % of participation initiation funds in participation accounts at participation banks or the lease certificates issued by these banks.

Based on the predefined asset allocation rules, we defined the category benchmark as BIST-KYD 1 Month Time Deposit Index (and BIST-KYD 1 Month Participation Account Index for participation initiation funds) as described in Table 3.24.

As observed in Figure 3.78, the initiation fund category has achieved returns above its benchmark and the risk-free rate of return. This is confirmed by the risk-adjusted performance measures in Tables 3.55 and 3.56 as per both equally and AuM-weighted data, respectively.

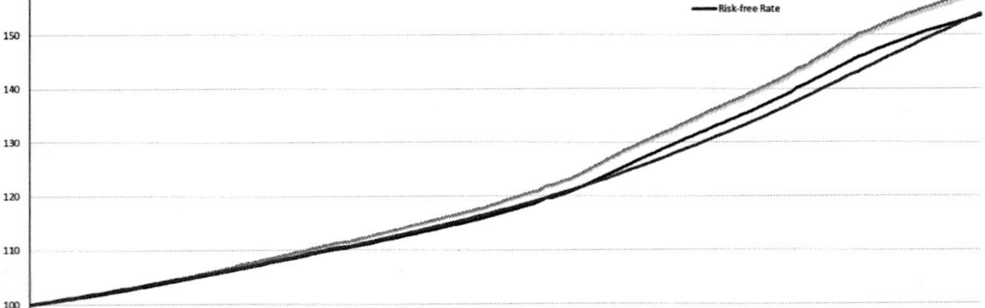

Figure 3.78: Initiations funds' performance vs benchmark (January 2017=100)
Source: Takas İstanbul, Borsa İstanbul, Finnet; indexed by the authors

Table 3.55: Initiation funds' performance (equally weighted returns)

Initiation Funds (Equally Weighted)	2010	2011	2012	2013	2014	2015	2016	2017	2018	2019
1-Year										
Sharpe Ratio	n.a	n.a	n.a	n.a	n.a	n.a	n.a	0.372971	0.567213	-0.206011
Treynor Ratio	n.a	n.a	n.a	n.a	n.a	n.a	n.a	0.000026	0.000492	-0.000172
Information Ratio	n.a	n.a	n.a	n.a	n.a	n.a	n.a	0.634024	0.485480	0.321861
Jensen's Alpha	n.a	n.a	n.a	n.a	n.a	n.a	n.a	0.000176	0.000197	0.000138
Sortino Ratio	n.a	n.a	n.a	n.a	n.a	n.a	n.a	1.906955	0.809609	0.624068
Omega Ratio	n.a	n.a	n.a	n.a	n.a	n.a	n.a	6.860254	3.546098	2.614513
3-Year										
Sharpe Ratio	n.a	n.a	n.a	n.a	n.a	n.a	n.a	0.185676		
Treynor Ratio	n.a	n.a	n.a	n.a	n.a	n.a	n.a	0.000119		
Information Ratio	n.a	n.a	n.a	n.a	n.a	n.a	n.a	0.464431		
Jensen's Alpha	n.a	n.a	n.a	n.a	n.a	n.a	n.a	0.000144		
Sortino Ratio	n.a	n.a	n.a	n.a	n.a	n.a	n.a	0.885760		
Omega Ratio	n.a	n.a	n.a	n.a	n.a	n.a	n.a	3.732446		

Source: Authors' calculations

Table 3.56: Initiation funds' performance (AuM-weighted returns)

Initiation Funds (AuM-Weighted)	2010	2011	2012	2013	2014	2015	2016	2017	2018	2019
1-Year										
Sharpe Ratio	n.a	n.a	n.a	n.a	n.a	n.a	n.a	0.434897	0.602437	-0.181894
Treynor Ratio	n.a	n.a	n.a	n.a	n.a	n.a	n.a	0.000035	0.000520	-0.000152
Information Ratio	n.a	n.a	n.a	n.a	n.a	n.a	n.a	0.714604	0.583218	0.389915
Jensen's Alpha	n.a	n.a	n.a	n.a	n.a	n.a	n.a	-0.000316	0.000340	-0.000314
Sortino Ratio	n.a	n.a	n.a	n.a	n.a	n.a	n.a	2.498200	1.063979	0.790217
Omega Ratio	n.a	n.a	n.a	n.a	n.a	n.a	n.a	9.321062	4.428901	3.254627
3-Year										
Sharpe Ratio	n.a	n.a	n.a	n.a	n.a	n.a	n.a	0.218765		
Treynor Ratio	n.a	n.a	n.a	n.a	n.a	n.a	n.a	0.000145		
Information Ratio	n.a	n.a	n.a	n.a	n.a	n.a	n.a	0.545616		
Jensen's Alpha	n.a	n.a	n.a	n.a	n.a	n.a	n.a	0.000001		
Sortino Ratio	n.a	n.a	n.a	n.a	n.a	n.a	n.a	1.128723		
Omega Ratio	n.a	n.a	n.a	n.a	n.a	n.a	n.a	4.717542		

Source: Authors' calculations

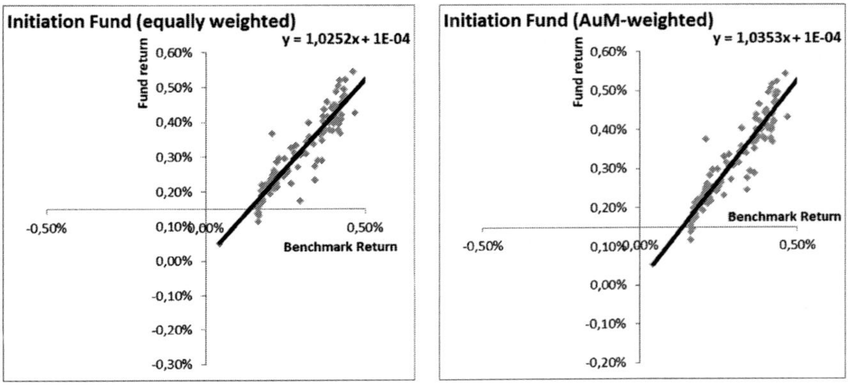

Figure 3.79: Initiation funds' Treynor ratio graphics
Source: Authors' calculations

In annual analysis, in the first two years, initial pension funds returned positive (above 1 Omega) ratios vis-à-vis all measures as per both equally and AuM-weighted data (ignoring the negligible negative Jensen's alpha). In 2019, however, the absolute risk-adjusted measured became negative (though the Treynor ratio is negligible), indicating the fund category returned below the risk-free rate of return.

In the only 3-yearly analysis all measures yielded positive results as per both equally and AuM-weighted data.

The Treynor ratio scatter diagrams demonstrate that there is a strong positive relationship between the funds' aggregate return and the category benchmark (Figure 3.79).

The Jensen's alpha graphs illustrate that the fund category generated positive alpha before May 2019 as per both equally and AuM-weighted data. Then the Jensen's alpha graph stayed below zero line till the end of 2019 when it just leveled out (Figure 3.80).

The Omega ratio graphics exhibit that the funds category's possibility of yielding a positive return compared to the category benchmark is 74 and 79 % as per equally and AuM-weighted data, respectively (Figure 3.81).

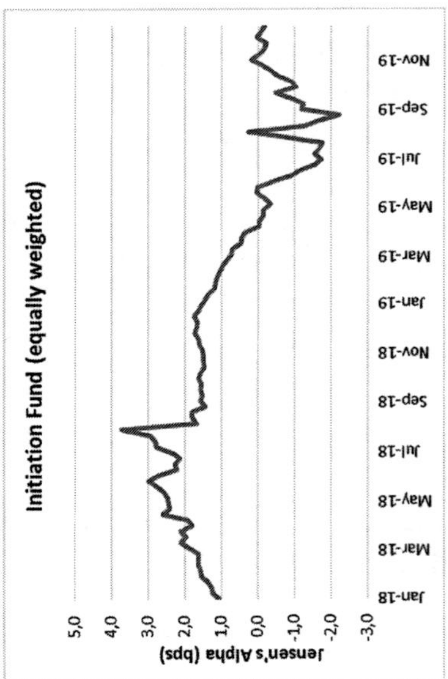

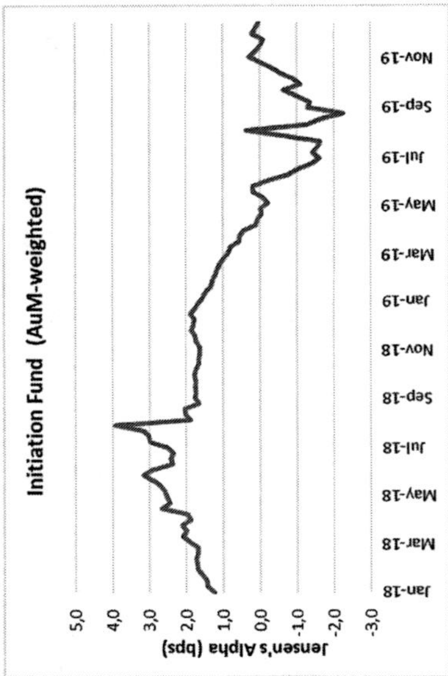

Figure 3.80: Initiation funds' Jensen's alpha ratio graphics
Source: Authors' calculations

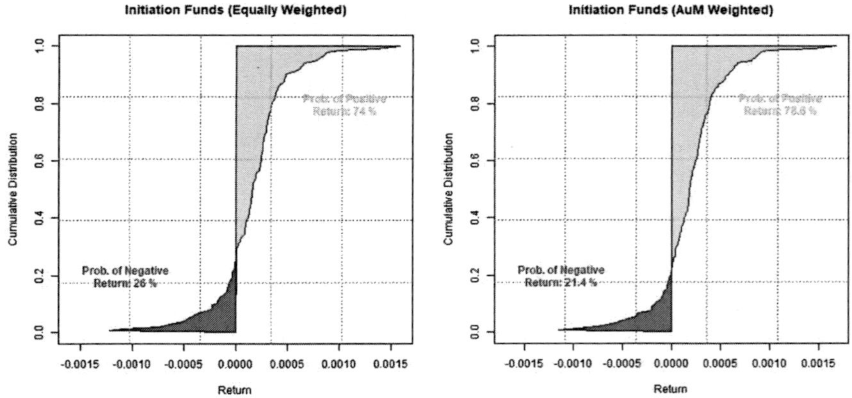

Figure 3.81: Initiation funds' Omega ratio graphics
Source: Authors' calculations

3.2.13 Initiation participation funds

We explained the establishment of participation initiation pension funds above.

This fund category has performed well above its benchmark, but we cannot state the same in comparison to the risk-free rate of return (Figure 3.82). This is due to nature of participation funds' being non-interest bearing.

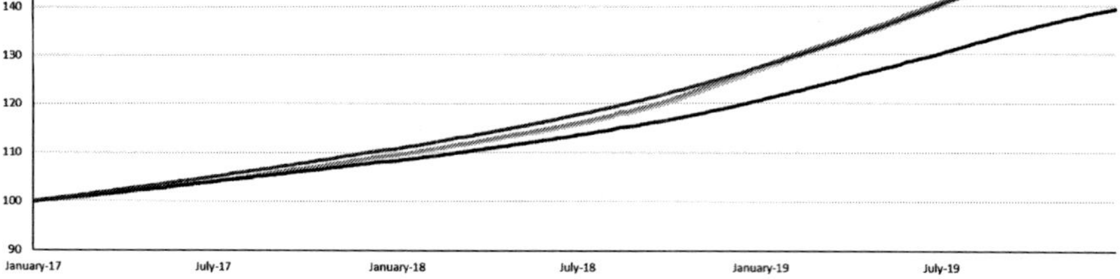

Figure 3.82: Initiation participation funds' performance vs benchmark (January 2017=100)
Source: Takas İstanbul, Borsa İstanbul, Finnet; indexed by the authors

Table 3.57: Initiation participation funds' performance (equally weighted returns)

Initiation Participation Funds (Equally Weighted)	2010	2011	2012	2013	2014	2015	2016	2017	2018	2019
1-Year										
Sharpe Ratio	n.a	n.a	n.a	n.a	n.a	n.a	n.a	-0.845059	0.169671	-0.332424
Treynor Ratio	n.a	n.a	n.a	n.a	n.a	n.a	n.a	-0.000084	0.000069	-0.000157
Information Ratio	n.a	n.a	n.a	n.a	n.a	n.a	n.a	0.519373	1.167365	1.264041
Jensen's Alpha	n.a	n.a	n.a	n.a	n.a	n.a	n.a	0.001358	0.001407	0.001248
Sortino Ratio	n.a	n.a	n.a	n.a	n.a	n.a	n.a	1.350324	17.372524	10.993843
Omega Ratio	n.a	n.a	n.a	n.a	n.a	n.a	n.a	4.140970	123.968855	39.861120
3-Year										
Sharpe Ratio	n.a	n.a	n.a	n.a	n.a	n.a	n.a	-0.179221		
Treynor Ratio	n.a	n.a	n.a	n.a	n.a	n.a	n.a	-0.000096		
Information Ratio	n.a	n.a	n.a	n.a	n.a	n.a	n.a	0.924885		
Jensen's Alpha	n.a	n.a	n.a	n.a	n.a	n.a	n.a	0.000861		
Sortino Ratio	n.a	n.a	n.a	n.a	n.a	n.a	n.a	6.181412		
Omega Ratio	n.a	n.a	n.a	n.a	n.a	n.a	n.a	21.627339		

Source: Authors' calculations

Table 3.58: Initiation participation funds' performance (AuM-weighted returns)

Initiation Participation Funds (AuM-Weighted)	2010	2011	2012	2013	2014	2015	2016	2017	2018	2019
1-Year										
Sharpe Ratio	n.a	n.a	n.a	n.a	n.a	n.a	n.a	-0.650739	0.269559	-0.266280
Treynor Ratio	n.a	n.a	n.a	n.a	n.a	n.a	n.a	-0.000068	0.000107	-0.000125
Information Ratio	n.a	n.a	n.a	n.a	n.a	n.a	n.a	0.560191	1.319849	1.370364
Jensen's Alpha	n.a	n.a	n.a	n.a	n.a	n.a	n.a	-0.006069	-0.002618	-0.002357
Sortino Ratio	n.a	n.a	n.a	n.a	n.a	n.a	n.a	1.221219	36.423147	17.117131
Omega Ratio	n.a	n.a	n.a	n.a	n.a	n.a	n.a	4.573255	263.651049	61.234270
3-Year										
Sharpe Ratio	n.a	n.a	n.a	n.a	n.a	n.a	n.a	-0.102624		
Treynor Ratio	n.a	n.a	n.a	n.a	n.a	n.a	n.a	-0.000061		
Information Ratio	n.a	n.a	n.a	n.a	n.a	n.a	n.a	1.007961		
Jensen's Alpha	n.a	n.a	n.a	n.a	n.a	n.a	n.a	-0.001443		
Sortino Ratio	n.a	n.a	n.a	n.a	n.a	n.a	n.a	5.648623		
Omega Ratio	n.a	n.a	n.a	n.a	n.a	n.a	n.a	25.213007		

Source: Authors' calculations

In the annual analysis, the first year (2017) yielded negative absolute risk-adjusted return measures (i.e., negative Sharpe and Treynor) but positive relative measures and measures of downside risk and higher moments (above 1 Omega ratio) as per both equally and AuM-weighted data (Tables 3.55 and 3.56). In 2018, all measures are positive (and Omega above 1) as per both equally and AuM-weighted data (ignoring negligible negative Jensen's alpha). In 2019, the results are like the ones in 2017, but higher positive ratios (and lower negative Sharpe ratios). The extraordinarily high Omega ratios in all three years are noteworthy.

In the only 3-yearly period analysis, the Sharpe and Treynor ratios are negative (though the Treynor ratio is negligible) while all others are positive (and Omega ratios well above 1).

The Treynor ratio scatter diagrams demonstrate that there is a strong positive relationship between the funds' aggregate return and the category benchmark (Figure 3.83).

The Jensen's alpha graphs illustrate that the fund category generated positive alpha during all its existence (Figure 3.84).

The Omega ratio graphics exhibit that the funds category's possibility of yielding a positive return compared to the category benchmark is 86 and 88 % as per equally and AuM-weighted data, respectively (Figure 3.85).

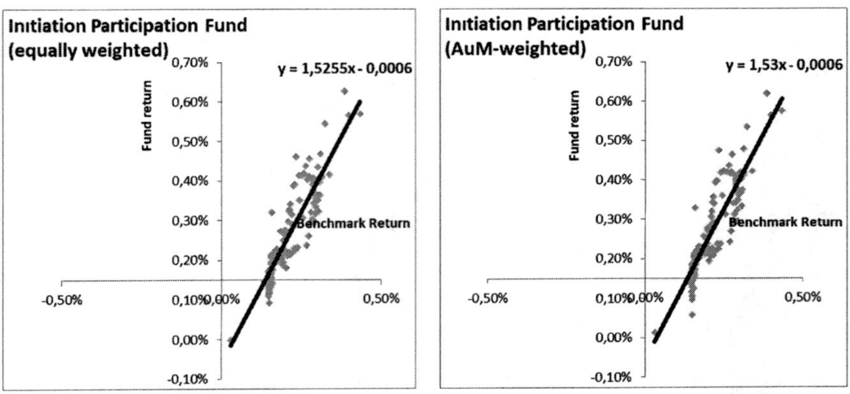

Figure 3.83: Initiation participation funds' Treynor ratio graphics
Source: Authors' calculations

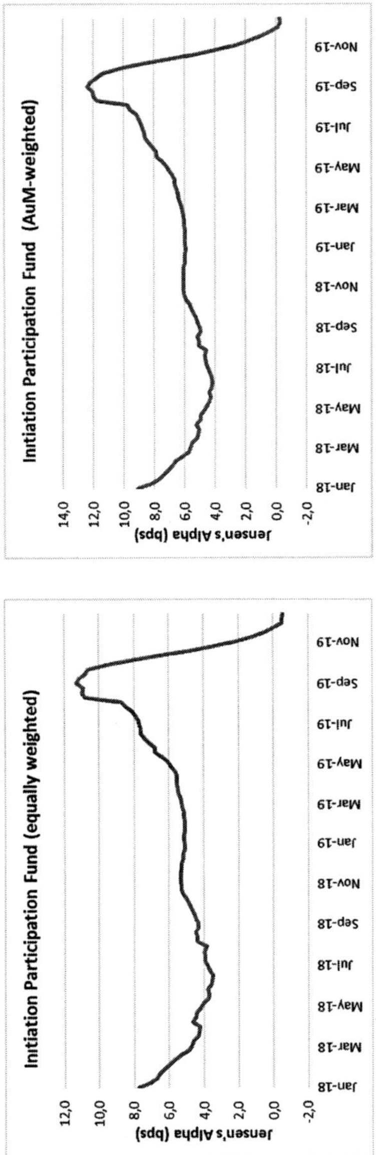

Figure 3.84: Initiation participation funds' Jensen's alpha ratio graphics
Source: Authors' calculations

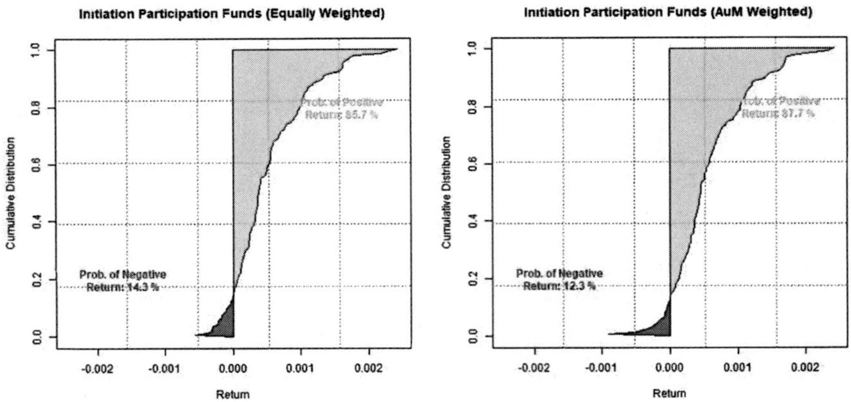

Figure 3.85: Initiation participation funds' Omega ratio graphics
Source: Authors' calculations

4. Results

In Sections 3.1 and 3.2 above, we analyzed each fund category's risk-adjusted performances using six different single-index models. The weekly returns data of 10 years analyzed by both taking into consideration the fund sizes (AuM-weighted) and not (equally weighted) between 2010–2019 (examined in annual, in rolling 3-yearly and 5-yearly, and a decade-long time horizons) reveal that none of the fund categories can deliver persistent risk-adjusted performance results in terms of absolute risk measures (i.e., vis-à-vis the risk-free rate of return) or in terms of relative returns (i.e., via-a-vis the benchmark return) or in terms of higher moments (i.e., in relation to downside risk).

In those analyses, the starting point of view has been the fund categories. Now we shall summarize the results with three different points of view: (1) the time horizon, (2) the single-index models, and (3) the same fund categories among mutual and pension funds.

4.1 Results comparison vis-a-vis time horizon

There is no evidence that the risk-adjusted performances are better in the long run. There is one exception though: equity pension fund category where in 6 of 8 3-yearly periods, 5 of 6 5-yearly periods, and finally the decade-long period yields positive (and above 1 in case of Omega) risk-adjusted returns especially based on equally weighted returns data while half of the annual periods' return performance is negative (and below 1 in case of Omega) in all measures.

4.2 Results comparison vis-a-vis single index models

There is no fund category which always beats *the risk-free rate of return*. The closest are three pension fund categories, namely (i) gold funds, which yield positive Sharpe and Treynor ratios in all annual periods other than 2014 and in all longer time horizons including the decade-long one, (ii) foreign currency denominated government bonds funds, which yield positive Sharpe and Treynor ratios in all annual periods other than 2010 and in almost all longer time horizons, and (iii) initiation funds, which yield positive Sharpe and Treynor ratios in all annual periods other than 2019 and the 3-year period of their existence.

There is no fund category which always beats its *benchmark*. The closest is the equity mutual funds category which beats the benchmark in 7 of the 10 annual periods, in 7 of the 8 3-year periods, in all 5-year periods, and finally in the decade-long period both based on equally and AuM-weighted returns. Fixed income mutual funds and participation mutual funds categories beat their benchmarks in about half of the annual periods but in most of the longer time horizons and finally in decade-long analysis, but only as per AuM-weighted returns analysis. Among 13 pension fund categories, the following six have beaten their benchmarks more than 50 % of the analyzed periods: (i) Gold pension funds only as per Jensen's alpha and based on AuM-weighted returns, (ii) initiation pension funds in all periods, (iii) initiation participation pension funds in all periods, (iv) government contribution funds in most of the periods but as per information ratio only, (v) equity pension funds in half of the periods, and (vi) foreign currency denominated government bonds funds only as per Jensen's alpha and based on AuM-weighted returns.

There is no fund category which always yields successful returns in terms of *higher moments*, i.e., positive Sortino ratios or above 1 Omega ratios. It is noteworthy that equity mutual funds, and participation mutual funds yield positive Sortino and above 1 Omega ratios in almost all longer time horizons, i.e., 3-yearly, 5-yearly periods, and finally in the decade-long analysis. It is more so for fixed income mutual funds based on AuM-weighted returns. Five of the 13 pension fund categories yield successful results in terms of higher moments in most of the periods, especially the longer time horizons: (i) initiation, (ii) initiation participation, (iii) government contribution, (iv) government contribution participation, and (v) equity pension funds.

4.3 Results comparison of the same mutual and pension fund categories

There are four fund categories which we can compare their "mutual" and "pension" versions with each other as they share the same investment strategy and hence the same benchmarks: (1) gold funds, (2) fixed income funds, (3) equity funds, and (4) money market funds (please see Tables 2.4 and 2.5 for the relevant benchmarks). The main difference would be in the management fees applied being a lower rate for pension funds (please see Table 2.8 for management fee comparisons).

Gold mutual funds and gold pension funds exhibit almost the same risk-adjusted performance results. They could not beat the benchmark at all. They beat the risk-free rate of return in all annual periods other than 2012, 2013, and 2014. This performance is reflected in 3-yearly and 5-yearly analysis and in a decade-long analysis as well. No size effect is observed. Gold pension funds' risk-adjusted returns are higher than those of mutual gold funds. This result can be explained by the lower management fees in pension funds.

Fixed income mutual and pension funds exhibit different risk-adjusted performance results. Fixed income pension funds cannot beat the benchmark ever based on equally weighted returns. However, we observe positive Jensen's alphas for years 2012, 2014, 2016, and 2019 when the analysis is run with AuM-based returns indicating a size effect. Fixed income pension funds can only beat the risk-free rate of return in years 2012, 2014, and 2019. Fixed income pension funds cannot yield successful results in longer time horizons; other than positive Jensen's alphas in 2012–2014, 2014–2016, and 2012–2016 periods and only as per AuM-weighted returns, all risk-adjusted return measures are negative (and Omegas below 1) in longer time horizons yielding all negative decade-long results as well. On the other hand, fixed income mutual funds have beaten the benchmark and the risk-free rate of returns especially in longer time horizons of 3- and 5-years. The risk adjusted returns are higher with AuM-weighted data indicating a size effect favoring the larger funds such that while the decade-long analysis yields all negative results with equally weighted returns, it is vice versa with AuM-weighted returns. Although the management fees are lower in the fixed income pension funds, the performance of fixed income mutual funds is clearly higher. We can track the reason in the asset allocations: while there is a 28 % allocation to private sector bonds and a 42 % allocation to T-bills in mutual funds, the same allocations are 1 % and 73 %, respectively, in pension funds.

Equity mutual funds and equity pension funds exhibit almost the same risk-adjusted performance results. There are two exceptional periods: (i) In 2016, while mutual funds yield positive results in all measures, pension funds yield positive result only in Omega measure and negative ones in all others. (ii) In 2011–2015 period while mutual funds yield positive results in all measures other than the absolute performance measures, pension funds yield positive result only in Jensen's alpha measure and negative ones in all others. Other than these, they beat both the benchmark and the risk-free rate of return one year and fail the other year consecutively starting with a success year in 2010 and repeating the success year in 2017. This pattern coverts into more successful periods in longer time horizons, i.e., more successful periods in 3-year and 5-year time horizons. In a decade-long analysis, equity mutual and pension funds beat both the benchmark and the risk-free rate based on all risk-adjusted measures. No size effect is observed strong enough to alter the sign of the results. Equity mutual funds' risk-adjusted returns are higher than those of equity pension funds although the management fees of pension funds are lower.

Money market mutual and pension funds exhibit almost the same risk-adjusted performance results. They could beat neither the benchmark nor the risk-free rate of return in annual periods until 2017 (with one exception when the money market pension funds beat the risk-free rate of return only in 2015). This performance is reflected in 3-yearly and 5-yearly time horizon analysis, i.e., only in the last two periods of each time horizon positive results are yielded. In a decade-long analysis, the results are negative in all risk-adjusted return measures (and lower than 1 in Omega measures). No size effect is observed strong enough to alter the sign of the results. Money market mutual funds' risk-adjusted returns are higher than those of money market pension funds although the management fees of pension funds are lower.

Considering these findings, we regret to state that the fund management industry in general failed to deliver a persistent satisfactory risk-adjusted performance whereas we expected otherwise. The results are mainly consistent with both academic and research papers that value creation is limited in Turkish fund management industry.

References

Books

Elton, E. J., Martin, J. G., Brown, S. J. & Goetzmann, W. N., 2010. Modern Portfolio Theory and Investment Analysis. 8th Edition, NJ: Wiley & Sons.

Periodicals

Barber, B., Huang, X., & Odean, T. (2016). Which Factors Matter to Investors? Evidence from Mutual Fund Flows, Review of Financial Studies, 29 (10), pp. 2600–2642.

Berk, J. & van Binsbergen, J. (2015). Measuring Skill in the Mutual Fund Industry, Journal of Financial Economics, 118 (1), pp. 1–20.

Bilici, N. (2016). Debt Crises or Debt Fools (!), International Journal of Public Finance, 1 (1), pp. 109–121.

Boratav, K. (2019). Capital Movements and Five Crises in Turkey, Journal of Work and Society, 1 (1), pp. 311–323. https://calismatoplum.org/Content/pdf/calisma-toplum-1781-51d7ce8e.pdf.

Carhart, M. (1997). On Persistence in Mutual Fund Performance, Journal of Finance, 52 (1), pp. 57–82.

Cremers, M., Fulkerson, J., & Riley, T. (2020). Benchmark Discrepancies and Mutual Fund Performance Evaluation, Journal of Financial and Quantitative Analysis, forthcoming, https://ssrn.com/abstract=3173437.

Elton, J. E. & Gruber, M. J. (2020). A Review of the Performance Measurement of Long-Term Mutual Funds, Financial Analysts Journal, 76 (3), pp. 22–37.

Fama, E. & French, K. (1992). The Cross-Section of Expected Stock Returns, Journal of Finance, 47 (2), pp. 427–465.

Fama, E. & French, K. (2015). A Five-Factor Asset Pricing Model, Journal of Financial Economics, 116 (1), pp. 1–22.

Jensen, M. (1968). The Performance of Mutual Funds in the Period 1945–1964, Journal of Finance, 23 (2), 389–416.

Jensen, M. (1969). Risk, the Pricing of Capital Assets, and the Evaluation of Investment Portfolios, The Journal of Business, 42 (2), pp. 167–247.

Keating, C. & Shadwick, W. F. (2002). A Universal Performance Measure, Journal of Performance Measurement, 6 (3), pp. 1–33.

Kuzubaş, T. U., Saltoğlu, B., Sert, A., & Yüksel, A. (2019). Performance Evaluation of the Turkish Pension Fund System, Journal of Capital Markets Studies, 3 (1), pp. 18–33.

Sharpe, W. F. (1966). Mutual Fund Performance, Journal of Business, 39 (1), pp. 119–138.

Sharpe, W. F. (1994). The Ratio, Journal of Portfolio Management, 21 (1), pp. 49–58.

Sortino, F. A. & van der Meer, R. (1991). Downside Risk, Journal of Portfolio Management, 17 (4) pp. 27–31.

Treynor, J. L. (1965). How to rate mutual fund performance. Harvard Business Review, 43, 63–75.

Other sources

BDDK News Bulletin, April 2020.

BIST-KYD Indexes Main Rules, https://www.borsaistanbul.com/files/bist-kyd-endeksleri-temel-kurallari_14082017.pdf.

Central Bank of Republic of Turkey, CBRT.

Capital Markets Board of Turkey, CMB.

Central Securities Depository of the Turkish Capital Markets, CSD.

Global Financial Institutions' Assets. 2020. https://www.statista.com/statistics/421221/global-financial-institutions-assets-by-institution-type/

Itts to GDP ratio by country. 2020. https://www.statista.com/statistics/368648/europe-investment-funds-assets-to-gdp-ratio-by-country/

Le Sourd, V. (2007). Performance Measurement for Traditional Investment: Literature Survey. https://www.researchgate.net/publication/292032684_Performance_measurement_for_traditional_investment_Literature_survey.

Marriage, Madison. Banks Embrace "the Age of Asset Management", Financial Times. 2015. https://www.ft.com/content/40c39d3e-9440-11e5-b190-291e94b77c8f.

OECD, Pension Markets in Focus 2020, https://www.oecd.org/pensions/pensionmarketsinfocus.htm.

Oxera Consulting LLP, 2016. The Contribution of Asset Management to the UK Economy. https://www.oxera.com/publications/the-contribution-of-asset-management-to-the-uk-economy.

Pension Markets in Focus, OECD. 2020. https://www.oecd.org/pensions/pensionmarketsinfocus.htm.

SPK Monthly Statistics, April 2020.

TCMA (2020). Turkish Capital Markets-December 2020. https://www.tspb.org.tr/wp-content/uploads/2020/12/Turkish_Capital_Markets-202012-TR.pdf.

TYKD, Pension Funds' Performance Report (2018), http://www.tkyd.org.tr/assets/raporlar/EYF_Performans_2018_Aralik-9a85f5af46e7a0be5591aefad0dc3890.pdf.

World Economic Forum.

www.Statista.com.

List of figures

List of tables